un
puzzling
hebrews

Dedicated to the memory of Dr. Dwight A. Pryor.

Remember your leaders who taught you the Word of God. Reflect on the results of their lifestyle and emulate their faithfulness.

CONTENTS

Introducing
Hebrews
The Anonymous Letter

A long time ago in a church far, far away....

A half-empty church in a small city struggled to start the evening service as the weight of the room's negative space bore down on them. The service never could get off the ground anymore since it appeared from the size of the room that the rest of the congregation should be arriving any minute. Those in attendance knew that was untrue. No one else would be coming. It was harder and harder to start each week.

Silence echoed off the walls—walls that surely could remember a full gathering clamoring with activity and life. But that was a long time ago. Even the tiny congregation had a hard time recalling those memories. How long had it been? Months? Surely longer than that, but could it have been years? No one wanted to admit these thoughts, but they were all thinking them.

It had been so long since things were normal, since things were safe. The room was so much fuller back then. There was real risk now. It wasn't safe to be in church anymore. Their fears loomed larger than their desire to worship God. Was the risk worth it? What if my neighbors knew I was here? What if the public officials found out?

This room used to be full of worshippers who never asked questions like these. Such thoughts would have been entirely foreign to them. But that was a long time ago. Faithfulness had ground to a halt. Energy was gone. Fear filled the room. Silence had become the loudest sound.

Without warning the silence was suddenly broken. A man emerged from the auditorium's back door. Gasping with surprise, the church stared in confusion at the unpredicted site. The man in the back of the room had captured all attention. After standing surprisingly still, the intruder charged forward toward the front of the room, all without a word.

As he neared the front of the room, all eyes were fixed on him. Recognition began to set in. It was Fidelis, an old friend whom they had not seen in many years. Doubt also crept in. Could it really be him? No one had seen him in years, and he lived quite a journey away. Why had he returned? As they pondered these questions, Fidelis reached the front of the room.

He took his place behind the podium, and stared out over the congregation. His face showed a worrisome care and his body seemed bent from a heavy burden. The near-empty room and blank faces were to blame. Without a word, he removed a scroll from his coat, unrolled it, and began to read:

"God, who previously spoke in many different ways to our ancestors through the prophets, spoke to us at the end of these days through his Son."

HEBREWS, I HARDLY KNEW YOU

This is of course the opening of The Letter to the Hebrews, dramatically presented in a reconstruction of what its original reading may have looked like. It's easy to open the Bible, read a few verses, and forget that this letter was originally written to real people with real problems. This letter, under the inspiration of the Holy Spirit, was written by a real author to help them in their time of need. Hebrews was not written to be an academic or theological treatise (although it contributes to theology greatly). Like most of the New Testament letters, it was written for a particular group of Christians to address a particular need.

Hebrews is known for its puzzles. Unlike most other books of the Bible, we don't know the exact circumstances that prompted its writing. We don't know who the original audience was. We also don't know who wrote these words, despite 2,000 years of wondering. For these reasons, Hebrews is most famous for what we don't know rather than for what we do know.

This book is not designed to solve these puzzles, as they are largely unsolvable. However, with a careful reading of the letter, there is much we can know and *Unpuzzling Hebrews* is intended to help. At the heart of Hebrews is a message that matters deeply to Christians today. In fact, it may be the most important book for the present church.

Perhaps you noticed some similarities between the opening narrative and our current circumstances. Would it surprise you to know I wrote these words years before pandemic lockdowns emptied churches? My goal was to dramatize the situation facing the original audience in a way that would incite emotion and connection, but the world has changed since then. The world that encircled this ancient audience is more and more similar to the world that surrounds us today. Hopefully you enjoyed meeting Fidelis and his audience because we will be returning to them at the start of each chapter.

THE ANONYMOUS AUTHOR

We will spend more time talking about these circumstances in a minute, but let's look at the author first. For all of church history, Christians have tried to guess who wrote this letter. Even the earliest Christians who discussed the authorship of Hebrews were puzzled. There is no evidence that even these ancient believers knew who the author was, so these discussions appear to be nothing more than guesses. Perhaps good guesses, since they're based on what we find in Hebrews itself and what we know of the early church, but, at the end of the day, they're only guesses.

The most important thing to keep in mind is that the author was known to the original audience. In fact, that is part of the problem. He was so well known by them that he didn't have to sign his name in order for them to know who wrote it. As we will learn in the pages to follow, this small group of believers desperately needed these words. They needed a passionate and challenging message to spur them in the right direction. The intimacy of the language suggests that when they received the original letter, they knew exactly who it was from.

It is reasonable to ask then, what can we know about the author? If his true identity is hidden behind this puzzle, what can we learn if we try to unpuzzle it? First off, the author does refer to himself with a masculine participle in 11:32, so we can be confident in referring to him as male. Most of the time though, he refers to himself in the plural. Often the plural includes himself and the audience showing that he identifies with them and their plight. Look at how he does that in 4:14: "*We* should maintain *our* commitment to Jesus the Son of God since *we* have him as a great high priest who has gone beyond the sky." Both uses of "we" in that verse include the author along with the audience.

However, there are occasions when the plural cannot include the audience, such as these:

- *We* have a lot to say about this but it's hard to explain given that *you* have become lazy listeners. (Hebrews 5:11)
- *We* will help *you* carry on, assuming God allows. (Hebrews 6:3)

In these texts, the "we" cannot include the audience since they are referred to in the same verses as "you." Some have understood this to imply that Hebrews has multiple authors. This line of thinking certainly makes sense, but can we press it any further to know more about them? I think these words from the end of the letter help fill in some of the missing pieces. In 13:18, the author asks the audience to "Pray for *us*," but in 13:19, he says, "*I* specifically encourage *you* to pray that *I* can return to *you* sooner."

The reference to praying for "us" in 13:18, then shifting to a specific individual in 13:19 stands out and perhaps offers some assistance with our goal to unpuzzle this behind-the-scenes detail. We can see here that a single author is actually penning the letter, but he is doing so as a representative of a church who is rooting for this audience to take these words to heart.[1] So, the author is part of a larger community, emotionally connected to this audience, but geographically separated from them —a sister church so to speak.[2]

What else can we perceive about the author from this letter? While it is true even in translation, the remarkable skill of the author is unmistakable in the original Greek text of Hebrews. Hebrews may be the finest use of Greek in the entire New Testament. He repetitively demonstrates throughout the letter a high level of skill in rhetoric, composition, and vocabulary.[3] It is quite possible the letter took a long time, maybe months, to plan out before actually drafting it (This is not to discount the inspiration of the Holy Spirit in and through his letter).

In addition to masterful skills in composition, the author is extremely familiar with his Bible. He weaves quotations, references, and allusions together as naturally as taking a breath. It is estimated that over one hundred of these occur within his letter.[4] This would definitely lend credit to the belief that he is a leader within his congregation and may have considered himself a leader, in some capacity, of the audience first reading this letter.[5]

The letter itself reveals much about this man, but can it help identify him any further? The author does provide a hint about his backstory in Hebrews 2:3, where he indicates that he is not an eye witness of Jesus but learned of him from those who were. This would seem to rule out this man being Paul[6] or one of the other Apostles. Paul makes a big deal about his personal and direct relationship to Jesus in his other writings so it would be out of character for him to downplay it so notably here.

With all of this in mind, where does it leave us? We certainly can't solve it, but can we unpuzzle it at all? Throughout Christian history those with the same puzzle pieces have offered many guesses. These guesses include Barnabas, Apollos, Luke, Clement, and even Priscilla and Aquila. However none of these picks are better than a blind guess. We are left to say with Origen, "But who wrote the epistle, in truth God knows."[7]

But is that really the case? Remember the audience had no doubts about who this author was. They knew exactly who it was, probably from the second that the deliverer read its first words. In the mind of the author, writing his name was unnecessary. What if that choice was not only his, but a deliberate omission encouraged by the Holy Spirit? The Spirit inspired these words like the rest of the Bible; what if the choice to leave this letter totally anonymous was part of God's purpose?

Sure, that is interesting, but why would that be the case? What do we gain spiritually by *not* knowing the author? What possible advantage could there be to something like that? Before we can answer that question, we need to look closer at why this letter was written and what situation faced its audience when these words were first read.

X=WHY?

There are as many theories on why Hebrews was written as there are theories on its authorship. Maybe even more. While I love reading the perspective of scholars who have made this letter their life's work, I much prefer to look at Hebrews itself to find this answer. Trying to find this answer is a lot like eavesdropping on a phone conversation. Is anyone willing to admit they do that? Regularly when I'm on the phone, my daughter makes guesses about who I'm talking to or what we're talking about while I make wild gestures for her to be quiet. The letter itself only presents one side of a conversation, so we are left to fill in the gaps.

When we encounter the words in 1:4 that the Son "has become superior to the angels to the same degree that the role he has received is more distinguished than theirs," it would be easy to surmise that the letter is about not worshiping angels, like what is warned against in Colossians. But as we read on, the angels fall away from the subject matter and never re-enter the discussion. As we enter chapter 3 and see that Jesus "deserves more glory than Moses," we could guess that there is an unhealthy obsession with Moses, but that is also never developed.

As the author goes on, he discusses Aaron, the Levitical priesthood, the Tabernacle, the Sinai Covenant, sacrifices, blood, altars, and the list goes on. He seems to be all over the place, leaving us helpless to guess what he is trying to get across. But wait! Do all of these facets combine together in any way? With a list so diverse it seems impossible, but could they all be parts of a greater discussion? The angels are mentioned as giving the law to the people and Moses was the mediator of the first covenant, so those fit together. Aaron and the Levitical priests also functioned as the staying power of the covenant ensuring that the people's shortcomings were atoned for with the appropriate sacrifices. And the Tabernacle was the sanctuary, the holy place of the covenant where this atonement would take place. Now the purpose falls into place. Hebrews is comparing facets of the first covenant with the same components of the new covenant.[8]

Well then, case closed. Hebrews is about how the new covenant is superior to the old covenant. Great job everyone, you can probably close the book now.

But, what about Hebrews 11? It's the most famous chapter in Hebrews, but it isn't about the first covenant or the new covenant. How can we make sense of that? Something more has to be going on then. The author is definitely talking about the covenants, but he has to have some greater purpose in mind. He must have some bigger picture he sees them fitting into.

The best way to look for a letter's purpose is to look at what the author tells the audience to do. When he gives directions, imperatives, and commands he is revealing what he expects the audience to take away from his writing. Let's look at some of these.

- Make sure to prevent there from being in even one of you, a heart corrupted by unfaithfulness that causes you to turn your back on the living God. (Hebrews 3:12)
- We should maintain our commitment to hope without hesitation because the one who promised is faithful. (Hebrews 10:23)
- You shouldn't throw away your confidence since it comes with a great reward. (Hebrews 10:35)
- You have to endure since God is training you like sons and daughters. (Hebrews 12:7)

These verses seem to be doing the same thing as Hebrews 11, just in a different way. Whereas these directions tell us what to do, Hebrews 11 shows us. The author is urging his audience to maintain faithfulness to God no matter what. He is urging them to stick with it through thick and thin, good times and bad, for richer or poorer. The imperatives explicitly say that, but the narratives recounting the examples found in the "Hall of Faith" demonstrate what it looks like.

This is why Hebrews appears to be about two different things—why the letter can turn from academic theology to emotional pleas on a dime. He is challenging his audience to stick with it, to remain faithful no matter what the cost, and he shows the importance of doing so by comparing the two covenants. Because the new covenant is superior to the first and because it offers greater benefits, we must not come up short in our faithfulness to God.[9] Ultimately, the author has two inter-related goals in mind:

1. to demonstrate that the new covenant is superior to the old and thus worthy of greater attention and faithfulness and
2. to showcase that the new covenant offers greater access to God to enable faithfulness in the midst of persecution and difficulties.

Why does the author need to do this though? What is happening with his dear friends that has prompted him to put together such a magnificent composition balancing these two challenging topics? We know from the letter that the audience previously suffered much for their relationship to God. The author, talking about the audience's past, says in 10:32, "when you first saw the light; you endured a tough fight in your suffering." We aren't told specifically how long ago this was, but it seems to have been many years prior.

With all of these details, we can start unpuzzling the picture. This small group of believers received the gospel from one of the Apostles at some point in the past. They quickly accepted Jesus as Messiah and were willing to suffer all manner of difficulty as part of their love for him. They were mocked and ridiculed, they had their property seized, possibly including their homes or businesses. Some of their members were even imprisoned. Throughout this time, they remained passionate for their Savior! They even chose to extend themselves further and help other Christians who were also being persecuted. Lastly, during this time, the leaders of the community had died. We don't know how, but we know the original leaders from this time were not alive when Hebrews was written.

After this trying time, there was a respite, some sort of break from the persecution. We don't know how long it lasted, perhaps years. It was certainly enough time that the author could declare the audience should be experienced teachers by now. Without warning, the difficult times re-emerged. At the time of writing, it seems the threat of persecution was larger than the actual persecution itself. This small group of Christians, gripped by fear of having to go through persecution again, was tempted, not to apostatize or walk away from their faith; they were tempted to slow down, hold back, or keep quiet. They just wanted to coast for a little bit and let the hard times pass them by. They could worship God quietly; they didn't have to let anyone know they were Christians. They could lie low for a little while and perk back up later when things were not so scary.

This is why Hebrews was written.[10] The author unashamedly answers their probably unspoken thoughts by eliminating this option altogether. We don't get to lie low, slow down or hold back when the subject is our relationship to God and his Son. We don't get to pick how much it costs to follow Jesus; we just have to be willing to pay anything and everything. This reminds me of Gandalf's response to Frodo in *The Lord of the Rings*. When Frodo laments that he wished the ring had never come to him, Gandalf wisely replies, "So do all who live to see such times. But that is not for them to decide. All we have to decide is what to do with the time that is given us."[11] The same is true for us. The world outside our windows may soon be a place where it costs more to follow Jesus than it did twenty years ago. But we don't get to choose how much it costs. We just have to write the check.

To summarize, our author was a passionate leader in a sister church to our audience. He was geographically separated but emotionally connected. He heard of the rising threat of persecution where they were located and was told the church wasn't doing well. They were overcome with fear and despair. Many members had stopped attending. There was an unwillingness to be publicly recognized as being Christians. This sister church, and specifically the author, knew they had to do something to help. They knew there was real risk with slipping away and they were unwilling to let their friends go down without a fight.

So, why is Hebrews anonymous? In view of all this, why would God withhold the name of this author? Perhaps the reason is so that we can imagine this letter as coming from someone we know who would risk everything to come get us when we were drifting from shore. We can insert the name of the person who would write a letter to us if they were concerned about our walk with the Lord. A passionate, pull-no-punches, hold-nothing-back, leave-it-all-in-the-ring kind of letter. One that addresses us honestly, shows us tough love, and points the way forward out of the dark. This is how I read Hebrews. I invite you to read it the same way.

Since this is the perspective this commentary will follow, referring to the author in vague terms seems inappropriate, while referring to him as "the author of the letter to the Hebrews" is cumbersome and gets old fast when you have been teaching on Hebrews for over a decade. Many years ago, I decided to give the author a personal name. Since he is well known for his role as an author, I named him Arthur. Originally, I did it as kind of a joke, but after many years it grew on me. Now I don't even think about it when I refer to him by this name. In fact, it was difficult for me to make it this far into the book and not call him Arthur. From here on out, Arthur will be used anytime the author is being referenced.

EVIDENCE LOCKER

Before we move on from here, we should ask if we can use this reconstruction to align Hebrews to any particular setting within First Century Christianity. In our journey to unpuzzle this letter, can we have any degree of confidence when it was written or where it was originally sent? These questions are a little easier to answer. As for the location of its audience, there is growing conformity among scholars that the letter was written to Rome. At the end of the letter, Arthur sends greetings from "the Italians." It is possible that Arthur is in Rome and he is sending greetings to an audience elsewhere, but it is more likely the Italians are outside of Rome sending their greeting back with this letter.[12]

As for the date, it is not quite as easy to pin down, but I have been convinced the circumstances best align to the early part of the reign of Emperor Domitian. This would mean Arthur wrote Hebrews sometime in the 80s A.D., making it one of the last New Testament books to be written. During this time in Rome, Christians often met in small groups that were loosely connected as part of the wider church in Rome. It is likely that Hebrews is to a specific one of these small groups, likely only including one to two dozen members.

Lastly, we should look at the title itself. Does that shed any light on the audience? It is acknowledged that nothing in the letter demands a specifically Jewish audience. Some have even speculated that the title "Hebrews" was added at a later point based on its subject matter. The problem with that approach is that all ancient Christians who refer to the title use "Hebrews." If the letter circulated without a title and one was later added, it would be strange that no other titles were used. So, was the audience Jewish? Probably not exclusively. We know other churches at the time were made up of both Jewish and Gentile believers, and there is no reason not to assume the same of this audience. Why is it called "To The Hebrews" then? Would it surprise you to learn that an ancient synagogue in Rome has been unearthed that bore the name, "Synagogue of the Hebrews"? I haven't found a scholar fully convinced this housed the original audience of Hebrews, but it aligns well with all of the details.[13] If so, this small gathering of Christians likely met in the original synagogue from when they first heard the news of Jesus, the long-awaited Messiah. This is where they stood the test under an earlier persecution and also where they were now starting to show cracks in their faith as new threats of persecution loomed. I will continue to refer to the letter as Hebrews throughout this book, but I put forward that a better title would actually be "The Anonymous Letter."

SAFETY BRIEFING

As we start out on our journey of unpuzzling Hebrews, I hope you are starting to get a sense of how important this letter is, both to Christian history and to our present predicament. I first became enamored with it nearly fifteen years ago, and I have kept it in consistent study ever since. At first, it was merely an academic interest. I enjoyed studying the Bible, and it was fun to dig deep in a single New Testament book. Over time, as my family and I encountered financial hardships and health crises, it became a source of strength in difficult times. Throughout those years, I found comfort not only studying Hebrews but also teaching through it in many churches. However, when the world began changing and more and more Christians felt confronted with the notion that the cost to follow Jesus may be going up, I felt moved to commit this message to a book.

I am glad to have you with me on this journey to unpuzzle Hebrews, so I want to take a short moment here to lay out how the rest of the book will go. It was my intention not to spend much time introducing the letter so this section has been kept as brief as possible. I want you to enjoy the richness of God's Word, so my goal was to get to it quickly. The remainder of the book will be a verse-by-verse commentary through the entire letter. The commentary will be broken up over five chapters following the structure of the letter which immediately follows this introduction.

Each chapter will begin by continuing the narrative of Fidelis and his friends. After that there will be a short section, Inner Piece (get it? like a puzzle piece), where we will look at what we have learned so far and summarize how the current section of Hebrews fits into the letter holistically. Then the full text of Hebrews will be presented paragraph by paragraph and followed by commentary on it. Each chapter will end with a final section, Piece of Mind (continuing the puzzle piece puns), which contains the chapter's endnotes offering additional insights to go deeper into Hebrews. Unless otherwise indicated in the bibliography, works cited or referenced are identified with the author's last name and page number. The full reference is found in the bibliography.

The commentary will be based upon a new translation of Hebrews created for use in this book. While many traditional translation practices were followed, you will notice that the sentence structure and flow will follow typical American English style. Places where the translation notably differs from modern English versions will be fully explored and discussed in the commentary. You can rest assured that the highest commitment to accuracy was sought when producing this work.[14]

There will be infrequent digressions within the commentary to cover a particular topic that warrants a brief detour. This was done to keep the introduction succinct and to ensure the material occurred in tandem with its association in Hebrews. An example is Arthur's use of the Bible which occurs as a digression prior to the commentary on 1:5–14.

You may have already noticed, but throughout the book you will find less-than-serious headings. This was done so you can get the full experience of what it would be like talking about Hebrews directly with me and also to force a few chuckles (or eye rolls if you are my wife) in between very serious and often challenging words.

Lastly, I hope you have a sense of how important Hebrews is. An early version of this book had the title, "Why Hebrews Matters Most." While that is not the title I went with, it is a sentiment I still hold to. This letter was beloved in the ancient church and its message is more important now than ever before. Ultimately Hebrews is a letter—as much fun as it is to study in depth, its message was meant to be ingested in a single sitting. If you have never done this, I encourage you to do so. The complete translation is found after the commentary and is presented without headings or verse references to encourage uninterrupted reading.

I look forward to joining you on this journey of *Unpuzzling Hebrews*.

PIECE OF MIND

1. Daniel Wallace is a great example of a scholar who proposes multiple authors being behind Hebrews, see Wallace 396–397.
2. I use the term sister church for ease of reference. Technically it should be sister synagogue since Arthur refers to their gathering with a form of the word for synagogue in 10:25. At this time, both church and synagogue refer to the people gathered rather than the actual building. Later distinctions applied synagogue to a Jewish gathering that didn't hold to Jesus as Messiah.
3. See Koester 96: "Hebrews' vocabulary is high and varied, including 154 words not found in other NT writings."

4. Based on *Hebrews* by George H. Guthrie in *Commentary on the New Testament Use of the Old Testament* edited by G.K. Beale and D.A. Carson, see page 919.

5. The possibility of Arthur seeing himself as a present leader of the community is inferred from his flow of thought in chapter 13. He goes from discussing obedience to the present leaders to the prayer request for himself in 13:17–19, see Lane lxi.

6. Many Christians find value in the King James ascription of authorship to Paul, but this is a preservation of the authorship tradition identified by Jerome in the fourth century Latin Vulgate translation of the Bible. For clarity, I am not saying that Paul *could not* have written Hebrews, but that evidence of the letter itself and Christian history point away from this conclusion.

7. Cited from Attridge 1. The citation is originally from Eusebius' Ecclesiastical History 6.14. Origen probably did not mean to imply that the author was unknown, but only the penman. Origen likely believed Paul to be the author, just not the actual person physically writing the letter, see Black, David Alan. "Origen on the Authorship of Hebrews."

8. See *Inventing Hebrews: Design and Purpose in Ancient Rhetoric* by Michael Wade Martin and Jason A. Whitlark.

9. I highly recommend the video overview of Hebrews done by Bible Project, I actually have the official poster hanging in my office as I write this. https://www.youtube.com/watch?v=1fNWTZZwgbs

10. For excellent works evaluating the purported background of Hebrews, I highly recommend the following: *Resisting Empire: Rethinking the Purpose of the Letter to "the Hebrews"* by Jason A. Whitlark; *Suffering In The Face Of Death: The Epistle to the Hebrews and Its Context of Situation* by Bryan R. Dyer; and *Hebrews 1–8 WBC 47a* and *Hebrews 9–13 WBC 47b* by William L. Lane. I particularly enjoy the work of Whitlark, here is a great quotation regarding the circumstances of the original audience, "Hebrews was written as a "word of exhortation" (13:22) to encourage covenant fidelity in the face of suffering ... Such suffering, along with the ongoing derision and shame that the members of the community experienced, was 'threatening to take the heart out of them.'" Whitlark 2.

11. *The Lord of the Rings* quotation is from *The Fellowship of the Ring* by J.R.R. Tolkien. Houghton Mifflin, 1994, page 50.

12. Support for a Roman destination is also found in Arthur's term used for "leader" in chapter 13 (verses 7, 17, and 24). This Greek word also occurs in other Roman Christian works and is not commonly used of Christian leadership in the New Testament. Further support is also found in that Hebrews is first quoted by Clement, a famous Roman church leader of the first and second century, in First Clement.

13. See Bruce 13. Bruce identifies his doubts to this link but does not explain his reservations further.

14. For those interested, the base text used for the translation of the letter found in this book is the Tyndale House Greek New Testament published by Crossway. There are a few occasions in which alternate textual decisions are reached based on my comparative research into the Hebrews textual tradition.

THE LETTER TO THE HEBREWS

I. The Son (1:1–2:18)

  a. Jesus & Angels (1:1–14)

  b. The Great Salvation (2:1–4)

  c. Jesus & Angels Redux (2:5–18)

II. The Word (3:1–6:20)

  a. Jesus & Moses (3:1–6)

  b. The Unfaithful Example (3:7–4:13)

  c. The Great High Priest (4:14–16)

  d. Jesus & Aaron (5:1–10)

  e. A Brief Detour (5:11–6:12)

  f. The Faithful Example (6:13–6:20)

III. The Priest (7:1–10:18)

  a. Meet Melchizedek (7:1–10)

  b. High Priest Comparison (7:11–28)

  c. The Covenant Comparison (8:1–13)

  d. Holy Place Comparison (9:1–28)

  e. Covenant Sacrifice Comparison (10:1–18)

IV. The Faithful (10:19–12:29)

  a. The Great Reward (10:19–39)

  b. In Faithfulness (11:1–40)

  c. The Great Crowd (12:1–17)

  d. Two Mountains (12:18–29)

V. The End (13:1–13:25)

  a. Pleasing Service (13:1–17)

  b. Closing Remarks (13:18–25)

THE SON (1:1–2:18)

ORIGIN STORY

FIDELIS LEFT HOME OVER THREE WEEKS AGO. THE JOURNEY was never an easy one, three days on a merchant ship and over two weeks in a caravan. He was always on the road, so he had grown accustomed to uncomfortable accommodations. The difficult part? Not knowing what awaited him when he got there.

Fidelis had last visited these friends five years ago, and from everything he had heard, he didn't know quite what to expect. These concerns were only intensified by the letter he was going to read them. He had helped write it, but that only made his nerves worse. There was some really challenging things to say, and this letter would demand all of his skills as an orator to give it just the right heart. It was easier to believe God was in these words before, but now he was overcome with doubt as the time to face his friends grew close.

Preoccupied with this thought, he tripped over a loose stone on the roadway. Words from the letter flashed before his mind:

"We should give it all we've got to enter that place of rest so that no one goes down due to the same kind of disobedience."

This tough love seemed like a better idea when he was five hundred miles away. Fidelis pulled himself up and dusted off his tunic. He was getting close now; soon the message would be delivered, and it would all be in the hands of God.

He saw the sun lowering behind the mountains and realized he was late. He had planned to stop by Calvus' house before the service, but he must have lost more time than he thought going around that sheep pasture. The congregation, at least what was left of them, was probably already gathered.

Fortunately, he was close. He tightened his belt and ran the rest of the way. Candlelight glowed from the window; the service must have already started. It was now or never.

He whispered a prayer and opened the door with more strength than he should have. It seemed to crash open under the force of his push. Once inside, all eyes were on him. Sixteen people. That's all. This room used to be bursting with life, but it seemed empty now — in more ways than one.

Fidelis drew a deep breath. Without hesitation, he walked to the front. He had no idea what he had interrupted, but he didn't care. He had a job to do, and he was going to make sure it got done. This letter might be the last chance for his struggling friends before they crossed the point of no return. He wasn't going to let that happen.

He broke the seal of the scroll, his only traveling companion for the last three weeks. He started to read:

"God, who previously spoke in many different ways to our ancestors through the prophets, spoke to us at the end of these days through his Son."

INNER PIECE

Hebrews At A Glance
I. The Son (1:1–2:18)
a. Jesus & Angels
i. 1:1–4
ii. 1:5–14
b. The Great Salvation
i. 2:1–4
c. Jesus & Angels Redux
i. 2:5–9
ii. 2:10–13
iii. 2:14–18
II. The Word (3:1–6:20)
III. The Priest (7:1–10:18)
IV. The Faithful (10:19–12:29)
V. The End (13:1–13:25)

Arthur's mastery of language and rhetoric are on full display as he commences his passionate letter. The first major section of Hebrews includes chapters 1 and 2.[1] From its first words, Hebrews invites the listener on a journey. Arthur traverses the covenant history of God and his people, going all the way back to eternity past. He focuses the spotlight on Jesus and what he means to God's people, both in the past and in the present.

Arthur uses this first major section of text to engage his audience, both with the dizzying effect of circumnavigating all of biblical history, but also by building rapport with them. We don't know how long it's been since he has communicated with them, but it must have been some time.

The audience likely hasn't verbalized their encroaching fears, they don't see themselves on the verge of apostasy, but Arthur sees their situation much more seriously than they do. They may not be on the verge of apostasy, but they are drifting in the wrong direction. Arthur works within this dissonance throughout his entire letter. He leverages the idea that his perspective on the riskiness of their actions (and inactions) doesn't match their own point of view. Here in the beginning of the letter he plays a positive hand. He knows the audience highly regards Jesus, at least mentally, so he uses his opening paragraphs to exalt him as high as language allows.

At the beginning of chapter 2, he will start to reveal his concerns, but he'll quickly return to discussing Jesus. The subtlety is indicative of his skill. After this first section, Arthur will quickly throw his audience into the deep end with a biblical analogy intended to kick off his full intent of deeply challenging this small group.

For now, he begins with mystery, not revealing his hand. The audience is lured into the discourse with strong affirmations of the faith they inwardly honor as they anxiously listen to where this letter will lead.

Let's begin our journey unpuzzling Hebrews by looking at the first two chapters. We will review the text in depth, paragraph by paragraph, looking at each verse in detail.

JESUS & ANGELS: 1:1–4

[1:1]God, who previously spoke in many different ways[2] to our ancestors through the prophets, [2]spoke to us at the end of these days through his Son. He appointed the Son as rightful owner of everything, after all it was through him that God created the universe. [3]The Son is the tangible expression of his presence and the physical representation of his essence. Even now he sustains the universe by his powerful word. After purifying our sins,[3] he sat down next to the Majesty[4] in heaven.[5] [4]He has become superior to the angels to the same degree that the role he has received is more distinguished than theirs.

Arthur wastes no time beginning his masterpiece. He starts at a breakneck pace in which he immediately dives into a recapitulation of biblical history before advancing into an exploration of the nature of the Son of God and his relationship with the Father. It is clear from the beginning that we are reading something truly special. Arthur's mastery of language and rhetoric are on full display as he begins his passionate letter. He omits the customary pleasantries that typically open letters from the time period. We see these features on display in the other letters of the New Testament, but Hebrews explodes out of the starting gate.

These first four verses form a single sentence in the original Greek. Numerous times throughout the letter Arthur will use a long sentence to present tightly packed material.[6] This functions like a shaky camera action scene in which the senses are hyper-stimulated with content as you struggle to get your bearings through the relentless pace. In consideration of English style this run-on sentence is broken up into several sentences in the translation above. In Arthur's thought, he saw this opening paragraph in two units. The first half (verses 1 and 2) focuses more strongly on God whereas the second half (verses 3 and 4) focus more closely on Jesus.

God

The first words of Hebrews use poetic alliteration, which is not possible to reproduce in English, but in the first sentence, five words start with the P sound. The immediate usage of alliteration is strategic, but also indicative of Arthur's intentions. He plans for the letter to be read publicly by a trained orator (I have named him Fidelis in our narratives). Arthur's unmatched literary talent is deserving of the same masterclass-level expertise in the person he designated to travel to our audience and provide this much needed encouragement.

If you are comparing my translation to other newer versions of the Bible, you'll find an immediate distinction. My translation begins with God, rather than "Long ago" or "In the past" which most newer versions use. There is a critical reason why I have opted against this even though "God" is not the first word in the Greek text. The reason is the rhetorical usage of the alliteration. In the Greek text the word God occurs right in the middle of the P alliteration. Three Ps occur before it and two more occur after it.

This dynamic usage of alliteration forces an emphasis on the word "God" as the reader (and listeners) take immediate notice of the first word to break the alliterative cycle. Having the alliteration repeat immediately after adds further intensity to the emphasis. Arthur wants us to see God in big bold text. Since English readers are not used to this style of emphasis, recreating the alliteration becomes unnecessary. Instead we can capture the sense by putting God at the beginning of the sentence.

Arthur then advances to tell us about God. He is the God who speaks. He previously spoke through the prophets, likely not an allusion to any specific instance in the past, but a cumulative reference to the entire period before the New Testament. And he is speaking to us now through Jesus. This simple description of God as the "God who speaks" says so much about his character. God wants to be known. He has spoken throughout all of human history. Left on our own, we would be helpless to find God, but we are not on our own. God wants us to find him, he wants us to know him, so he is the God who speaks.

Another immediate distinction you might notice in my translation above is the designation of the present as "the end of these days" rather than the more familiar "these last days."[7] This distinction is critical, as we will find later in the letter, but Arthur purposely doesn't use the more traditional phrase, "last days," like other Old and New Testament authors. Time will factor significantly into the letter, and this mysterious claim that we live at the end of these days invites intrigue. What are these days? This is a question he will answer later, but for now it will be helpful to present this temporal anomaly visually. We will come back to this table throughout the book as Arthur defines his perspective.

Past	Present	Future
These days	The end of these days	After these days

Many translations add the word "but" in between the first speaking of God through the prophets and his second speaking through Jesus, but no such contrast is found in the Greek text. The current speaking of God in Jesus is not in contrast to his prior speaking, it is the natural evolution of that process.[8] The permanent and final method in which God has chosen to engage with humankind is through his Son. As we will find to be true every time the new covenant is compared to the former, there is an infinite improvement in quality, but there is also a commensurate increase in responsibility.

God Spoke	
In many different ways	[With singular definition]
Previously	At the end of these days
To our ancestors	To us
Through the prophets	Through his Son

Arthur then moves on to describe God's actions in reference to Jesus. For now, Jesus is referred to simply as Son. Arthur holds off utilizing the name Jesus until Chapter 2, but he assumes you know he is referring to the historical Jesus when he calls him by this title. Arthur makes an assertion, one that he will support with Scripture in the back half of Chapter 1, that God has appointed Jesus as the rightful owner of the universe and that Jesus was involved with God in creating the universe.

"Rightful owner" is typically rendered as "heir" or "inherit" in traditional English versions of Hebrews, but I think an alternate path is helpful. In our modern usage, we typically think of the process of inheriting as taking place after the death of a parent. For us, you really aren't an heir until after their death. This was not the case in the ancient world, and this is obviously impossible in the relationship of God the Father and God the Son, since God the Father cannot die. In the ancient world the firstborn son was known as heir his whole life. This position of honor imbued him with legal rights and authority that were not true of his younger siblings. This is the sense Arthur intends to convey. Jesus occupies a privileged position of authority over all of creation, a position which includes his legal or rightful ownership of everything God has made.

Arthur logically connects this thought to Jesus' role in creation. Other New Testament authors also present Jesus as being involved in the creation act, but Arthur will actually support his claim using Scripture to prove that Jesus participated with God in creating the universe.

Arthur uses Jesus' partnership role in creating the world as a hinge to transition his focus more fully on the Son.

Yet God, through Jesus, created more than just the earth. Arthur actually told us that he created the universe. The Greek word behind "universe" can refer to both time and space.[9] Since the translation "space/time continuum" is too nerdy, universe will have to do. This is just the first time that Arthur will blend the concepts of time and space in his letter, so we will return to this topic later as he expands upon it.

Jesus

Arthur continues his award-winning, run-on sentence by extolling Jesus with images defining his exalted relationship with God. The letter proclaims that Jesus is "the tangible expression of his presence and the physical representation of his essence." This is an attempt to present the images Arthur is conveying rather than a literal rendering of the words themselves. Typically, these two descriptions are brought into English as something like "the radiance of his glory" and "the imprint of his nature." I opted to represent the mental image more clearly to drive home the point of what he is saying.

When Arthur calls Jesus the "radiance of his glory," he uses the word "glory" in its Old Testament sense that we see represented here:

> Then the cloud covered the tent of meeting, and the glory of the LORD filled the tabernacle. And Moses was not able to enter the tent of meeting because the cloud settled on it, and the glory of the LORD filled the tabernacle. (Exodus 40:34–35 ESV)

Here, and many other times in the Old Testament, "glory" refers to God's presence. The radiance of his presence then is what the senses experience of his presence. As the radiance of the sun allows us to see the light and feel the warmth of the sun, Jesus, as the radiance of God's presence, is the tangible expression of God whom we can see and feel.

Arthur conveys a similar idea with Jesus as "the imprint of his nature." The Greek word behind "nature" or "imprint" means, "what stands underneath." In this context, it means God's character, nature, identity, or essence; what and who God really is. The image being conveyed then is like a rubber stamp pressing ink onto a page. In the same way that the stamped image perfectly represents the stamp, Jesus perfectly represents God to us. Thus, Jesus is the physical representation of the God who is otherwise invisible. These two ideas work together to exalt Jesus far beyond what is true of any other man who ever lived because he is more than a man. Jesus presents God to us in a way more intimately and more accurately than any former revelation of God ever could.

Next Arthur tells us that Jesus sustains the universe by his word. This continues the theme of Jesus' involvement in creation and extends that fact all the way to the present. Just like God's Word, all of creation responds to Jesus' authority and he uses this power to sustain it. The Greek word means to literally carry something. Far from being the watchmaker who created the clock, wound it up, and walked away, God, through Jesus, is intimately involved in the universe's continued progress. Progress implies a goal. Jesus isn't just holding up the universe like the mythical Atlas; he is carrying it to its scheduled destination. Arthur will have a lot to say about this destination as his letter progresses.

The discussion then advances to Jesus' work on the cross. This will feature prominently into the discussion later in the letter, but for now it is vaguely mentioned as "purifying our sins." This is designed to create dynamic tension with what follows. Jesus is the one who made purification for sins, but now he is the one sitting next to God in heaven. This is traditionally expressed as "at the right hand," but I have always been uncomfortable with this literal rendering. Not only do we lack the same sense of prestige associated with one's right hand that was found in the ancient world, but it is worth noting that God doesn't actually have a right hand, or a right side.[10] The point of the expression is that Jesus is sitting in the highest position of honor next to God on his throne. There is no need to imagine a second throne for Jesus, he sits on God's throne as we are shown in Revelation 3:21 (ESV):

> The one who conquers, I will grant him to sit with me on my throne,
> as I also conquered and sat down with my Father on his throne.

This is absolutely remarkable to think of. When Hebrews was written, Jesus walked the earth only fifty years earlier. At that time, you could have passed Jesus on the street and thought him an ordinary man, but now he sits on the literal throne of God reigning over all of the universe. This reference to Jesus on heaven's throne is the first of what will become many references to Psalm 110— a Psalm that both Arthur and we will discuss all throughout our journey.

Arthur concludes his run on sentence with a summarizing thesis. Jesus "has become superior to the angels to the same degree that the role he has received is more distinguished than theirs." The statement invites curiosity as well as wonder. The first listeners wondered what it meant that Jesus "has become superior," wasn't he always superior?[11] And why angels? What do they have to do with anything? Before they can process these questions, the listeners are compelled to worship as they contemplate this distinguished role that Jesus now occupies. The word "role" is traditionally translated as "name," but the Greek word is more expansive in its definition than "name" is in English.[12] The name or role Jesus has received is that of Son.[13] The exalted role, prophesied in the Old Testament, is now occupied by Jesus. It is no longer vacant, there is a man sitting on the throne of God, but not just a man, he is the physical representation of God's presence for us.

DIGRESSION: LADIES & SEPTUAGINTS

Have you ever read a powerful story in the Bible and imagined what it might look like as a scene in a movie? There are so many visually captivating stories in the Bible that make this act of imagination almost impossible to avoid. The event of God coming down on Mount Sinai, the story of Abraham and Isaac, or David and Goliath are all punctuated by visual storytelling. We can even imagine what camera angle would work best, when the musical score should swell, or what facial expressions the actors should convey.

Would you be surprised to learn that we find a similar theme in the way ancient believers read their Bibles? Obviously, they didn't have movies as the primary point of reference in entertainment, but they did have the theater. Now, plays in the ancient world had an element in the production that is not true of today's theater. In the ancient world, scripts didn't identify the speaker of dialogue. That sounds crazy but it's true.[14] When a producer would put on a play, he would interpret the script and identify what characters should say what lines. In most cases this is not a problem since the scene itself and the context make clear who should say what line, but there are occasions in which the creative team has to make a decision, which may affect how a scene is played out.

Ancient readers of the Bible brought this line of thinking with them when they approached Scripture. They interpreted the text and asked who might be saying this and when did they say it? They created theatrical backgrounds to particular biblical texts that imagined a verse being spoken by God or the Messiah, or the Holy Spirit.

This is exactly what we find when we approach Hebrews. Arthur never quotes the Old Testament as a written document like Paul uses "It is written." He always identifies his direct quotations of Scripture as being spoken. Using this form of interpretation, he paints a picture of a certain member of the Trinity speaking words within a particular setting.

For Arthur, the Bible is a script, and he is interpreting what characters are saying the lines. He then uses the results to make theological conclusions on the relationship within the Godhead. Arthur reads the Bible as an opportunity to eavesdrop on heaven and overhear God talking.[15] This might sound complicated, but trust me, it will make sense as we begin to apply it to the citations that fill up the rest of Chapter 1.

Before we can proceed though, we also have to look at the particular Bible being used by Arthur and his audience. They used a Bible that slightly differs from the text we open today. Typically, Old Testaments in modern English versions of the Bible are translated from Hebrew manuscripts, but that is not the case with Arthur. His Bible was a Greek translation of a Hebrew text which today is called the Septuagint.[16] It will be helpful to take a minute here and discuss this text before we proceed to Arthur's litany of quotations from it.

The name Septuagint comes from the Greek word for "Seventy" and for that reason is often abbreviated with the roman numerals LXX. The reason this translation is known as "The Seventy" is due to the interesting, yet entirely unlikely, legend of its origin. The story goes that in the third century BC, King Ptolemy of Egypt desired to place the Torah, the five books of Moses, into the famous Library of Alexandria. Since he was unable to read Hebrew, he ordered the production of a Greek translation. The task was undertaken by seventy Rabbis who worked the task completely independent of each other and after seventy days, each had completed an exactly identical translation.

This legend is certainly a fascinating story, but it's incredibly difficult to believe. However, the story does have some validity, and there are important points to consider before we dismiss it entirely. The first point is that no other story exists explaining how the Septuagint came into being. Second, the legend is supported as fact by many ancient sources including Josephus, the great Jewish historian of the first century A.D. and the early church father, Justin Martyr. Lastly, the legend itself references verifiable historical people, places, and events.[17]

Despite all this attestation and evidence, there is an easy explanation for why this story gained such widespread notoriety. The Septuagint was the only Bible available for the Greek-speaking population of the Jewish people. This first major translation of the Bible came at a key time in history when the Jewish people were spread across the world. They desired a story that gave validity to their text in the same way that the Hebrew Torah had divine approval as being delivered by God to Moses. This fable provided an inspirational confirmation that they were truly reading the authentic Word of God.

By the time we arrive at Arthur composing this letter, he was a part of a community that had used the Septuagint, in virtual exclusivity, for more than two hundred years! It was the text used in school; it was the Scripture they memorized at home; it was the version read at Synagogue each week. And it's how Arthur quotes the Bible throughout Hebrews.

So why does this matter? I wish I could tell you that the Septuagint, like the fable describes, is a perfect translation of the Hebrew Bible and that no differences exist in Septuagint manuscripts, but that is far from true. As we encounter quotations from the Old Testament, we will be confronted with the reality that the verses do not always match the text we open up to. There are many differences in word choices and indeed entire verses found in the Septuagint which are not found in our Hebrew-based Old Testaments. We will look at these distinctions more in depth as we reach relevant quotations. By and large, the Septuagint is a strong translation which deserved the acceptance it received by the early church of this period.

With that background on the method of interpretation employed by Arthur and the biblical text he used, we can proceed back to the remainder of Hebrews chapter 1.

1:5–14

*1:5*Did God ever say to an angel, "You are my Son; today I have crowned you king"? Or, "I will be his Father and he will be my Son"? *6*On the contrary, when he presents the Firstborn into the heavenly world,[18] he declares, "All of God's angels must worship him." *7*When talking about the angels, God says, "He turns his angels into the wind and his ministers into fire." *8*But he says to the Son, "God, your reign is forever and ever, and your rule is characterized by justice. *9*You value what is right instead of what is wrong,[19] and that's why God, your God, has crowned you Messiah with a joyous celebration rather than your partners." *10*He also says to the Son, "Lord, in the beginning you established the earth, and you made the sky with your hands. *11*They will both wear out like clothing and come to an end, but you will continue on. *12*You will wad them up like an old shirt, and just like clothes, they will be replaced[20] with something new. You, however, are the same, and your lifetime will never end." *13*Has God ever said to an angel, "Sit next to me until I pile your enemies under your feet"?

*14*Aren't the angels just ministering spirits sent to serve those who are about to receive salvation?

Arthur quickly turns to his Bible in order to justify the dramatic statements made about Jesus in the opening paragraph. In this paragraph he will quote seven texts, coming mostly from the Psalms.[21] He is continuing to move at breakneck speed, assuming you can keep pace with him as he works quickly to establish the biblical reality of the assertions he has made so far.

What is the point of the quotations though? Using this perspective of eavesdropping on heaven, Arthur is inviting us into a throne room scene in which Jesus is being coronated as king. Remember, part of the goal of this method of reading the Bible is not only to establish what character was saying the lines, but also what made them say it. Arthur compiles seven texts in which God is talking and interprets them as being spoken in relation to this celebratory coronation ceremony.[22] We will look at each verse individually to see how Arthur draws this context from the text itself.

Psalm 2:7 (Hebrews 1:5)

The first quotation is introduced with a rhetorical question, "Did God ever say to an angel?" Why angels? We remarked before about how the entrance of angels into the discussion seems out of nowhere. Arthur leaves this as a mystery for now, but he will answer that question in chapter 2. So, what is it that God has never said to an angel? "You are my Son; today I have crowned you king."[23]

If you are comparing my translation to others, you will quickly notice a key difference. Most translations render the second part of the sentence with something like, "Today I have begotten you." This is not a mistranslation on my part, but it is an attempt to prioritize the context. The original setting of Psalm 2 is that of a coronation of Israel's king. The words originally applied hyperbolically to a real human king over God's people. The king understands his role as being a representative of God to the people. In a way he becomes the son of God as part of this royal identification.[24] This is metaphorically true of Israel's historical kings, but it is literally true when talking about Jesus. After being raised from the dead and exalted to heaven, Jesus is invited by God to sit down on his throne and receive the nations as a heritage and the ends of the earth as a possession like Psalm 2 goes on to say. He is crowned king of the universe by God himself.

This is not meant in any way to nullify the church fathers' discussions on the eternal generation of the Son, but it is meant to honor the context of the Psalm. The Psalm is describing a royal coronation and that is how Arthur reads it.[25] These are the words of God to his Son as he crowns him king!

That does fit the scene Arthur is describing, but how did he know this was God talking? This question will be harder to answer in later quotations, but in this verse, we are explicitly told that it is God talking. Right before the text quoted, Psalm 2:7 says, "The Lord said."

2 Samuel 7:14 (Hebrews 1:5)

Arthur links the next quotation to the first as another thing God has not said to angels. The quotation comes from 2 Samuel 7:14 and is another verse connected to Israel's monarchy. This verse, also featuring the royal connection of a father-son relationship between God and king, is part of the oracle of the prophet Nathan to King David. God is prophesying about the future son of David who we now know as Solomon. Just like above though, what is metaphorically true about Solomon having a father-son relationship with God as part of his royal role, is literally true of Jesus. Arthur puts these words in the mouth of God at the throne room coronation of Jesus.

We also see something of Arthur's incredible knowledge of his Bible. Keep in mind that his Bible had no verse references, he had no concordances or search tools. He had to know these verses and connect them in his mind in order to draw out this interpretation. He does this consistently. All throughout his letter he links verses together through common words and contexts to draw out depths of meaning not apparent in the individual verses themselves. This passage also references the Exodus (2 Samuel 7:6), which will become a dominant theme in

Hebrews in chapter 3. Arthur's mastery of the Bible allows him to link these themes by weaving citations together.

Deuteronomy 32:43 LXX (Hebrews 1:6)

For the next quotations Arthur reveals his hand. He shows that this throne room scene is the setting of the Father's words. Arthur simply says, "when he presents the Firstborn into the heavenly world."[26] He makes clear he is inviting his original audience, as well as us, into this royal coronation ceremony in the heavenly world. But why does he call Jesus the Firstborn?

As we discussed above when talking about Jesus being the rightful owner of the universe, the role of heir in the ancient world did not take effect after the death of the father, but was a privileged position all throughout the life of the firstborn son. Arthur identifies that Jesus occupies this privileged position. But there are two more reasons why Arthur calls Jesus Firstborn.

1. This is a reference to the prophetic words of Psalm 89:27 (ESV), "And I will make him the firstborn, the highest of the kings of the earth." This allows Arthur the opportunity to allude to another Messianic Psalm reference. This Psalm also continues Arthur's trend of referencing topics he will cover later on which include Jesus being anointed (Messiah), resurrection from the dead, and an abiding covenant.

2. Arthur also means for us to make the logical deduction that if there is a "firstborn" there must be more born afterwards. We are those younger siblings in God's family. Our position may not be equivalent to the exalted status of "The Son," but I think it's pretty incredible that a nobody like me can be a part of God's family.

What is Arthur actually quoting here? This verse is the primary reason why I wanted to introduce the topic of the Septuagint. If you are reading a mainline version of the Bible, this verse won't be in there. It was found in Arthur's Bible in the Song of Moses and is Deuteronomy 32:43 in modern printings of the Septuagint.[27] Here it is compared:

Deuteronomy 32:43 ESV	Deuteronomy 32:43 LXX
Rejoice with him, O heavens; bow down to him, all gods, for he avenges the blood of his children and takes vengeance on his adversaries.	Heaven, you must rejoice with him and all of God's angels must worship him. Nations, you must rejoice with his people and all of God's children must strengthen themselves in him. This is because he will avenge the blood of his children and take vengeance on his enemies.

The Septuagint version of this text, that both Arthur and his audience read, contained this extra bit of text in which Arthur sees God addressing Jesus at this climactic throne room ceremony. But how does he know God said these lines? This is told to us in verse 37 of the LXX version, "The Lord says." Since the verse is understood as God talking, Arthur interprets that the only "him" that God could instruct angels to worship is the Son of God, Jesus. He aligns this verse with the preceding verses and identifies it as another thing God tells Jesus during this enthronement event. Note how the sentence above ends with a reference to Jesus' enemies. That is another example of Arthur's interconnected use of Scripture—this time a reference to the "enemies" which will also be mentioned in Psalm 110 below. It is probably also worth noting that this being the Song of Moses showcases the Exodus theme that was also a part of the greater context of 2 Samuel 7:14.

Psalm 104:4 (Hebrews 1:7)

Arthur switches gears now to highlight the contrast between Jesus in the role of Son and the angels in their divine service. He quotes Psalm 104:4 to accomplish this.[28] The first point to acknowledge is that this passage doesn't seem to indicate God is talking. Reading the context from verse 1, it seems to be nothing more than the prayer of the Psalmist.

Remember how I compared this method of looking for God talking to how we might imagine the Bible stories as movie scenes? Well, many interpreters were overzealous to find these occasions of God talking, and Arthur also shares that passion. Arthur notices the verbal shift from "you" to "he" and uses that transition to see that a new speaker, God, has begun talking.[29] He sees the Psalmist relinquish center-stage and turn the spotlight to God. See how it works:

Psalm 104:1–4 ESV	
Bless the LORD, O my soul! O LORD my God, you are very great! You are clothed with splendor and majesty, covering yourself with light as with a garment, stretching out the heavens like a tent.	The psalmist's prayer referencing God as "you."
He lays the beams of his chambers on the waters; he makes the clouds his chariot; he rides on the wings of the wind; he makes his messengers winds, his ministers a flaming fire.	God's response to the psalmist referencing a third character (Jesus) as "he."

That answers how Arthur interprets these verses as God talking about Jesus, but what do they mean? What does it mean that Jesus turns the angels into wind and fire? Arthur's interpretation works best with the Septuagint. In the original Hebrew, and translations based upon it (like the ESV above), the verse is saying that Jesus (or God) has power over the elements to the degree that the wind can be used as his messenger and fire as his servant. But the word order in the Septuagint makes it easier to understand it as talking about the angels rather than a nondescript messenger. This would then yield the meaning that Jesus has the power to turn the angels into wind and fire. It implies the angels are transient in their form and that they are subject to the authority of God's Son.[30]

Would it surprise you that this verse also connects to the Exodus? This will become an important theme in Hebrews, and Arthur is wasting no time alluding to its arrival. What is the connection? Arthur is going to identify that angels were present at the Mount Sinai event, and he sees in Deuteronomy a hint that they appeared there in the form of fire. The Lord came "from the ten thousands of holy ones, with flaming fire at his right hand" (Deuteronomy 33:2 ESV).

Psalm 45:6–7 (Hebrews 1:8–9)

The next two citations are introduced again as direct dialogue from God to the Son. In the first one he speaks the words of Psalm 45:6–7. Just like Psalm 104, Arthur detects God speaking by the verbal change that occurs after verse 1. The shift from "I address my verses to the king" in Psalm 45:1 (ESV), to "You are" in verse 2 signals to Arthur that a new speaker emerges. We are now eavesdropping on God talking to the Son.

Just like in Psalm 2 and 2 Samuel 7, this psalm is a royal psalm about a human king of Israel, and the language that is hyperbolically true of the ancient kings is literally true of Jesus. The most notable of these hyperboles is God calling the king, "God." When referring to the human king, it is a term of exaltation, not an ascription of divine status, but with Jesus it is literal. As the second person of the Trinity, he can correctly be called, God. This is the only occasion in which the title God will be applied to Jesus in Hebrews and one of the only occasions in the entire New Testament. The rarity doesn't make it any less true, it only points to the fact that God is most commonly used to reference God the Father rather than any other person of the Trinity.

The divine identity of Jesus is not the primary reason for the quotation though. Arthur wants to demonstrate the eternal nature of Jesus' reign. This coronation scene is one that will never be repeated. Jesus is being made king permanently and his reign will never come to an end. We can be confident that Jesus' reign will bring about true justice, not the off-brand version that was peddled in the Roman world surrounding the original audience or that surrounds us in our world today.

Arthur continues the quotation to identify the Son as also being the Messiah. Other translations typically use the word "anointed." In the Old Testament kings were anointed with fine oils as part of their coronation ceremony. This verse is describing the same occasion for Jesus, but he is not just another anointed one, he is *the* Anointed One, the Messiah (the title Messiah, means the anointed one). God is putting his personal seal of approval on Jesus as King and Messiah for God's people. The quotation goes on to say that God has made Jesus the Messiah instead of any of his partners. Who are his partners? This is another question Arthur invites us to ponder, which will we come back to when we look at Hebrews 3.

Psalm 102:25–27 (Hebrews 1:10–12)

Arthur pairs the use of Psalm 45 with a quotation of Psalm 102:25–27. This is another text where it is hard for us to detect how Arthur interprets God as the speaker of these verses. Unlike in the prior verses, a verbal shift is not the answer. The Septuagint has a different translation of the original Hebrew in verse 23 than our modern English versions have.

Psalm 102:23 ESV	Psalm 102:23 LXX
He has broken my strength in midcourse;	He answered him in the way of his strength,

In our versions of the Psalm, the psalmist is still speaking in verse 23, but in the Septuagint version, it comments that God is going to answer him. Arthur (and his audience) would have then understood the following verses to be God talking. And does ever he have something to say! Not only does God refer to Jesus as Lord, he also tells us that Jesus was involved in the very creation act at the beginning of time. He then goes on to say that Jesus will live forever. Unlike the present creation which is subject to decay and death, Jesus's lifetime will never end.

Psalm 110:1 (Hebrews 1:13)

Arthur introduces his next quotation with the same rhetorical question that he used in verse 5. He is about to tell us something God would never say to an angel. These words can only be true of Jesus. Arthur ends his round of quotations with Psalm 110. As many have noted, Psalm 110 is absolutely central to Hebrews. It is hard to overemphasize how critical a piece it plays in his understanding of Jesus and our relationship to him. For now, he just quotes verse 1, but he will go on to include verse 4 later in the letter. Verse 1 tells us, "Sit next to me until I pile your enemies under your feet."

The verse is easily identified as the direct speech of God by looking at the text that immediately precedes the quoted portion, "The Lord said to my Lord." This Psalm of David easily ensnares the attention as much now as it did when David originally wrote it. This Psalm is the most quoted text in the New Testament, and that probably goes back to Jesus' use of it in his ministry:

> "Now while the Pharisees were gathered together, Jesus asked them a question, saying, 'What do you think about the Christ? Whose son is he?' They said to him, 'The son of David.' He said to them, 'How is it then that David, in the Spirit, calls him Lord, saying, "'The Lord said to my Lord, "Sit at my right hand, until I put your enemies under your feet"'? If then David calls him Lord, how is he his son?' And no one was able to answer him a word, nor from that day did anyone dare to ask him any more questions" (Matthew 22:41–46 ESV).

I mentioned earlier how remarkable it is to think that Jesus is sitting down next to God, but it is worth mentioning again. Jesus is sitting on the throne of God. This fact will play into how Arthur understands our relationship to God, but for now he uses this verse to close out the throne room scene. Jesus has taken his seat on the throne next to God— a seat no angel and no other man has ever been invited to sit on.

Arthur finishes this paragraph with a thesis statement. The angels are "ministering spirits sent to serve." This language recalls his use of Psalm 104. The word translated "wind" there is also the same word translated "spirit" here, and the word translated "serve" here is a synonym for the word translated "ministering" there. The angels' role is a far cry from the prestigious and honorific role occupied by the Son. They are servants, but he is king. But is it curious that the angels serve "those who are about to receive salvation"? I mean, haven't we already been saved? Don't we possess salvation as a present reality? This is another puzzling remark that we will unpuzzle as we continue on.

THE GREAT SALVATION: 2:1–4

*2:1*This is why we must really pay attention to what we have heard so that we don't get distracted. *2*After all, if the message God spoke through the angels became binding so that every violation received a rightful punishment, *3*how will we escape punishment if we disregard such a great salvation? God initially spoke of this salvation through the Lord which was confirmed for us by those who had heard him. *4*God verified their testimony with many powerful miracles and by distributing the Holy Spirit just like he wanted.

Arthur spent fourteen verses in chapter 1 building rapport with the audience by acknowledging their shared appreciation of the Son, but he cashes all of that in as he transitions to chapter 2. He grinds the gears as he rapidly and unexpectedly transitions from the celestial throne room coronation to an abrupt challenge: "This is why we must really pay attention to what we have heard so that we don't get distracted."

Some translations choose to render the warning as "drift away" rather than "get distracted." It is possible that Arthur intended a metaphor of a boat slipping away from the shore, but it is more likely that he used the underlying Greek word as a reference to Proverbs 3:21 LXX, "My son, don't get distracted. Instead focus on my counsel."

Remember, Arthur and the audience likely have a different perspective on their circumstances. They see themselves taking a short break, holding back for a little while, but he sees them drifting backward into distractions. This dissonance between their two perspectives best overlaps in this warning. All of the other warnings in Hebrews are immediately followed by comforting words from Arthur; he feels the threat doesn't readily apply to them. But he doesn't do that here. This is indicative of where they really are spiritually. Perhaps they would even concede that they have become distracted. They have been distracted by fear of what it means to follow Jesus when the world around them is inflicting pain. Their focus has shifted from their heavenly Lord, and they have become distracted with their earthly circumstances.

This is a very telling reminder for us too. Even without the present situation of our world, we have no end to the number of distractions that grasp our attention. Unlike no generation before us, we are bombarded with interruptions, I mean *notifications*, that prevent us from deeply focusing on anything for more than just a few minutes. We are always connected, but what are we *connected* to? This book is a direct result of God convicting me to divert my attention away from distractions. In fact, this book would have never been a reality had I not deleted my YouTube account and sold my Nintendo Switch.

Why is it that we have to really pay attention to the message we have heard? Arthur answers that question by also answering why he chose to compare Jesus to the angels in chapter 1. They both bore a message from God to his people. The message from the angels is the Law of Moses, the first five books of the Bible. Deuteronomy 33:2 (quoted earlier) formed the scriptural basis for the understanding that the angels served as the intermediary between God and Moses when the Torah was delivered. This vague allusion in Deuteronomy was fleshed out into a full-fledged tradition by the time of the apostles. It is mentioned by Paul in Galatians and most notably by Stephen in the book of Acts. When talking about Moses, Stephen tells us, "This is the one who was in the congregation in the wilderness with the angel who spoke to him at Mount Sinai" (Acts 7:38 ESV).

Arthur uses this fact to express the severity and urgency of earnestly paying attention to the message from God presented in his Son. If the role Jesus occupies is altogether superior to the role of the angels, then the message of Jesus must be altogether more important than the message of the angels. This fact comes with a warning label. If disobeying the message from the angels brought punishment, then a more severe punishment must await those who disregard the saving message of Jesus.

The next sentence of the paragraph goes on to summarize how this critical message reached Arthur and the audience. God gave the message through the Lord (Jesus) and it was later communicated to the audience through his eyewitnesses, most likely referring to the apostles. Arthur positions himself along with the audience as second-hand believers who didn't know Jesus personally. They may not have had the benefit of knowing Jesus personally during his time on earth, but they did witness powerful miracles during the ministry of the apostles, which they understood as God authenticating their witness.[31]

He then identifies that God further supported the message of Jesus by "distributing the Holy Spirit." Some translations understand this as a reference to the gifts of the Holy Spirit, but it is more likely that he is talking about the gift of the Spirit himself.[32] This is not to discount that the Spirit bestows gifts, but to connect Arthur's words here with Old Testament prophecy. Joel tells us that, "It shall come to pass afterward, that I will pour out my Spirit on all flesh" (Joel 2:28 ESV). Arthur sees the beginnings of fulfillment taking place with the gift of God's Spirit upon the church.

Arthur doesn't just tell us that God distributed the Holy Spirit though. He says that he did it "just like he wanted." Modern English versions typically translate this as "according to his will." This traditional translation sometimes pushes our minds towards understanding "God's will" as an impenetrable matter. The Greek word has the simpler meaning of "what he wants." God wanted to distribute the Holy Spirit. He wanted his people to be quickened with the life of the third person of the Trinity, just like he said above in the prophetic words of Joel.[33]

What is this message that God spoke in his Son? It probably is not a literal teaching from Jesus we find in the Gospels. Every time Arthur quotes Jesus in Hebrews, he quotes him saying text from the Old Testament. The message then is not likely any direct dialogue we can find, but the cumulative scope of his entire earthly (and now heavenly) activity. God spoke to us through Jesus, not just through his impactful teaching, but primarily through his actions. Through Jesus' life, death on the cross, burial, resurrection, ascension, and enthronement, God has preached the message of the new covenant to us. This message is simply too important to devalue it with distractions. We must pay attention to what God is saying in his Son.

JESUS & ANGELS REDUX: 2:5–9

2:5Now we are talking about the future world, which God did not subject to angels. 6On the contrary, one of them declared somewhere, "Why do you think about man and why do you care about the son of man? [7]You ranked him lower than the angels for a little while; you crowned him with nobility, [8]and you subjected everything under his feet." Now when it says he subjected everything to him, it means he left nothing unsubjected to him. But for right now, we don't see everything as being subjected to him. [9]However, we do see Jesus, the one who was ranked lower than the angels for a little while because he suffered death and who is now crowned with nobility so that he could experience death[34] for everyone as an expression of God's grace.

With the comparison of the message from Jesus and the message from angels now resolved, it would seem that Arthur should move on from this topic to the next covenant comparison, but that doesn't happen until chapter 3 with the entry of Moses into the conversation. Why does Arthur continue to dwell on the topic of angels?

Remember from the introduction how we talked about the purpose of Hebrews? Arthur's two primary goals in his writing are:

1. to demonstrate that the new covenant is superior to the old and thus worthy of greater attention and faithfulness and
2. to showcase that the new covenant offers greater access to God to enable faithfulness in the midst of persecution and difficulties.

Both of these goals are on full display in Chapter 2. The first one was in focus in 2:1–4, and the second one enters into focus now. Let's look at what he has to say so that we'll connect the dots before the chapter is through.

Arthur acknowledges he is talking about the "future world." This future world of 2:5 is the same as the heavenly world of 1:6 where Jesus has been crowned king. For us it's a future reality awaiting fulfillment, but for Jesus it is a present reality. There is a mingling of time and space where what will be true for us in the future, Jesus sitting on the throne, is true in heaven now. Comprehending a God who transcends space and time can be confusing. We can understand a good deal though, so let's look closely at what Arthur tells us.

When Arthur says that the future world has not been subjected to angels, he implies that the current world is subject to angels. This was commonly held in the Jewish world of Arthur's day, and it is based on LXX version of Deuteronomy 32:8. "When the Most High divided the nations, when he separated the sons of Adam, he set the borders of the nations based on the number of God's angels." Remember when we discussed the universe in 1:2? There we talked about how time and space would be important topics for Arthur. For ease of presentation, we can look at time and space graphically with space on the horizontal axis and time on the vertical axis. Keep this in mind as we will return to it throughout this book.

Time/Space	Earth	Heaven
Present	Subject to angels	Subject to the Son
Future	Subject to the Son	Subject to the Son

Arthur progresses to quote the Bible to prove his point and continue his discussion about the angels. Again, he quotes the Bible as a spoken document. Remember our discussion of eavesdropping on heaven from Arthur's quotations in chapter 1? Are you ready to let it get more complicated? Remember how we compared this approach to reading the Bible to an imaginative movie scene? Well Arthur has the same scenic goal in mind. Chapter 2 now presents the responses of the characters involved to what God has said. He expands the cast of characters and offers them the spotlight. He is continuing this throne room scene but now turning the focus to the angels and Jesus for their dialogue.

He lets the angels go first and they proclaim the words of Psalm 8 at this coronation event.[35] This is not only a response to what God said about them, but also an appropriate exclamation as they watch Jesus take his seat on God's throne.

God about the angels	An angel's response
All of God's angels must worship him.	Why do you think about man and why do you care about the son of man?

In its original context Psalm 8 is probably about the general role of humanity over creation, but placed in the mouth of an angel at the coronation of Jesus it becomes a summary for his past, present, and future. The angel tells us three things about Jesus:

1. He was temporarily ranked lower than angels
2. He is crowned with nobility
3. Everything is subjected under his feet

Arthur finds in this Psalm an encapsulation for the entire Jesus story.[36] But there is one point of tension he wants us to notice. He reveals this tension when he says that "everything" means "everything" in 2:8. Do you see the problem this poses with what was said about Jesus in chapter 1? How can everything be subjected to Jesus as Psalm 8 says, if Psalm 110 says that everything is being subjected to him?

Psalm 110	Psalm 8
Sit next to me until I pile your enemies under your feet.	You subjected everything under his feet.

How can everything be subjected under Jesus' feet if God is in process of subjecting his enemies right now? Arthur answers us straightaway. "We do see Jesus, the one who was ranked lower than the angels for a little while." Arthur means to tell us that only the first two statements of Psalm 8 have actually transpired. Jesus was ranked lower than angels when he suffered and died and he is now crowned with nobility as he sits next to God on his throne, but everything is not yet subjected to him. This is a promise yet to come. Right now, we are in the "Today" of Psalm 2, not in the future of Psalm 8.

Let's examine this graphically to make the point clearer:

Past	Present	Future
Cross	**Today**	**Future World**
Jesus lower than the angels	Jesus crowned with nobility, waiting until his enemies are under his feet	Everything subjected to Jesus

Arthur read his Bible extremely closely to reach conclusions like this. The word order and tenses of the verb play into his discussion. Why does this matter though? Why does this interesting interplay between Psalms and the chronology it weaves make a difference any more than academically? It matters a great deal. We are invited to serve Jesus, not in a world that has already been subjected to him, but one in which his enemies still roam. We can't expect easy street knowing that the process of this submission is not complete. Arthur is both challenging and encouraging his audience. He shows tough love in challenging them to buck up and accept that it costs something to follow Jesus, and we don't get to set the price. But he encourages them (and us) with the reminder that this "today" won't last forever. Jesus is sitting next to God *until* he piles all of his enemies under his feet. We live in a world still full of Jesus' enemies. Cancer, hate, depression, murder, persecution, abortion, idolatry, tyranny, and the like are still a present reality, but not for long. God has promised there will be a day when all of the enemies are slaughtered and their dead bodies are piled in a heap at Jesus' feet. This is perhaps a more violent reading of Hebrews than you have heard before, but this is the future that awaits God's enemies. It is the future Arthur desperately wants to ensure doesn't await his audience.

Arthur concludes this paragraph with a short, but impactful, summary of what we hear God preach in the cross. In the cross we hear God's grace, we see God's love for us—and for everyone—on full display. But as we have come to expect from Arthur, he doesn't linger here. He presses on to the next thing he wants to say.

2:10–13

*2:10*Now God is the source and goal of the universe so it makes sense for him to qualify the pioneer of their salvation through suffering, ultimately leading many sons and daughters to nobility. *11*After all, the one who makes holy and those being made holy all come from a single ancestor, which is why he is not ashamed to call them his brothers and sisters. *12*He says, "I will proclaim[37] your name to my brothers and sisters and praise you in the middle of the family gathering."[38] *13*He also says, "I will depend on God." He then goes on to say, "I am here with the children God has entrusted to me."

The next paragraph opens with another thesis statement. Arthur tells us that God has qualified the pioneer of our salvation through suffering. A remarkable statement, but he doesn't stop at that. He adds that this qualification process results in many sons and daughters being led to nobility. Let's unpack these two in order.

What in the world does it mean that God has qualified him with suffering? And why is Jesus called the pioneer of their salvation? Modern English versions typically use "perfected" rather than qualified, but qualified is more in line with the sense being conveyed here. The underlying meaning of the Greek word is bringing something to a goal or destination. When referring to Jesus it speaks of his qualification to occupy the role of Son that God has appointed him to. Jesus as our representative (and high priest as we will see in the next paragraph) became qualified for this role through his loving and self-sacrificing actions on the cross. This willingness to suffer and die for humanity has qualified Jesus to serve in a role no one else is qualified to perform. I purposefully overlooked the first words of this paragraph, "God is the source and goal of the universe." The connection of God being the source and goal of the universe and his actions qualifying Jesus with suffering are designed to create conflict in the rational mind. It wouldn't make sense to us to choose a path of suffering if one could be avoided, but this is a stark reminder that God's thoughts are above ours.

Why is Jesus called the pioneer of salvation? This will be the first of many times Arthur invites us to see Jesus as experiencing the salvation that awaits us as God's sons and daughters. Jesus of course doesn't need to be saved from sin like we do, but his journey mirrors the future that we face. We will arrive where he is; we will spend eternity with God just like Jesus. Jesus experiences our future in his present. More than just a pioneer though, Jesus is a trailblazer. He has opened the path that makes it possible for us to follow him. Salvation is thus equated with nobility. Other translations use "glory" here, which makes it easy to see heaven as the reference, but more is meant than just heaven. We are being led to our heavenly home, but Arthur is pointing back to Psalm 8. Jesus is not going to rule the future world in isolation; he invites us to this nobility as well.

Arthur goes on to restate his thesis from above. So he can be doubly sure you understand what he means, he restates it with different words. He tells us that the one who makes us holy (Jesus) shares the same ancestor as those who are being made holy (us), which means he is obliged to call us his siblings. I do like the present implications of this restatement though. In the original thesis he uses salvation and nobility which are future oriented, but here he says we are "being made holy," we are in process of becoming holy. The full reality of being saved lies in the future, but as God transforms us in holiness now, we see the beginning points of being made ready for it.

This process of being made holy, being fit for service, being qualified for nobility, fits with the meaning of Psalm 110 too. Jesus is sitting next to God *until* his enemies are piled under his feet. We participate in this process of putting his enemies under his feet as we progress in our journey to holiness. When we conquer the enemies of lust, greed, selfishness, and hate in our lives, we add to the pile. We slay an enemy that gets laid at Jesus' feet. Psalm 110 is not just the demonstration of the present, nor just a promise of future fulfillment; it's a challenge to become warriors of holiness, ultimately fit for nobility in the future world.

Before we go on to the quotations Arthur will levy in support of his twofold thesis statement, we must ask who is this ancestor that we all share? It is without question Abraham. We can be certain of this because Arthur calls believers the "descendants of Abraham" in the next paragraph showing he has Abraham on his mind. Later on, he will call

Abraham "the one" (11:12), which is the same word translated as "single" here. While it could be argued Adam is a more logical selection since he is truly the ancestor of all humanity, all humanity is not what Arthur means. Here he is referring to the family of the faithful, God's sons and daughters. Abraham, as Paul concludes as well, is the father of not only all Israel, but faithful Gentiles too.

We can now progress to the Old Testament quotations Arthur uses to prove his thesis. He quotes three verses that are collectively designed to accomplish three purposes:

1. Serve as Jesus' responses to what God said to him in Chapter 1[39]
2. Prove that Jesus identifies God's people as his siblings
3. Prove that these siblings are being led to nobility

We will highlight each individual quotation and how it contributes to these purposes, but let's first look at how each statement aligns to the prior statements from God.

God to the Son	The Son's response
You are my Son; today I have crowned you king... I will be his Father.	I will proclaim your name to my brothers and sisters.
God, your reign is forever and ever... Lord, in the beginning you established the earth.	I will depend on God.
Sit next to me until I pile your enemies under your feet.	I am here with the children God has entrusted to me.

Psalm 22:22 (Hebrews 2:12)

The first thing we hear Jesus say in Hebrews is a quotation from Psalm 22. Most of us are familiar with this Psalm from its haunting opening, "My God, my God, why have you forsaken me?" (Psalm 22:1 ESV). This opening verse is spoken by Jesus during the crucifixion in the Gospel accounts, but Arthur quotes further down in the Psalm.

Based on its use in the Gospels, it is safe to understand these words as being spoken by our Lord, but how do we know they were spoken at the enthronement? The first half of the Psalm is a highly detailed description of the suffering he experienced, but in verse 22 the tone of the Psalm radically changes. Instead of recounting the horrors of the cross or crying out for deliverance, the promise of praise is uttered. Arthur understood this shift from a negative to a positive tone to indicate that God's deliverance occurred in between these two verses.

Psalm 22 LXX	
22:21, "Save me ..."	Jesus' prayer for God's intervention
In-between verse 21 and 22	God intervenes and raises Jesus from the dead, exalts him to heaven, and crowns him king.
22:22, "I will proclaim your name to my brothers and sisters"	Jesus' promise to praise God for his intervention and enthronement

What are we supposed to take away from this text? First it is a clear occasion in which Jesus refers to his "brothers and sisters," so that solidifies Arthur's point that we are in the family of God. But how does it function as a response from the Son back to the Father?

When Jesus assumes his role as Son and king, Jesus responds to his Father with words of praise. He promises to praise God's name in recognition of receiving this universal rule. But why does it say, "will"? Why does Jesus say that he *will* praise God, why doesn't he do it right away? Jesus' promise is to praise God to us. He wants us to hear his song of worship to God, but we aren't there. That is, we aren't there *yet*. This verse is how Arthur can conclude that God is leading *many* sons and daughters to nobility.

Since these words were spoken by Jesus *after* the crucifixion, he logically infers that there has to be a time when we are with Jesus in order to hear him sing this song. This is another example in which Arthur uses the smallest of details from his Bible to reach massive conclusions for us.[40]

. . .

2 Samuel 22:3 / Isaiah 8:17 / Isaiah 12:2 (Hebrews 2:13)

The next quotation, "I will depend on God," is harder to pinpoint because these Greek words occur in three different places in Arthur's Bible. Before we look at these texts, we can answer how this exclamation from the mouth of our Lord functions as a response to his Father.

According to Arthur's presentation of this throne-room scene, God tells Jesus that his reign and life are to last forever. Jesus, hearing these words, responds back to God with his promise to depend on God in his performance of these duties. The humility of Jesus is on full display, which also reminds us that Jesus, despite being exalted to heaven, is still a biological person. He is in a resurrected body, but it is a human body nonetheless. Jesus takes this opportunity to promise God he will look to him as he oversees the governance of the universe. This also continues proving Arthur's point that Jesus is our elder brother. It is only in his humanity that he identifies his trust and dependence on God[41] (it is certainly not in his deity that he needs to do this) so this continues proving that Jesus can accurately call us his siblings.

How does Arthur assign these Old Testament words to Jesus at the coronation ceremony? This question is harder to answer since any of the above three texts could be the one Arthur is referencing. In 2 Samuel, David is praising God with a song after delivering him from Saul. In Isaiah 8:17, the prophet calls God's people to perseverance while they wait for God's promised salvation. In Isaiah 12:2, he declares words that will be proclaimed upon God's final salvation. Which one is it? Yes. Arthur has purposely quoted this text in a way that allows it to be any one of these. Just like if I told you a Star Wars quotation, "I have a bad feeling about this." This single line occurs in all of the original trilogy movies, and any astute fan would quickly realize I cited a line that comes from each movie. Arthur, to the same effect, quotes words that bring all three contexts to mind in a way that referencing just one of them could not do.

Isaiah 8:18 (Hebrews 2:13)

Arthur then goes on to quote Isaiah 8:18, an easy connection to make from the immediate context of Isaiah 8:17 above. It is easy to understand Jesus as the speaker of these words due to the enigmatic introduction found in the LXX, "One will say." Similar to the citation of Psalm 22, the use of "children" creates the family connection that Jesus shares with us. As in Psalm 22 above, the declaration that Jesus is "here with" them implies that there has to be a future occasion in which he will be with him.

Furthermore, this quotation works as a response to God's invitation for Jesus to take his seat. Jesus responds back to God with the certainty that others will join him in this rule. Just like he says in Revelation:

"I will grant him to sit with me on my throne, as I also conquered and sat down with my Father on his throne" (Revelation 3:21 ESV).

All three of these quotations are initially introduced with the remark that Jesus is not ashamed to call us his brothers and sisters. This is an example of litotes, using a double negative to express a strongly positive statement. This technique is found in English today but is not as widely used as in ancient rhetoric. The thought being expressed is more than just not being ashamed, it is that he "is proud to call us brothers and sisters." However, I have chosen to preserve the litotes since the word choice is intentional. Arthur is subtly hinting that his audience is ashamed to call Jesus their brother. By their willingness to pull back from public recognition of Jesus, they have, perhaps inadvertently, indicated they are ashamed of their faith. Arthur's skillful use of shame here chides them to rethink this course of action and proudly identify with Jesus who has willingly identified himself with them.[42]

2:14–18

[2:14]So, given that the children are composed of flesh and blood, he took on the exact same condition.[43] He did this so that, by dying, he could disarm the devil, who has the power of death, [15]and liberate everyone who was enslaved to the fear of death throughout their lives. [16]After all, it's obviously not angels that he helps, quite the contrary, he helps the descendants of Abraham.[44] [17]This being the case, he had to become exactly like his brothers and sisters so that he could become a merciful and faithful high priest[45] to make atonement for the sins of the people in the service of God. [18]Now he is able to help those in the midst of temptation because he was tempted[46] when he suffered.

Hebrews goes on to describe this family connection between Jesus and us more clearly. Using the term "children" from Isaiah 8:18, he makes an obvious deduction: Jesus can't be a part of our family if he isn't flesh and blood. He also can't redeem the family if he isn't flesh and blood. Jesus joined the human family at the incarnation to fulfill this mission. He was born to die. But by his death he disarmed the devil. This term "disarm" is key. Some translations use destroy; while it is accurate to say that Jesus' death will ultimately destroy the devil, it isn't true yet. For now, his power is abated, his main weapon has been taken from him. He can no longer swing the sword of death against the church. Because of Jesus' death, we will rise again—the devil has been disarmed.

This is excellent theology, but also practical advice. He is reminding his audience in the midst of persecution and pain that their enemies, Jesus' enemies, can't keep them down. There is no reason to fear death because our Savior has already conquered death. He offers liberation from the fear of death so we can serve him, even if it costs us our lives.

Arthur then makes a summary statement that resolves this discussion of the angels. Jesus is here, not to help the angels, but to help God's people. He was born to die, but he died to live. He now lives in heaven and serves as our high priest. His life and death qualified him for this high priestly role in a way that proves his faithful and merciful character. Arthur subtly mentions the atonement again, but this time with slightly more detail than the prior "purifying our sins" in 1:3. He now connects the dot of Jesus' death to this purification of sins, but he leaves this as a central topic for later in the letter.

Chapter 2 concludes with a perfect reminder for those in the midst of life's hardships. Jesus can help. Since he experienced pain, suffering, temptation, and death, he is fully equipped to help us through our challenges in life. This is the power of the New Covenant priesthood. Jesus sits next to the Father and serves as High Priest on our behalf. Arthur is doing more than just academically comparing covenants, he is offering hope to his audience. They have access to God that was never true in the

Old Testament period. As long as Jesus is on the throne, we have all that we need to endure hardship and persevere through pain. This may not make a good Hallmark card, but far more beneficial is the knowledge that there is nothing we can experience in life that Jesus is not infinitely qualified to help us through.

PIECE OF MIND

1. There are a variety of ways to structure Hebrews; different methodologies yield different results. For the purpose of this commentary, the structure has been developed from the perspective of the audience. I conducted several uninterrupted readings of Hebrews looking for transitions in topic, theme, or tone that would be immediately perceptible to a listening audience. The structure used in this commentary is based on that research.

2. A literal translation would be "In many parts and in many ways." Throughout Hebrews, Arthur uses nearly synonymous terms together for poetic and rhetorical effect. Since a distinction in meaning is not intended, the translation in this book will routinely leverage a single English word when this technique is present in the Greek text.

3. Arthur pulls the wording "purifying sins" in 1:3 from Exodus 30:10. This passage in Exodus is referring to the Day of Atonement which will feature prominently in the letter later on.

4. Arthur uses Majesty as a name for God. He found this title in his Bible at Deuteronomy 32:3 and 2 Samuel 7:21, both of which he cites in chapter 1.

5. Here Arthur uses a distinct word for "heaven." It literally means "on high," and is pulled from Psalm 113:4.

6. Arthur uses a long sentence in 1:1–4 to grip the audience's attention and set the tone for the highly technical letter that awaits them. He will reuse this technique again in 2:2–4, 3:12–15, 4:12–13, 5:1–3, and others.

7. Modern English versions typically translate the phrase in 1:2 as "these last days" rather than "the end of these days." The literal is to be preferred since it will feature into Arthur's theology later in the letter. For reference that this is the literal translation, see Attridge 35.

8. Madison Pierce, one of my favorite Hebrews scholars, has a great video on why "but" should not be included in Hebrews 1:1-2. https://www.youtube.com/watch?v=-kIE-IkL2io.

9. The decision to translate the literal Greek "worlds" as "universe" is due in part to this being the standard English translation used in Jewish prayers as well. The plural points to the fact that God, through Jesus, created two worlds and two times. He created an earthly world and a heavenly world and a present time and a future time. Arthur will expand on this concept throughout his letter.

10. The assessment that God doesn't have a right hand or a right side is based on passages like John 4:24, Colossians 1:15, and 1 Timothy 1:17 among others. The issue is complicated by other passages that do speak of God using anthropomorphic language (as in Exodus 24:10, Deuteronomy 33:27, and Isaiah 59:1). For our purposes in

Hebrews, God's right hand represents the prestigious place of authority where only Jesus is qualified to dwell.

11. Technically Arthur doesn't compare the name of the angels to the name of the Son as the translation indicates. The Greek text compares the name of Jesus to the angels *themselves*. This technique serves to heighten the value of Jesus. Just the name of the Son is superior to all of the angels! Arthur will use this technique again later on in Hebrews.

12. For the use of "role" as the translation of the term customarily translated as "name," see BDAG 714. One of the definitions for "name" is "office." This category of meaning led to the translation "role."

13. For the understanding that the name Jesus received is "Son," see Lane 1:25, "The writer now identifies that name ... as 'my Son.'"

14. For the assessment that ancient scripts lacked dialogue identification, see Pierce 6–8. Actually, just read her whole book; it's an excellent resource!

15. The technical name for eavesdropping on Heaven is Prosopological Exegesis. This comes from the Greek word for 'person' and highlights the need for interpreters to see what person or character a particular line of text is being spoken by. Eavesdropping is somewhat misleading since God intends for us to hear his revelation, but it conveys the thematic sense of us *overhearing* God talking in Heaven. There are two great works on Prosopological exegesis that I strongly recommend: *Divine Discourse in the Epistle to the Hebrews* by Madison Pierce and *The Birth of the Trinity* by Matthew Bates.

16. The Greek Bible used by Arthur will always be referred to as the Septuagint (LXX) in this book, though it is not the most accurate name for this text. It would be more accurately identified as "Old Greek." For ease of reference and alignment with the title used by modern scholarly resources, the name Septuagint is applied throughout this book. For those who intend to look up these verses in a Septuagint version of the Old Testament, note that the Psalms are numbered differently than our book of Psalms. In the LXX, Psalm 1 and 2 are combined into one which throws off the numbering of the entire Psalter (thus making Psalm 110 Psalm 109). For ease of reference, the standard numbering found in modern English versions is used throughout this book for both chapter and verse references to the Septuagint text.

17. The origin of the Septuagint is reported as fact in the ancient Letter of Aristeas (estimated to 150–100 BC), Josephus (Book 12 of his *Jewish Antiquities*), and Justin Martyr (1 Apology 31).

18. The literal Greek is simply an inhabited world. This has led some to see 1:6 as a reference to the incarnation, but it is best to see it as a reference to Jesus' exaltation. The same word occurs in 2:5, and in that case, it definitively refers to the future (or heavenly) world. Exodus 16:35 LXX also uses the word for the Promised Land. Later on, Arthur will conflate this heavenly world with the land promised to the patriarchs. The word has the meaning of "heavenly world" in Psalm 96:10 and Arthur will allude to this Psalm later in the letter.

19. The literal Greek is "You love what is right and hate what is wrong." The decision not to translate the literal terms "love" and "hate" was motivated by the fact that people are not the object described. In Jesus' kingly role, the Psalmist is telling us that he values justice. The English word "love," with its more sentimental meaning, is less conducive to this specific context.

20. In his quotation of Psalm 102 Arthur actually changes one word from his Bible to another (for those interested, he changes ἀλλάξεις into ἑλίξεις). This is done to incorporate yet another scriptural reference into his text. The words are essentially synonymous in meaning, but by changing it, he can import the context of Isaiah 34:4 into the

discussion. This is yet another way Arthur evidences his genius-level knowledge and handling of the biblical texts.

21. Arthur will routinely quote the Psalms throughout his letter. He quotes from them seven times in the first section alone. He is not unique in this, as Psalms is the most frequently cited book in the New Testament. The compressed and poetic language of the Psalms allowed it to function as a theology textbook for the early church.

22. See Harris 24: "The author of Hebrews understands the fulfillment of these OT prophecies to have occurred at the Son's exaltation."

23. Collectively angels are sometimes referred to as the "sons of God." This occurs most notably in Job. That is another reason it is helpful to translate 1:4 with "role" instead of "name." Jesus doesn't just bear the title "Son;" he occupies the role of "Son." This also helps support later statements in Hebrews that Jesus was God's Son before his enthronement. He has always been God's Son in a trinitarian way, but he is only now God's Son in the eschatological role prophesied throughout the Old Testament.

24. For a helpful summarization of the relationship between sonship and kingship in ancient Israel found in the Psalter, see Attridge 53–54.

25. See Bruce 54. This is not intended in any way to discount the work of the early church fathers to understand the "eternal generation of the Son" or "begotten not created." These Christian forbears were dedicated to the terminology employed in their Bibles to explain the concept of the Trinity and the relationship of the Son to the Father.

26. "When he presents the Firstborn into the heavenly world" parallels Deuteronomy 6:10 LXX (in addition to referencing Psalm 89), "when the Lord God presents you into the Land." The similarity is intentional and allows Arthur to again hint about the theme of the Exodus which will become prevalent beginning in chapter 3. The interplay between "the heavenly world" and "the Land" will function as a key part of his discussion there as well.

27. Technically the quotation is from Odes 2:43. Odes is a book appended to the LXX which compiles songs found elsewhere in the Bible. Odes 2 presents the Song of Moses which originally occurs in Deuteronomy 32.

28. Psalm 104 is attributed to David in the LXX, but not in the Hebrew text we have today.

29. The identification of a new prosopological speaker being identified by means of a verbal shift is further discussed in Bates 74–76.

30. Angels are also mentioned as changing into wind and fire in the pseudepigraphic work of 4 Ezra (see 8:21–22).

31. The same Greek words used to describe the miracles in Hebrews 2:4 are also used by Paul in 2 Corinthians 12:12 to denote the signs of a true apostle. A shortened version of the expression is also found regularly in the Old Testament to summarize the miracles associated with the Exodus (for example Exodus 7:3).

32. For a great summary of the Holy Spirit as being distributed in 2:4, rather than the spiritual gifts, I recommend this helpful video featuring Madison Pierce: https://www.youtube.com/watch?v=9d5G5_OHa00.

33. Joel's words themselves are likely intended to represent the prophetic fulfillment of Moses' prayer in Numbers 11:29 (ESV), "Would that all the LORD's people were prophets, that the LORD would put his Spirit on them!"

34. The literal Greek is that he "tasted death." The imagery is that of experiencing the full bitterness of it, rather than sampling it as the word "taste" can imply in English, see BDAG 195.

35. Most English translations of Hebrews 2:6 leave the subject as "someone," but there are many good reasons for believing an angel is in view. The context certainly points in

that direction, and angels also speak these words in the pseudepigraphal work of 3 Enoch (see 5:10).

36. See Cockerill 126–135. I highly recommend his commentary. Also of note, this interpretation of Psalm 8 is nearly identical to what Paul presents in 1 Corinthians 15.

37. In the Psalm 22 citation, Arthur changes one of the words (for those interested he changes διηγήσομαι into ἀπαγγελῶ) just like he did in 1:12. The purpose is the same, it imports the context of another biblical reference into the thought process. This time he pulls the word from Psalm 102 and Isaiah 12, both of which are quoted in Section 1.

38. The word translated as "family gathering" is the word typically translated "church" elsewhere in the New Testament. Since the context of the Psalm 22 citation is that of a family gathering, it is translated as such here.

39. For further defense of Jesus' quotes in 2:12–13 serving as a response to God, see Cockerill 142.

40. For more on the interpretation of Psalm 22 found in the commentary, especially the indication of an unspoken deliverance occurring in the middle of the Psalm, see Bates 136–140.

41. The reference to Jesus depending on God is also stated of Jesus at the cross in Matthew 27:43.

42. Most of the time the translation of Hebrews found in this commentary translates examples of litotes with the positive affirmation intended by the double negative response. This is avoided (as in this example) when the double negative captures contextual information lost when translated as a positive. The decision to translate litotes as a positive is due to the different way they are often used in English today. Today if we say, "I don't disagree" it doesn't necessarily mean, "I strongly agree" like it would in the ancient world, but something closer to "I mostly agree."

43. The tenses of the Greek verb used further support the theological ramifications of the incarnation. Humanity "are composed of flesh and blood" (perfect tense), but Jesus "took on the exact same condition" (aorist tense). People are bound to biology as an inescapable reality, but Jesus *became* human at a specific point in time.

44. Hebrews 2:16 is incredibly vague in the original text and could be understood as "After all, it's obviously not angels that the fear of death seizes; quite the contrary; the fear of death seizes the descendants of Abraham." This alternate approach is endorsed by Michael Gudorf in "Through a Classical Lens: Hebrews 2:16." While this view is intriguing, the occurrence of several key words in Isaiah 41:8–10 LXX support the position here and in all other modern English translations of Hebrews. The Isaiah 41 connection is missed by some since the verb used is slightly different. This is again an example of how Arthur imports the context of another passage, this time Jeremiah 31.

45. The phrase "faithful high priest" in 2:17 is drawn from 1 Samuel 2:35.

46. I've opted to use "tempt" in connection with Jesus (and its related forms) rather than "test." The belief that temptation is always sinful is problematic in view of English usage. In English, when we are tempted to do something, the element of volition is always present. Jesus experienced the same temptations we do, but he never succumbed to them by sinning.

THE WORD (3:1–6:20)

ONCE UPON A TIME

FIDELIS HAD BEEN READING FOR ONLY A FEW MINUTES, BUT he had grown more positive in his outlook. Perhaps it was due to the drama of his unplanned entrance or maybe it was because of the words themselves. Everyone was sitting on the edge of their seats, hanging on every word he read.

As he was reading, his eyes caught Livia. She was now ten years old, but she couldn't even read the last time he had seen her—or sit still for that matter. Her youthful enthusiasm seemed to radiate, though it didn't do enough to liven up the room. He was encouraged to see at least one member of this group was undeterred.

Livia was young, but not too young to notice that things had been different as of late. She was no stranger to hard times; her mom had been sick for many months. Since that time, she had been walking to church by herself; nothing could keep her from the songs and the stories. She knew not everyone here felt that way; she was observant beyond her years, plus it was obvious when so few people were meeting in such a large room.

Some in the church helped out at her home but not enough to

prevent most of the chores from falling to her while her father ran the shop. Church was her safe place, a respite from the difficulties that pervaded every other space she occupied. It's no wonder she came early and stayed late. She longed to get every possible minute out of the gathering as often as she could.

She hadn't remembered Fidelis, but knew he looked familiar. She heard Camilla whisper his name just before he started reading. She started sitting with Camilla when her mother became too ill to keep coming. She never asked if it was okay; she just felt comfortable with her and Camilla didn't seem to mind.

Her mother must have known Fidelis for a long time, because she remembered being told to pay attention any time he brings a letter, "You never know what our friends might need to tell us." Livia caught herself drifting back to those memories of her mother when she snapped back to Fidelis. She loved hearing about God's Son, but where was this all heading?

She knew she was about to find out, so she shifted in her seat and leaned forward as he read:

"This being the case, he had to become exactly like his brothers and sisters so that he could become a merciful and faithful high priest to make atonement for the sins of the people in the service of God."

Inner Piece

Hebrews At A Glance
I. The Son (1:1–2:18)
II. The Word (3:1–6:20)
a. Jesus & Moses
i. 3:1–6
b. The Unfaithful Example
i. 3:7–11
ii. 3:12–19
iii. 4:1–5
iv. 4:6–10
v. 4:11–13
c. The Great High Priest
i. 4:14–16
d. Jesus & Aaron
i. 5:1–4
ii. 5:5–10
e. A Brief Detour
i. 5:11–14
ii. 6:1–3
iii. 6:4–8
iv. 6:9–12
f. The Faithful Example
i. 6:13–20
III. The Priest (7:1–10:18)
IV. The Faithful (10:19–12:29)
V. The End (13:1–13:25)

In the first section of Hebrews, Arthur gains rapport with his audience by inviting the listener into the heavenly throne room for Jesus' coronation as cosmic king. He accomplishes this by allowing us to eavesdrop on heaven through creative interpretation of several Old Testament texts. He transitions in chapter 2 to a word of caution. This magnificent message comes with a warning label. It requires all of one's attention.

The message also comes with a threat. Punishment will be due and owing to the one who disregards this message of God through Jesus. Arthur finishes chapter 2 of his letter by illuminating the realities of the present time through a comparison of Psalm 110 and Psalm 8. We live in a world still full of God's enemies, but are promised a future when all of them will be defeated. In the final parts of chapter 2, Arthur comforts his audience with the realization of what we have in the present. We have direct access to God through Jesus who offers unlimited assistance to strengthen his people in times of need.

With that Arthur progresses to the second section of his letter which will extend from 3:1 all the way through 6:20. This entire section will revolve around the theme of the Exodus generation, which was repeatedly hinted at in the first section. Arthur will use this theme as an analogy with the audience's present predicament and challenge them to press forward in the midst of the rising cost of following God.

JESUS & MOSES: 3:1–6

[3:1]So, holy brothers and sisters, recipients of a heavenly[1] invitation,[2] contemplate Jesus the apostle and high priest whom we have sworn allegiance to. [2]Contemplate how he was faithful to the one who appointed him[3] just like Moses was faithful within his entire household. [3]He deserves more glory than Moses to the same degree that the person who builds a house has more respect than the house itself. [4]After all, every house is built by someone, but God built the entire universe. [5]Now Moses was faithful within his entire household as a servant[4] to put what God would say on record, [6]but Messiah is faithful as a Son over his household. We are members of his household if we don't let go of the confidence that comes from our hope.

Arthur begins the second section with a direct address to the audience, but not just any direct address. He summarizes the core elements of the first section with his word choices. When he calls them "holy" he recalls the thesis statement that we are "being made holy" from 2:11. When he calls them brothers and sisters, he points back to the use of Psalm 22 when Jesus identified God's people as his siblings. Lastly, the designation of the audience as those who have received a heavenly invitation calls to mind that he is leading "many sons and daughters to nobility." So is it an invitation *from* heaven or *to* heaven? Yes! God, through his Son, is inviting his people from his heavenly throne to join him in the heavenly world. It is up to us, as recipients of this invitation, to RSVP back to him.

This theologically dense designation of the audience leads into an imperative, something we are supposed to do as a result of everything we have seen in section 1. We need to contemplate Jesus. There are two aspects to what Arthur requests of us in this contemplation, so they are broken up into two sentences in the above translation. We will handle each individually here.

First, we are to contemplate Jesus in his person, that he is apostle and high priest. Hebrews is the only New Testament book that definitively identifies Jesus in either of these roles. It is certainly hinted at elsewhere, but it is on full display in this letter. What do these two terms communicate about Jesus and his relationship to his people? Apostle could be translated as "emissary" or "delegate." As our apostle, Jesus represents God to us.[5] On the flip side, as high priest, Jesus represents us to God. This twofold description[6] will later be condensed into Jesus being identified as the mediator of the new covenant. Jesus is the only one qualified to stand between us and God, completely capable of identifying with both parties in order to bring them together in relationship. Lastly, Jesus is identified as the one whom we have sworn allegiance to. Most English versions render this as "of our confession." While this is an appropriate translation since Arthur and the audience likely had a specific liturgical confession they regularly repeated as a congregation, the point is that this act of confession is a swearing of allegiance. Since congregational confessions are not as normative for Christians today, I elected to translate the sense rather than just the words themselves. This is the heart of what the audience felt as they recited these words at each meeting. When we accept God's salvation, we swear lifelong allegiance to him. When we worship him, we corporately renew it.

The next aspect of Jesus that we are to contemplate is that "he was faithful to the one who appointed him just like Moses was faithful within his entire household." The theme of faithfulness will dominate this section and indeed the entire letter. Loyalty to God is first emphasized in Jesus, but it was also found in Moses. It is later commanded of the audience and vicariously of us. The language of Jesus being appointed echoes a similar statement about Moses. In 1 Samuel 12:6 LXX, Samuel addresses the people with these words: "The Lord, who appointed Moses and Aaron, is witness."[7] The language of Moses being faithful is also from Arthur's Bible, being found in Numbers 12:7 LXX, "My servant Moses is faithful within his entire household."

Arthur goes on from here to compare the glory due to Jesus and Moses by leveraging the word "house." This comparison is achieved since the word translated "household" in 3:2 is the same word translated "house" in 3:3. Arthur uses the words from his biblical passage to assert that Jesus is worthy of more glory than Moses just like someone who builds a house deserves more glory than the house that was built. He further emphasizes this illustration by commenting that God is ultimately the source of everything that has been built and is therefore worthy of glory to an infinite degree.

Subject	Is worthy of more glory	Comparison
Jesus	>	Moses
House builder	>	A House
God	>	Universe

Arthur shows that his conclusion is reached by a careful reading of the text itself. Moses was faithful from *within* this household, but Jesus is faithful from *over* his household. Moses is not being denigrated in any sense; it is his faithful completion of the task assigned to him that makes this comparison possible. If anything, Moses is being exalted so that Jesus, who is above him, can be lifted up even higher! Moses' most important achievement is called out specifically. He put God's Word on record. As was identified in Section 1, God delivered the words of the Pentateuch, the Torah, the five books of Moses, to him via the angels, and Moses wrote it down for the people. Arthur then reaches a conclusion relevant to his audience. We are members of God's household.[8] The same household that Moses is within and the same household that Jesus is over. But this membership is conditional upon our holding onto the confidence that comes from our hope. Let's unpack that a little before we move on to another digression.

What is our hope? I chose to maintain the traditional translation here, but it should be acknowledged that the English word, "hope" has much against it as a viable translation for the underlying Greek word. The Greek term emphasizes a certain reality, whereas hope generally implies positive wishful thinking. Our hope is the source of confidence because it is certain. God will right every wrong, break every chain, and defeat every enemy. We don't hope for hope, we expect it! With this meaning in mind, the obvious result should be confidence. Confidence can also be translated as "boldness," but the sense of the underlying Greek word is "freedom of speech." Roman citizens were granted the ability to speak freely without fear of reprisal from the government (at least in theory) and it is this sense which Arthur means to convey. Perhaps a better illustration would be that our hope should generate the same feeling as being at home. The same way we can be ourselves in the comfort of our own home, our certain expectation of God's future fulfillment of his promises should equip us to be who we really are, his children. Arthur will return to these ideas, but first we must take a brief detour to look at the theme of the Exodus generation as a whole.

DIGRESSION: THE WRONG-HATTED THOUGHT

All throughout Section 1, Arthur hinted at the Exodus in preparation for the discussion that begins in chapter 3. Arthur paved the way for this topic when he referenced the angels transmitting the Torah to Moses in 2:2 and with his terminology that described the apostolic miracles in 2:4. He was preparing our minds for the emergence of this theme so it flows naturally as we proceed into Section 2 of the letter.

This section will be dominated by an analogy he perceives between the ancient Exodus generation and the first century setting of his audi-

ence. At the Exodus, God's people were witnesses to spectacular miracles. They saw the Nile turn to blood, frogs cover the land, and darkness
shroud the Egyptians. This experience was capped off with the death of
the firstborn within all of Egypt and the splitting of the Red Sea to see
them safely escape the tyranny of Pharaoh. They even looked on as the
sea came crashing down and the armies of Egypt were drowned in the
sea.

These visual displays of God's saving power are remarkable to think
about. Yet, what is even more remarkable is that the people who saw
these miracles, who experienced this salvation, didn't make it to the
Promised Land. Except for Caleb and Joshua, all of them died in the
wilderness as punishment for unfaithfulness. We can easily forget this is
the end of the story for the people who saw such a dramatic display of
God's miracles, but it is true. And this unhappy ending is precisely what
worries Arthur about his audience.

The parallels between the Exodus generation and believers are
unmistakable.[9] Both they and we experienced a past salvation act of
God. They were rescued from Pharaoh and Egypt through powerful
displays by God. We experience the death of Jesus applied to our sin
debts. They and we were invited to follow an intermediary figure to
receive ultimate salvation. This ultimate salvation is living forever with
God. Both of us have been invited to rest, which Arthur will have a lot
to say about as we progress.

	Exodus Generation	Christians
Initial saving event	Ten plagues and splitting of the Red Sea	Death and resurrection of Jesus
Invitation to live with God	Promised Land	Eternal rest
Faithful mediator to lead	Moses	Jesus
Result	Failure and death	Yet to be decided

In the next paragraph, Arthur will offer a lengthy quotation from
Psalm 95 which recounts much of the events of the book of Numbers
(especially chapters 13 and 14). He uses this quotation to set the stage
for the analogy. If it is possible for God's people in the past to come up

short and miss the destination, it is logical to deduce that the same is true for us.

This is the reason why he begins this section with a comparison between Moses and Jesus. This eliminates the option to blame the leader. Since both Moses and Jesus are faithful in their roles, the failure of the Exodus generation is not to be blamed on Moses. The blame entirely rests upon the people. The same is true for us. We have a great mediator, a worthy leader, who is ushering us into final salvation. If we fail, it won't be Jesus' fault—it will be our own.

This analogy is easy to draw within a culture dominated by the books of Moses. In the first century all Christians read the Torah every week. When they finished reading the last book, Deuteronomy, they rerolled the scroll and restarted in Genesis. This pattern repeated without end.[10]

How does this fit together? It is important to see that the book of Deuteronomy doesn't end the story that Genesis begins. The Torah begins with the fall of man, the banishment from God's presence, and a future promise to re-enter. When the Torah ends, the people are on the edge of the Promised Land still waiting to go in. Then you re-roll the scroll and restart the story in Genesis. This leads to a sense of anticipation for finality. It also makes this analogy much easier to convey. In many ways the people lived as though the Exodus never ended. With most of the Jewish people spread throughout the Roman world and with those in Israel under direct governance of Rome, it didn't feel like they ever actually entered the land God promised them. It was easy to feel like the children of the Exodus generation, those born as pilgrims hoping one day to reach the place God planned for them.[11]

This is exactly the plight Jesus came to solve. This is the story he brings to its climax.

The Unfaithful Example: 3:7–11

> *3:7*This is exactly why the Holy Spirit says, "Today if you hear his voice, *8*don't let your hearts be resistant like on the day when your ancestors rebelled in the desert. *9*This was where they skeptically tested me even though they saw my works for forty years. *10*That's why I was provoked by this generation and said, 'Their hearts are constantly wandering off*12* and they wouldn't learn my ways.' *11*So, when I was angry, I swore, 'They will never enter my place of rest!'"

Arthur sets up his analogy with a quotation of Psalm 95:7–11. Since this quotation serves as the backbone for the entire discussion that proceeds for the rest of this section, it will be helpful to look at each line individually. Before we do that, did you notice who was speaking? The Holy Spirit. Arthur is continuing to allow us to eavesdrop in on heaven, but this time we don't have to overhear the words—the communication is directed to us. From out of this throne room experience, the Holy Spirit offers a warning to God's people.

Today if you hear his voice

The quotation starts dramatically telling us that the following message is for today. Arthur will further develop this later on, but for now, note the conditional aspect. "If you hear his voice," implies it is possible to hear his voice. Remember from the very first verse of Hebrews (and the first book of the Bible) we are told that God is the God who speaks. He wants us to hear him, to know him. But we have to listen. Note also how the "if" doesn't have a following "then." Arthur will also make a big deal of this later on too.

Don't let your hearts be resistant like on the day when your ancestors rebelled in the desert.

The instruction that follows has to do with our hearts. Don't let your hearts be resistant. Modern English versions typically use "harden," but the sense is of obstinance. The refusal to open up one's heart to

God. This is what God finds wrong with the Exodus generation. It is helpful to note that "heart" means more than just the emotional center of a person, like we might use it today. In biblical terms, the heart is the totality of the inner person. The internal sphere of life where we think, feel, and make decisions. This is why we can't risk being obstinate. We can't be resistant to God and his word if we want to avoid the same end as the Exodus generation.

This was where they skeptically tested me even though they saw my works for forty years.

When the Exodus generation was in the desert they repeatedly demonstrated their lack of trust and commitment to God as they skeptically tested him. They complained about the lack of water in Exodus 17 and about food in Numbers 11. God miraculously provided both times. Finally they demonstrated their distrust of God in a single event. In Numbers 14, they refuse to trust that God would give them the land.

In view of all of the miracles they had seen up to this point, this is tantamount to treason. They saw the power of God strike down the Egyptians, the most powerful nations on earth at the time. They saw him split the mighty Red Sea and guide them across on dry land. God proved his authority over nature and nations. Doubt should have been impossible. Unfaithfulness should have been unthinkable.

That's why I was provoked by this generation and said, 'Their hearts are constantly wandering off and they wouldn't learn my ways.'

God goes on to say that he was provoked because of this generation. He was brought to anger because of their disloyalty. Sometimes it can be troubling to think of God getting angry. It doesn't help that the practicality of this is confusing since God exists outside of time. I think the lesson here is that God is not stoic, nor is he disconnected from our circumstances. We are made in God's image and thus we have emotions like he does. Our thoughts and feelings are representations of the source: God's emotions. He does exist outside of time, but he chooses to engage with us in the here and now and respond to us as we are. This makes the chastisement so much harder to hear. This people who saw God personally on Mount Sinai, this people who experienced miraculous saving power from his right hand, wandered away from him. They refused to learn his ways.

So, when I was angry, I swore, 'They will never enter my place of rest!'

The quotation (and the original Psalm) ends dramatically. Arthur brings us to this terrifying conclusion. God promises that the Exodus generation will not enter his place of rest. Some translations leave the term simply as "rest," but it is not the *state* of rest they are barred from, it is the *place* of rest. Isaiah uses the same word to describe God's heavenly abode, "Thus says the LORD: "Heaven is my throne, and the earth is my footstool; what is the house that you would build for me, and what is the place of my rest?" (Isaiah 66:1 ESV).[13]

Arthur's quotation of this text is designed to invoke intense introspection. The original audience, under threat of persecution, pain, and perhaps death, were taking their eyes off the God who saved them. The similarity of what transpired to the Exodus generation invites a nerve-racking uneasiness as we are left to wonder, is the same true of me?

3:12–19

*3:12*Brothers and sisters, make sure to prevent there from being in even one of you, a heart corrupted by unfaithfulness that causes you to turn your back on the living God. *13*To prevent this, encourage each other every single day, as long as today lasts, so that you don't let a single heart among you be resistant due to the seduction of sin. *14*After all, we have become Messiah's[14] partners but only if we stick closely to our original plan all the way to the end. *15*When it says, "Today if you hear his voice, don't let your hearts be resistant like when your ancestors rebelled," *16*who was it that heard God, but then rebelled? Wasn't it everyone who left Egypt under the leadership of Moses? *17*Who provoked him for forty years? Wasn't it those who sinned[15] and fell down dead in the desert? *[18]*If it wasn't those who disobeyed, who did he swear would not enter his place of rest? *[19]*So, we see that they couldn't enter because they were unfaithful.

Arthur reuses his direct address of the audience as "brothers and sisters." This is a reminder of Jesus' use of Psalm 22 quoted by Arthur earlier in 2:12, but it is also a reminder of the family relationship Arthur shares with the audience and that we share with believers today. Jesus' identification of us as his siblings does more than just establish a bond between us and him; it also establishes a family connection with Arthur and his audience and with you and me. Those who claim Jesus as their brother claim all other believers as their brothers and sisters. For Arthur, this family connection promotes the need for tough love. As a good brother, he can't sit by and watch his siblings slide backwards, drifting towards destruction. He has to do something, even if that something is difficult to do.

Arthur proceeds to his difficult task of challenging his dear listeners. He started with an overall imperative, built upon the example of the Exodus generation. "Make sure to prevent there from being in even one of you, a heart corrupted by unfaithfulness that causes you to turn your back on the living God." The audience is to avoid even a single member having a heart corrupted by unfaithfulness. The literal Greek is a "corrupt heart of unfaithfulness." The interplay of the terse expression is designed to denote that unfaithfulness is what causes a heart to become corrupt.[16] This was proved to be the case with the Exodus generation. God indicted them because their hearts were resistant and wandering away. This movement of the heart away from God is a descent into unfaithfulness that corrupts the heart.

He then provides guidance on how to avoid this from occurring. "Encourage each other every single day." This is applicable to us as much as it is to Arthur's original audience. So why doesn't it say weekly? Are they going to church every day? Yes! There is much evidence that early Christians met in some capacity every day, even if just to say a quick prayer together. Arthur will later confront the audience that they need to prioritize this practice, but it drives a hard distinction between them and our modern Christian world. For us, church is largely a consumer experience. We consume a time of worship and teaching. This is why it was so easy to be convinced that we could just have virtual church. I'll go on record as saying that it is impossible to fulfill this command in virtual church. It is only in close knit, personal, and tightly developed relationships that we can truly encourage and be encouraged. There is simply no other way to avoid hearts being corrupted by unfaithfulness.

Arthur further pushes his point by advising what the goal of all of this is. "So that you don't let a single heart among you be resistant due to the seduction of sin." This reinforces the connection with Psalm 95 by employing the same language used there. But this time Arthur rewords the origin of the corrupted heart. In his prior sentence it was corrupted by unfaithfulness; here the heart is made resistant due to the seduction of sin. He probably means for the two expressions to be synonymous, two different ways to say the same thing. The personification of sin as a force, as a power seeking to seduce followers of Jesus away from their Lord, is startling. Sin is looking for you, desperately making every attempt to allure you into its deadly grip. Its grip will leave your heart resistant to God's Word and ultimately corrupt it by committing spiritual adultery. This is doubly true when the price to follow Jesus is high. The answer: "Encourage each other every single day, as long as today lasts."

What does it mean, "as long as today lasts"? It is certainly an odd expression. Isn't it always technically today? Arthur means to draw a connection between this verse and the quotations from the first section. Do you remember the other verse that had the word "today" in it? "You are my Son; *today* I have crowned you king." That was his quotation of Psalm 2 from 1:5. Remember though that Arthur connected this verse with Psalm 110. "Sit next to me *until* I pile your enemies under your feet." The implication is that the today of Psalm 2 lasts for the duration of time that Jesus' enemies are being piled under his feet. Today is a ticking clock. One day the counter hits zero and today is no more. We then move into the period defined by Psalm 8, "You subjected everything under his feet." Arthur is keenly aware of eschatology. We have to live in light of eternity, knowing that at any time, today could be over. Perhaps it would be helpful to reexamine our chart from the last section. We can add another row with this warning.

	Past		Present	Future
Old Testament	**Cross**		**Today**	**Future World**
	Jesus is lower than the angels.		Jesus crowned with nobility, waiting until his enemies are under his feet.	Everything subjected to Jesus.
Exodus generation fails to listen to God's voice and is refused entry into rest.			We are presently invited to "hear his voice" and avoid the end result of the Exodus generation.	Those who do "hear his voice" enter rest with God.

Arthur then founds the expectation with another assessment of our relationship to Jesus. We are "Messiah's partners." Remember back in chapter one when he alluded to this? In his quotation of Psalm 45 in 1:9 he says, "[God] has crowned you Messiah with a joyous celebration rather than your partners." This uses both key terms we find there. Arthur is deeply indebted to his Bible; he constantly pulls terms from the text. What does it mean to be partners with Jesus? Similar to business partnerships today, it means we are in relationship together for a purpose. We have a family relationship as siblings, but we also have a business relationship as partners.

How do we know we are Messiah's partners? "If we stick closely to our original plan all the way to the end." A business relationship requires a purpose and a plan. There is no business without these two things. Some translations use the word "confidence" instead of "plan," but that meaning is not attested elsewhere and is a guess based on the context here. The word's primary meaning in the LXX is of a "plan" and that meaning fits best here too.[17] When we swear allegiance to Jesus, when we decide to turn our hearts to God, we make a plan to maintain that commitment for the rest of our life. To serve him, to please him, and to avoid sin. If we want to stay partners with Jesus, we have to stick closely to that plan even if the cost to follow him goes up.

Arthur rounds out this section with a series of rhetorical questions to bring home his point in citing Psalm 95. The point is introspection. He means for you to see the warning of the Psalm and look inward to ask if it applies to you. Are you in danger of unfaithfulness? He fears his audience is and he uses this section to challenge their preconceived notion that everything is okay in their relationship with God. He challenges us to do the same. So what does he ask us to consider?

"Who was it that heard God, but then rebelled?" This reminds us that the rebellion took place *after* they heard God's voice. Since we have also heard God's voice (in his Word), we are in danger of the same outcome if we rebel.

"Wasn't it everyone who left Egypt under the leadership of Moses?" He reminds us again that they had a faithful leader in Moses. It wasn't his fault; it was theirs. It won't be Jesus' fault if we come up short. It will be ours.

"Who provoked him for forty years? Wasn't it those who sinned and fell down dead in the desert?" He reminds us that unfaithfulness provokes God to anger. In this case his anger led to every member of the Exodus generation (other than Joshua and Caleb) falling down dead in the desert rather than entering God's place of rest.

"If it wasn't those who disobeyed, who did he swear would not enter his place of rest?" Ultimately, unfaithfulness is disobedience. It is spiritual adultery. The Exodus generation refused to trust God, they refused to obey God, so God made an oath they would not join him in his place of rest.

These questions can be tough to read as we ponder how they could apply to our lives. Arthur doesn't mean to frighten without purpose; he intends to scare his audience straight. He drives home the point with a final concluding thought: "So, we see that they couldn't enter because they were unfaithful." Unfaithfulness, exampled by their hearts' resistance to God's Word and their rebellious actions led to disaster. Don't let the same happen to you.

4:1–5

[4:1]Since the promise to enter his place of rest remains open, we should take it seriously[18] to prevent even one of you from missing out. [2]After all, we received an invitation to enter his place of rest just like they did, but the message they heard didn't benefit them because they didn't join in with those who responded in faithfulness to what they heard. [3]We will enter the place of rest because of faithfulness just like he said, "So, when I was angry, I swore, 'They will never enter my place of rest!'" Nevertheless, his works have been finished since the beginning of the world [4]considering he has declared[19] somewhere about the seventh day, "God rested on the seventh day from all of his works." [5]Yet in another place he says, "They will never enter my place of rest!"

Did the last paragraph depress you at all? Introspection is exhausting! Arthur begins transitioning to a more positive interpretation of Psalm 95 now. He starts with a thesis, "The promise to enter his place of rest remains open." He will go on to explain how he reaches this conclusion from the passage, but for now he sets an expectation for the audience, "take it seriously." We have to take it seriously that God is beckoning us to enter his place of rest. More than just for our benefit, when we take it seriously, we can have an impact on our entire community. Arthur goes on to found his argument on the analogy he has been building between the current circumstances of his audience (and us) and the Exodus generation. The next statement is complex, so let's break it into pieces to get the most out of it.

After all, we received an invitation to enter his place of rest just like they did,

This first part of the sentence was reworked to clarify the intention of the Greek text. Technically the original says, "We were evangelized." Typically, this word is translated with gospel or good news in modern English versions. This is problematic though for contemporary readers since we are preconditioned to think of the gospel as the message of Jesus' death and resurrection, typically paired with an invitation to accept him as savior. This cannot be the meaning here since Arthur will progress to say that this "gospel" was also given to the Exodus generation. With that in mind, it is best to see the Greek word in its sense of a positive message rather than the technical term "gospel." He is talking about good news, just not the specific form of it that we are used to when we hear the word "gospel." This is the good news of being invited to God's resting place. We have already seen that the Exodus generation received this same invitation as well.

But the message they heard didn't benefit them

However, the invitation didn't make a positive impact. They may have sent the initial RSVP but they don't make it to the actual event. They failed to make it to the place of God's rest. Arthur goes on to explain why.

Because they didn't join in with those who responded in faithfulness to what they heard.

The Exodus generation doesn't make it to the place of God's rest. We already know that is because they had a heart corrupted by unfaithfulness and they were seduced by sin, but Arthur gives another reason here too. They didn't join in, or team up, with those who did respond in faithfulness to the message. Who was it that did respond faithfully? There are two possible answers to that.

1. Arthur could mean to say that the Exodus generation should have listened to Joshua and Caleb who attempted to steer them in the right direction towards God's promises.
2. It is also possible that Arthur intends a less linear solution. He may mean they didn't join in with us, those who do remain faithful to God, since we will enter God's rest. This would then be cumulative for all believers past, present, and future who do choose to remain faithful to God throughout their lives.

Arthur then goes on to say, "We will enter the place of rest because of faithfulness." Arthur bolsters this claim with a reference back to the Psalm, "So, when I was angry, I swore, 'They will never enter my place of rest!'" How does this passage inform him that we will enter his rest?

Remember Arthur reads his Bible *very* carefully. Every word matters to him. When it says, "*They* will never enter," he understands that not only does this limit the application to a specific group, but it also identifies that there is a second group, a "We" who will enter it. The question then is, are you *they* or are you *we*?

Arthur has extreme confidence in his audience to rapidly deduce these intensely practical truths, but he is about to make the discussion even more complicated. "His works have been finished since the beginning." This is a reference to the creation story when God rested on the seventh day and instituted the Sabbath as is identified by the quotation of Genesis 2:2 that he employs.[20]

Do you see the conflict that is presented between the quotation from Genesis 2:2 and Psalm 95? Genesis says (Arthur sees the Holy Spirit to be speaking just like Psalm 95), "God rested on the seventh day from all of his works." Arthur understands that this resting never stopped. He just told us, "His works have been finished since the beginning." So if God started resting on the seventh day of creation week and he has been resting ever since,[21] how can Psalm 95 say, "This was where they skeptically tested me even though they saw my *works* for forty years"? How can the Exodus generation see God's works if he stopped working after the act of creation? This apparent conflict only appears when pairing these passages together, but it does appear to be a conflict nonetheless. The solution is that God is an infinite God. He can work and rest at the same time, albeit from two different places. God is working on earth, but he is resting in heaven. Arthur again blurs time and space when talking about a God who is outside of both. God's rest is a present reality for God now, but a future reality for us.

Time/Space	Earth	Heaven
Present	God is working	God is resting
Future	God is resting	God is resting

4:6–10

^{4:6}So, given that it is reserved for some people to enter it, and those who were originally invited failed to enter because of disobedience, he has scheduled a new date. ⁷The new date is today, which he said much later through David as quoted above, "Today if you hear his voice, don't let your hearts be resistant." ⁸Now, if Joshua had offered them rest, God would not have spoken about another date after these days. ⁹Then a Sabbath rest must be reserved for the people of God. ¹⁰After all, those who enter his place of rest also rest from their own works just like God did from his works.

Arthur takes the first line of this paragraph to summarize this discussion as it has unfolded so far. We know it is reserved for some to enter because "they" didn't enter. We know they didn't enter because of disobedience. We are told that this logically requires God to set a new date. The original Save the Date that was sent to the Exodus generation is invalid and a new date has been set. The new date is "Today." This is the "today" of Psalm 95 and Psalm 2. The time period in which Jesus is seated on the throne waiting for his enemies to be piled at his feet, is the same timeframe during which we have to respond to this invitation. We must choose to listen to the voice of God before it's too late!

Since Arthur already alluded to a heavenly rest being God's place of rest, he makes it unmistakable by saying Joshua did not give them rest since God is speaking about a time "after these days." This aligns to a phrase we saw back in 1:1–2. Remember our chart from back there?

Past	Present	Future
These days	The end of these days	After these days

We can now merge that chart with the chart we have been building so far and add in a new column with the creation period, since Arthur just reflected on God's rest at creation with the "place of rest" promised in Psalm 95. Let's look at it all together:

	Past		Present	Future
Creation	Exodus Generation	Cross	Today	Future World
	These days		The end of these days	After these days
		Jesus is lower than the angels.	Jesus crowned with nobility, waiting until his enemies are under his feet.	Everything subjected to Jesus.
God rests after his works of creation.	Exodus Generation fails to listen to God's voice and is refused entry into rest.		We are presently invited to "hear his voice" and avoid the end result of the Exodus Generation.	Those who do "hear his voice" enter rest with God.

Arthur summarizes his teaching with two succinct summaries:

1. A Sabbath rest must be reserved for the people of God.
2. Those who enter his place of rest also rest from their own works just like God did from his works.

With these two remarks he reminds us that this rest is a certain reality, promised by God in his word. But how does Arthur assert that this rest *must be* reserved? Remember how the quotation from Psalm 95 begins in 3:7, "*If* you hear his voice." The quotation starts with an *if*, but there is never a *then*. Arthur reads an unstated then from the argument of Psalm 95. If they didn't hear God's voice and they didn't enter his rest because of it, then we will enter his rest if we hear God's voice. God has sent the invitation; he has set the deadline to respond; will you send your RSVP? We have the opportunity to enter the same heavenly world that Jesus is now in and join God in his place of rest. We can't miss out like the Exodus generation did.

4:11–13

> *4:11*So then, we should give it all we've got to enter that place of rest so that no one goes down due to the same kind of disobedience. *12*After all, the Word of God is alive and effective. It is sharper than any double-edged sword. It penetrates all the way down to the border between soul and spirit and the border between joints and marrow. It is qualified to judge the thoughts and feelings of the heart. *13*Nothing created escapes his sight,[22] quite the contrary, everything is naked and vulnerable in front of the one who will judge us.[23]

The irony of Arthur's first words here is not lost. We have to give it all we've got, spare no effort, hustle, to enter that place of rest. We work now to rest later. Not just any rest, the resting place of God. The effort must be exhibited toward avoiding the same kind of disobedience that the Exodus generation exhibited. This is the disobedience of unfaithfulness, distrust, and disloyalty. It takes effort to avoid this with a world all around us urging us to give in. The same world surrounded Arthur's audience, and he is rooting for them to continue on the right path.

The next two verses (4:12–13) are some of the most famous verses from Hebrews. This inspiring exaltation of the Word of God is well known in Christian circles past and present. Would it surprise you that the Bible is not the primary meaning of "the Word of God" here? Of course, the Bible is the Word of God, but Arthur is referring to Psalm 95. This specific word from God is what he means to say is alive and effective.

He goes on to emphasize the danger found present in this word from God. It is sharper than any double-edged sword. It literally cut off their opportunity to enter God's rest.[24] More than that, this sword penetrates down beyond the realm of the natural. It goes down to the borderline between soul and spirit and the borderline between joints and marrow. Arthur purposely doesn't explain the difference between soul and spirit or joints and marrow. They are both (at least in their ancient context) intended to be nearly synonymous. Only God's Word can decipher the difference between them.

Arthur abandons the sword imagery and tells us the power of God's

Word, largely as a personification of God himself. The word is qualified to judge the thoughts and feelings of the heart. It knows if our hearts are faithful or unfaithful. It knows if we serve God or we serve man. This is proven to be the case with the Exodus generation. Their hearts were judged unfaithful and they were refused entry into God's rest. What will God's Word find in your heart?

A final statement brings this acclamation of God's Word to its terrifying conclusion. God sees everything—literally everything. Nothing in the realm of creation is hidden from him. He is the perfect judge, capable of weighing all the facts in his decision-making process. The word "vulnerable" is the Greek word from which we get our English word, trachea. Why would the word "trachea" be translated as "vulnerable" (or exposed like in many modern versions)? Two images lie behind the use of the word and its meaning here:

1. The image of a priest pulling back the head and exposing the neck of a sacrificial animal before making the killing slice.
2. The image of a gladiator pulling back the head of his opponent waiting for permission to make the killing strike.

Neither image is overly positive, but that is the point. In our relationship to God, we are entirely naked before him. One day we will stand before this God in judgment, completely vulnerable to him. Arthur warns his audience, and us, to keep this in mind at all times. Psalm 95 cut off the Exodus generation—don't let it cut you off too.

THE GREAT HIGH PRIEST: 4:14–16

$^{4:14}$So then, we should maintain our commitment to Jesus the Son of God since we have him as a great high priest[25] who has gone beyond the sky. ^{15}After all, we have a high priest who is more than capable of understanding our limitations since he was tempted exactly like us except that he never sinned. ^{16}So then, we should confidently approach God's throne, the source of grace, so that we can receive mercy and grace to help us in our time of need.

After a lengthy section of explanatory work on the analogy between the Exodus generation and the situation of Arthur's audience (as well as our situation), he transitions into a positive assessment of the benefits we have in Jesus. He introduces this theme with a command to "maintain our commitment to Jesus the Son of God." Other translations render it as "hold fast our confession," but remember the core element of "confession" is a declaration of allegiance. This is what he urges for his audience to do. In the midst of pain, persecution, and difficulties, we can't let anything come between us and Jesus. Why? Because he is our great high priest, not on earth, but beyond the natural order. He escaped the boundaries of the created order and sits with God on his throne.

Remember, Hebrews is about two things:

1. to demonstrate that the new covenant is superior to the old and thus worthy of greater attention and faithfulness and
2. to showcase that the new covenant offers greater access to God to enable faithfulness in the midst of persecution and difficulties.

The first of these goals was covered at length with the comparison of the first covenant participants (the Exodus generation) and now the second of these goals is evaluated. Jesus as our priest in heaven offers us unimpeded access to God through him.

Arthur stresses the remarkable quality that we have with Jesus functioning as our heavenly priest. He can fully understand our limitations. This is because in his time on earth, he faced the same temptations we do. The supreme distinction being he never succumbed to sin's seduction. It would be possible to claim that this makes Jesus less able to sympathize with us since we have sinned and he has not, but I think the opposite is the case.

Temptations increase in strength as we learn to battle against our urges, but as the difficulty rises, we succumb (assuming for a moment that we don't successfully pass the test). This means that when we succumb to temptation, we don't necessarily reach the strongest difficulty setting. Think about it like a video game. As you progress in a video game, the difficulty gets higher and higher as you face harder levels and boss fights. Until you reach the final boss, you don't know how hard the game as a whole will be. If you give up prior to beating it, you never faced all the challenges the game offered. Since Jesus never yielded to sin, he always faced temptation in its strongest form. This is why Jesus is supremely qualified to help us in temptation. He can identify with the raw human elements of temptation and knows what it is like to have physical limitations enhance temptation's call. Therefore, he beckons us to where he is, God's throne, to find strength to overcome.

We can confidently approach God's throne. Remember when we talked about confidence back in 3:6? It has the sense of being at home—the comfort of being who we really are and not hiding behind a mask. This is how we should approach God. I chose to keep the traditional "approach" for the court room imagery it offers. I served in jury duty while writing this book and the image of "approaching the bench" is a relevant cultural example for us. The judge has to beckon you forward to pass the bar and approach the bench. In Jesus, God is inviting us forward. We can approach him when we need strength to overcome our trials.

God's throne is described as the "source of grace," but then it says we receive mercy and grace from it. Arthur paints this picture that we always get more than we ask for when we approach God. We come for grace, but God heaps mercy upon us as well. God is always surprising us with his generosity! It should be no surprise then that he is always willing to help us overcome our trials and temptations. Brothers and sisters, remember to approach the throne when you are tempted. I promise, God will equip you with what you need to overcome.

JESUS & AARON: 5:1–4

> [5:1]Now every human high priest is appointed to represent humanity so that he can offer sacrifices for sins in the service of God. [2]He can be sensitive to the ignorant or wayward given that he is also burdened with limitations. [3]This is why he has to offer sacrifices for his own sins just like he offers sacrifices for the sins of the people. [4]Additionally, no

one picks himself for this honored position, but he must be invited to it by God just like Aaron was.

Arthur moves forward with the conversation about Jesus as our high priest, but he also redirects it back to the Exodus generation. He now compares Aaron, the high priest of that time, with Jesus. Arthur uses this first paragraph to summarize the general qualifications of being a high priest and he will use the next paragraph to showcase the specifics of Jesus as a priest.

Arthur begins by using the expression "human high priest." Some translations use the word "mortal" to eliminate the ability of this referring to Jesus, but that is a misunderstanding. This verse does apply to Jesus. He is a human high priest, and the point of this paragraph is to establish key characteristics of all high priests to then prove that Jesus has all of these qualifications in the following paragraph.

The general statement of "every human high priest" leads into Arthur's general job description for the role: "Every human high priest is appointed to represent humanity so that he can offer sacrifices for sins in the service of God." This forms the overview for what both Aaron and Jesus were expected to do in the role of high priest. They have to represent humanity, offer a sacrifice for sins, and do it all in service to God.

Arthur draws this out further by advising that high priests can be sensitive to "the ignorant and wayward" since they are also burdened with limitations. We already saw that, during his time on the earth, Jesus shared the limitations that come with being human, and that he is understanding towards us because of his humanity. However, this is mostly about Aaron as is indicated by the word choices of "ignorant" and "wayward." These two terms are forms of the same words used in God's indictment of the Exodus generation.

Hebrews	Psalm 95
Ignorant	They wouldn't learn my ways
Wayward	Their hearts are constantly wandering off

Arthur drives his next point further in a way that only applies to Aaron and his order of priests, as we will come to see when the conversation of Jesus' priesthood progresses. Aaron, and the priests descended from him, sin and therefore must offer sacrifices for their own sins before they can offer sacrifices for the sins of the people. Lastly, we are reminded that no one can nominate himself for the role of high priest. God must select the high priest directly.[26]

5:5–10

[5:5]This being the case, Messiah didn't promote himself to the position of high priest; quite the contrary; he was promoted by the one who told him, "You are my Son; today I have crowned you King." [6]He goes on to say in another place, "You are a priest forever in the Melchizedek tradition." [7]During his natural life, Messiah offered loud and tearful prayers to the one who could save him from death and God answered him because of his devotion. [8]Despite the fact that he was his Son,[27] he learned obedience from what he suffered. [10]Since[28] he was qualified, God named him high priest in the Melchizedek tradition, [9]ultimately becoming the basis for eternal salvation to everyone who obeys him.

Arthur shifts from more general dialogue on the role of high priest to the specifics of Jesus as a priest. He ended the last paragraph by acknowledging that Aaron didn't nominate himself as high priest, and he shows the same is true of Jesus. Jesus was promoted to the high priesthood by God himself, as was Aaron.

Arthur finds this promotion by linking Psalm 2 and Psalm 110 which he quoted earlier. He already established that these verses were spoken by God at the enthronement ceremony for Jesus. The verses are linked together by their shared use of the direct address "You."[29] Although Arthur did previously quote Psalm 110:1, he now quotes verse 4, "You are a priest forever in the Melchizedek tradition." In the connection of Psalm 2 and Psalm 110 we have a clear picture of Jesus as a reigning king and a royal priest. Each word of Psalm 110:4 will feature into Arthur's discussion later on so we will go into much greater depth as his analysis takes shape at that point. For now, Arthur is content to tell us more of Jesus' natural life. Because of the in-depth view we are granted into Jesus' life, let's look at this part in detail.

Messiah offered loud and tearful prayers

In this tightly compact section, Arthur starts by telling us that the Messiah (Jesus) offered loud and tearful prayers. The use of the word "offered" serves to embed this declaration into the priestly discussion at hand. Since God saying to Jesus, "You are a priest" takes place chronologically after this event, it is probably not seen as a literal priestly offering, but a foretaste or hint at Jesus' priestly identity that follows his ascension.

When did this happen? When did Jesus offer loud and tearful prayers to God? It is possible to see an allusion to the Garden of Gethsemane, but Arthur doesn't identify this with any specific moment of Jesus' life that we know from the Gospels. He only tells us that it happened during his "natural life." Since there are no other occasions in Hebrews where specific events from the life of Jesus are discussed, it is probably not best to see a single event in mind. This is a general description of the suffering Jesus experienced during his time on the earth.

This also best aligns with Arthur's presentation of Jesus through Old Testament imagery that we have seen so far. Every time Arthur tells us something personal about Jesus, he does so through references to his Bible. This presentation of Jesus connects us to the lament psalms in which we see the psalmist in desperate prayer with God. Look at these examples from Psalm 116 (ESV):

- The snares of death encompassed me; the pangs of Sheol laid hold on me; I suffered distress and anguish. Then I called on the name of the LORD: "O LORD, I pray, deliver my soul!"(116:3–4)
- For you have delivered my soul from death, my eyes from tears, my feet from stumbling; I will walk before the LORD in the land of the living. (116:8–9)

- Precious in the sight of the LORD is the death of his saints. (116:15)

To the one who could save him from death

This next line is the centerpiece of the whole discussion. We have to look carefully at what we are told. Jesus prayed to the one who could save him from death. As soon as we hear these words in English the Gethsemane event is put right back in front of our eyes, and we hear Jesus say, "Father, if you are willing, remove this cup from me. Nevertheless, not my will, but yours, be done" (Luke 22:42 ESV). We hear Jesus looking to God for a way to avoid death. This is difficult to construe though with what follows. We will be told in the next point that whatever Jesus prayed, God answered it.

Note exactly what it says. It says, "save him from death," not "prevent him from dying." Jesus was not praying that God would allow him to avoid death—far from it! He was praying that God would rescue him from out of death. This is the message that Arthur's audience needed to hear. As they are overcome with fear and panic at the threat of mounting persecution, they needed to see how Jesus responded to the same threat. Jesus trusted his life to God. And Jesus trusted his resurrection to God. It is okay for this trust to be expressed in "loud and tearful" prayers since such praying is still trusting him nonetheless. Jesus was willing to follow God all the way to death, because he knew that physical death is not the end of the journey for those who are faithful to God.

And God answered him because of his devotion.

Arthur then tells us that God answered Jesus prayer. Jesus prayed to be rescued from the state or realm of death and God powerfully responds through the resurrection. We are also told why God does this. He answered Jesus because of his devotion. In this verse, Jesus serves as our example for a wholly-devoted relationship with God.

. . .

Despite the fact that he was his Son, he learned obedience from what he suffered.

The text now draws out the seemingly illogical interplay found between Jesus' intensely intimate relationship with God and the actual events of his life. Arthur draws out the theological explanation by saying "he learned obedience from what he *suffered*." In his full humanity, Jesus surrendered himself to the experiential nature of suffering and, as a result, he learned obedience through it.[30] We are afforded the same privilege. Persecution, pain, and difficulties are the only way to measure the extent of our devotion to God. Arthur uses Jesus as an example for his audience to focus upon as they evaluate how dedicated they truly are to the God they serve.

Since he was qualified, God named him high priest in the Melchizedek tradition

We again see qualification language used of Jesus but this time in his role as high priest. Jesus' willing submission to suffering and death infinitely qualified him for this role as eschatological and heavenly priest. We will look more closely at the figure of Melchizedek when Arthur returns to him in Section 3.

Ultimately becoming the basis for eternal salvation to everyone who obeys him.

For now, Arthur is content to keep Jesus in the spotlight by summarizing the result of Jesus' obedience on our behalf. The word translated as "basis" means "legal grounds." Jesus is the firm footing upon which we can receive eternal salvation. The phrase "eternal salvation" is drawn from Isaiah 45:17 (ESV), "Israel is saved by the LORD with everlasting salvation." This again shows how Arthur is constantly overflowing with references to his Bible.

I love the use of obedience in this passage. It helps to know that the words translated as "obey," (5:9) "obedience," (5:8) "answered," (5:7) and "listen" (Deuteronomy 18:15) are all based on the same Greek root. This creates a flow of thought that directly connects this passage to

Moses' prophesy of the Messiah in Deuteronomy 18:15 (ESV), "The LORD your God will raise up for you a prophet like me from among you, from your brothers—it is to him you shall listen." Remember when Arthur said that Moses was faithful to record God's Word? We see that on full display here. Hundreds of years earlier, Moses let us know how important it would be to obey Jesus, and now we know those who do are granted an eternal salvation![31]

With that overwhelmingly positive paragraph end, Arthur now transitions into the strongest warning that will be found within his letter.

A Brief Detour: 5:11–14

> [5:11]We have a lot to say about this but it's hard to explain given that you have become lazy listeners. [12]You should be teachers by now, but you need someone to reteach you the very basics about what God has said. You have regressed to needing milk and can't handle solid food. [13]After all, nursing babies are not prepared to discuss righteousness since they are just babies. [14]Solid food is for grownups who have conditioned themselves to tell the difference between what is helpful and what is harmful.

Arthur returns to his direct address, but not with words of comfort this time. The tone is a night and day transformation from the glowingly positive remark just made. Remember the two goals Arthur has for his letter:

1. to demonstrate that the new covenant is superior to the old and thus worthy of greater attention and faithfulness and
2. to showcase that the new covenant offers greater access to God to enable faithfulness in the midst of persecution and difficulties.

He just spoke at length on the amazing benefits we have with Jesus as our high priest, and he is going to talk about them even more in the next section. It is because these benefits are so amazing that he can't risk his dear friends missing out. He is willing to challenge them, to show them tough love in these paragraphs, when the fortifications of their faith seem to be falling down.

He immediately says he wishes that he could go on about the topic of Jesus' priesthood, but he can't because they are "lazy listeners." The original audience was likely taken aback by what is essentially an insult. He goes on to express disappointment with their progress in that they should be teachers but they have not progressed beyond needing teachers themselves. This is awkward to listen in on as the conversation grows in intensity. We only see one side of the story, but this continues to paint the picture of a group pressed into panic by the threat of persecution. As a response, they have slipped away from honoring their obligations to the Word of God and have fallen behind. Keep in mind that at this time people don't own personal copies of the Scripture. The community's Bible is found at their place of worship, which we know is not being attended as it should be.

Arthur then progresses further with his disappointment at their current state by comparing them to a nursing infant. The comparison is out of place in English, but was a common image in rhetorical dialogue in the ancient world. The imagery makes more sense in the ancient world where infants usually nursed into early childhood, much longer than in our world today.

He says that they have regressed to needing milk and can't handle solid food. Paul uses this same technique in 1 Corinthians 3:2 (ESV), "I fed you with milk, not solid food, for you were not ready for it. And even now you are not yet ready." Arthur begins to blur the lines between the metaphor of the baby and milk with the true situation when he says that babies are "not prepared to discuss righteousness." This is the exact problem he is aiming to solve. He needs them to be able to discuss righteousness.[32]

Wait, what is righteousness? At its core righteousness is a relational word. The idea present in the Greek word is having a right relationship with God.[33] It can take on the concepts of justification, but it also can have the sense of doing what pleases God. Just as having a right relationship with your spouse has associated actions that keep the relationship healthy, the same is true in our relationship with God. That is the sense here. The audience hasn't been doing what it takes to keep their corporate or individual relationships with God in a healthy place.

Arthur also uses the next sentence to blur the lines between the metaphor's image and the real situation now facing his audience. He says, "Solid food is for grownups who have conditioned themselves to tell the difference between what is helpful and what is harmful." The blunt tone is still present as Arthur effectively states that the audience has failed to demonstrate that they have attained Christian maturity.

Do you see why he took five chapters to get to these words? This is really hard stuff to have to say to someone you care deeply for. Christian maturity is marked by the ability to tell the difference between what is harmful and what is helpful. It is possible to translate the expression as "good and evil" or "right and wrong," but there is a greater degree of maturity found in comparing "helpful and harmful." The prior terms are usually used in abstracts, cases when good is always good and wrong is always wrong. It is certainly an act of maturity to know the difference and live accordingly, but it is even more notable when using the terms "helpful and harmful."

This higher degree of maturity is seen in Arthur's Bible. Look at Deuteronomy 1:39 (ESV), "And as for your little ones, who you said would become a prey, and your children, who today have no knowledge of good or evil, they shall go in there. And to them I will give it, and they shall possess it." The knowledge of good and evil, or rather the absence of it, is used to describe *children* as old as nineteen. It takes more than Sunday School answers to know what is truly helpful for oneself and for others. This is the depth of maturity Arthur is pressing his audience toward.

In both the ancient context of the audience and our modern context, we are surrounded by a culture that doesn't know the difference between right and wrong and that certainly doesn't know the difference between what is helpful and harmful. In fact, they preach that wrong is right. For the audience, their world was overrun with the worship of idols. This worship, at best, was spiritual adultery, but even worse, it included drunkenness, sexual perversion, and all kinds of other sins. Our world's flaws may not be as intrinsically connected to idolatry, but the same sins persist. It takes great maturity to recognize sin within oneself and even more maturity to know what to do about it. It demands great maturity to help our Christian brothers and sisters identify areas of opportunity in their lives and assist them in maturing beyond them. The reward is worth it for those who fight to escape immaturity, and our communities desperately need people who will.

6:1–3

*6:1*This is why we should advance beyond the initial lessons about Messiah and carry on towards the destination. We shouldn't have to start from scratch by reteaching you about repentance from dead works, faithfulness to God, *2*purification instructions, the laying on of hands, resurrection from the dead, and eternal judgment. *3*Although we will help you carry on, assuming God allows.

Arthur drops the metaphor but continues the same theme. He urges them to press on from something and toward something. He wants them to advance beyond the "initial lessons about Messiah." This is equivalent to the phrase in the last paragraph, "the very basics about what God has said." I have a joke in my house where I tell my kids they will have to go to remedial classes in heaven if they don't learn God's Word here on earth. Arthur is saying something similar here but it doesn't seem to be a joke. They have to press on from learning the basics of God's Word and move toward the destination. The word translated as "destination" is the same word translated as "grownups" in 5:14. This double meaning serves to cap off the metaphorical comparison between nursing infants and those capable of eating solid food, and it exposes the sense of what Arthur is trying to tell them.

The word "destination" is also the same word translated as "qualified" when talking about Jesus' role as high priest. The expansive meaning of the word makes it difficult to grasp all of the nuance with a single English word, so one was not sought. What is meant by destination? It's where we're headed. Just like in Bunyan's *Pilgrim's Progress* we are headed for the Celestial City. Destination is a catchword in early Christianity that includes everything associated with God remaking the world the way it should be—no sickness, no death, no sin, resurrection bodies, and most of all, a world with unimpeded access to our God and our Savior. As we progress in our Christian walk, this is where our focus must lie.[34]

In fact, the destination is the whole reason we endure. There is a subculture on the internet that strives for discipline, productivity, and stoic endurance of life's pain. As much as it might be possible to learn helpful practices, our goal is different. We don't endure pain, persecution, and difficulties to show that we are tough or to be unaffected by the outside world. We do it because the destination is worth it. We are willing to suffer pain, torment, and death on account of our God because no suffering on earth can compare to the joy that awaits us when we see our savior and God.

Arthur chides his audience again by saying he shouldn't have to start from scratch in teaching them these basics again, yet he lists what he has in mind before expressing his intent to do just that. The list is broken up into three sets of two interconnected items; let's look at the list before we proceed to the last sentence of the paragraph.

Repentance from dead works & faithfulness to God

The first two items on the list cover the entry point into our relationship with God. They are two sides of the same coin more than they are separate entries. Repentance is changing your mind about sin and turning from it. Arthur chooses not to use the word "sin" though. He uses "dead works." Dead works is used as a technical term for any action associated with the worship of idols.[35] He is challenging his audience not to be corrupted by the idolatrous world around them. In tandem with the turning away from idols and sin, we turn toward God, and that turning is marked by a commitment to be faithful to him and his expectations for us.

Purification instructions & the laying on of hands

The next two items are more liturgical in nature.[36] It isn't exactly clear what the first item refers to. It is a similar word to "baptism," but not one that is used elsewhere in the New Testament for the Christian practice. It seems best to say that whatever purification instructions are, it at least includes baptism as we think of it. This combined with the "laying on of hands" and described as an "initial lesson" most likely refers to the ritual acts associated with welcoming in a new member to the congregation. The modern-day equivalents would be something like baptism and the "right hand of fellowship."

Resurrection from the dead & eternal judgment

The last two are distinctive elements of theology within Judaeo-Christianity. At its biblical root, our beliefs are not about going to heaven when we die. That is certainly a part of the biblical teaching, but the emphasis is always on the resurrection. The reuniting of soul and body into resurrection life. The theatrical trailer for the resurrection is already playing in cinemas in the resurrection of Jesus and we await the day of its release. The day of resurrection is preceded by "eternal judgment." Everyone—big and small, young and old, rich and poor, good and bad—will stand before God in judgment. These are basic doctrines of both Jewish and Christian faith, certainly something this church-going audience had not forgotten. So why does Arthur say all of this? They weren't living like it was true. It doesn't look like you believe in the resurrection if you are too scared to leave your house. It doesn't look like you believe in eternal judgment if you are obsessed with the things of this world (especially dead works). This is how Arthur perceived his audience and why he challenges them with this recounting of "the basics."

The final line of this paragraph reverts to a positive before the difficult words found in the next paragraph. Arthur confirms that he, and the community behind him, will help his audience carry on. Technically the verb, "carry on" is passive. Something to the effect of "We will help you be carried on" is more literal. The sense is that ultimately God is the one who advances our relationship with him. The paragraph closes with the unexpected phrase, "assuming God allows." Why wouldn't God let them carry on? Wouldn't he always want people to grow in their faithfulness to him? This mystery is answered in the next paragraph with some of the most terrifying words found in the entire New Testament.

6:4–8

[6:4]Now for those who have already seen the light, tasted the heavenly gift, shared the Holy Spirit, [5]tasted how good God's Word is, experienced the miracles of the future universe, [6]and have fallen back, it is impossible to reinstate them to repentance again since they are recrucifying[37] the Son of God and making a mockery of him. [7]After all, soil that gets frequent rainfall and produces useful crops for those who tilled it, receives a blessing from God. [8]However, if it produces thornbushes, it is worthless and in danger of being cursed. It is destined to be set on fire.

These words are a challenge in every sense of the word. They challenge us doctrinally, practically, and contextually. We are going to discuss these challenges at length in the digression that follows the commentary on the next paragraph, but for now we need to look at the verses themselves. After making his bold and challenging assertions in the first part of the paragraph, Arthur uses imagery to clarify his point. For that reason, unlike how we examined previous passages, it is helpful to look at the clarifying imagery first before we tackle the theological assertion that precedes it.

In 6:7–8, Arthur paints a picture of a plot of land that has been given all the proper prerequisites to produce a bountiful harvest. It got all the water it needed and it was properly tilled and cared for. Arthur then shows us two possible futures. In one future the soil produces crops and is blessed by God. In the other future it produces thornbushes and is on the verge of being cursed and set on fire.[38] This is exactly where Arthur sees his audience. They are at the crossroads. Either future is possible.

The Day of Judgment	
Cursed soil destined for fire	Blessed soil

With that imagery in mind, let's look at the theological description of this crossroads. Rather than continuing the use of "we" and "you" from the prior verse, Arthur shifts to the general "those." He is making an assertion, a truism. As we will find in the next paragraph, he doesn't actually think this destiny awaits his friends, at least not yet. The distance established by shifting from "you" to "those who" helps alleviate the passage's intensity, but not by much. This still remains the most threatening and fear inducing passage in the New Testament.

So what is Arthur describing? He undertakes to describe what he will refer to metaphorically as the soil that received rainfall and careful tilling. He is describing people whom God invested in. We will look more closely at each of the benefits received in the upcoming digression, but for now we can safely say they should have everything needed to produce a bountiful harvest for God. But that isn't what happened. Thornbushes are all that grew up. They fell back from their relationship with God.

So many commentators assume this is a reference to apostasy, that Arthur is warning his audience of the irreversible effect of renouncing one's faith. In view of all that we have learned about the circumstances of the audience, apostasy is not Arthur's main concern. They are not on the verge of recanting their connection to Jesus; they are slowing down, pulling back from publicly identifying with God and his Son. The price to follow Jesus has gone up, but they haven't signed the check for the new amount yet. If that is the case and apostasy is not in view, why is it impossible to restore them?

This assertion certainly seems like an extreme and unfounded one to make. How can he say it is "impossible"? He has a reason that we will see in the digression, but for now we must make certain he does really mean "impossible." Some have tried to understand this to mean "really difficult" or "impossible with man, but not with God." As nice as that sounds for either of these to be the meaning here, Arthur really means "impossible." For those who have received these blessings from God, it is impossible to be restored to a repentant life. It is impossible to the same degree that it is impossible for God to lie (6:18). Arthur will use the same word to denote the complete and utter impossibility in both instances.

We'll get to how Arthur reaches this conclusion, but let's look at his justification. If it were possible to be restored to repentance, this would be equivalent to yanking Jesus off of his throne, nailing him back on the cross, and publicly laughing at him. This is absolutely unthinkable in every sense of the word. For those who have experienced these benefits, if they fall away, restoration is truly impossible. They are destined to be set on fire.

6:9–12

> [6:9]Beloved, despite the fact that we are talking like this, we are certain of a better outcome for you, one that includes salvation. [10]After all, God is fair[39] so he will not ignore your loving support which you have shown for his name when you cared for the saints both now and in the past. [11]However, we want each of you to show the same level of effort towards the future fulfillment we hope for,[40] all the way to the end. [12]This is so that you can emulate those who inherit what is promised because they persevered faithfully instead of becoming lazy.

Fortunately, the dark and stormy tone of the last paragraph gives way to a sunny day as Arthur dramatically shifts gears. This is the one instance of "beloved" in the entire letter and this is definitely the place to use it! After seemingly threatening his friends with the fires of hell, he now pulls them from the fire and places them safely in the bounds of God's love. For most of the translation, I have used vocabulary customarily used today, but I chose to keep the more traditional "beloved" here. I am not often annoyed with modern English versions, but I deeply dislike the use of "dear friends" here in many contemporary translations. In English "beloved" is the past participle that describes an object of one's love.[41] I would accept "dear friends" if it was talking about Arthur's love for the audience, but it isn't. The audience is loved by Arthur, but they are beloved because they are loved by God. We are God's beloved. You, reading this now, are God's beloved. That is what the audience needs to hear as Arthur transitions into his confidence-affirming paragraph.

Arthur acknowledges that he is being overly harsh, but he lays down his hand and tells them he is certain that their future is the same as the soil that produced crops. They are to experience God's salvation.

Remember in Hebrews, salvation is always looked at as a future reality. As much as we are saved now, Arthur sees the full application of this term applying when all enemies have been piled under Jesus' feet and we live in resurrected bodies ready to worship him for all time.

Arthur justifies his confidence in their salvation by advising that God (and Arthur himself) has not ignored how they have lovingly cared for God's people in the past and present. Is this surprising to hear? For six chapters Arthur has challenged this audience that they are not living up to their commitment to their God and their Lord, but now we are learning they have been and are continuing to run a ministry supporting underprivileged believers. If I told you this Sunday your church would hear from a group of Christians in the throes of persecution, who had weathered prior persecution, and who now managed a soup kitchen to take care of struggling community members, wouldn't you be excited to hear them teach? Yet Arthur tells us that they aren't qualified to teach anyone, they need someone to teach them!

Arthur alleviates the oddities of this new information (at least in part) in his next sentence, but let's look at a few features first. The opening comment of this line stresses that God is fair. Just like we hear from Abraham, "Shall not the Judge of all the earth do what is just?" (Genesis 18:25 ESV). Arthur isn't overlooking the true state of his friends' relationship with God, and he tells them God is not overlooking it either. It is unclear what exactly is meant by "loving support," but the underlying terms in the Greek traditionally translated as "work" and "love" imply that some kind of material care is intended. Whether it is food, clothing, or some other need being met, Arthur's audience is committed to helping their wider Christian community.

More than just committed to the Christians themselves, we are told they offer this "loving support" for "his name." God's name means his character. The audience has demonstrated their love for who God is by mirroring his compassion and love for needy Christians in their area. Arthur calls these local Christians, "saints." I debated whether to use this traditional term or to use the more consistent "holy ones" in view of earlier uses of the same word. I chose to go with "saints," but it is worth noting here that we are saints, or holy ones, because Jesus is making us such, as we learned in 2:11.

The final two sentences evidence Arthur's concern for the audience. What is it he is nervous about, and what does he want them to do? Let's look closely at each part of the first sentence before we cover the last sentence of this paragraph.

We want each of you

Arthur, and his community, wants every member of their sister church to move beyond their fear, accept the rising cost to follow Jesus, and demonstrate their faithfulness to God. Based on this line, we can know that some members of the community are at greater risk than others, but Arthur's heart is to see every member step up to their God-ordained challenges.

To show the same level of effort

What does he want each member to do? To show the same level of effort. The same as what? It isn't specified here, but he means the same level of effort that they previously showed when subjected to persecution in the past. This will be further developed later in the letter.

Towards the future fulfillment we hope for

The audience's willingness to endure their present pain, persecution, and difficulties will be directly proportionate to their level of certainty in the future we hope for. Remember in the Bible, hope doesn't mean optimism or wishful thinking; hope is the certainty that God will fulfill his promises. God has promised that there will be a day when all of the forces of sin, evil, and death will be laid at Jesus' feet. To the extent we believe that, we can endure the hardships imposed upon us.

All the way to the end

The Christian life is not a sprint though. It is a marathon race. We have to show this level of effort in our blessed hope all the way to the end of the race. Until we reach the end of our life or until we reach the destination promised by God, we have to keep going no matter what we face.

Arthur rounds out this paragraph with a summarizing remark. All of this adds up to the ability to emulate those of the past who did inherit the things promised by God. They did this by persevering and by not becoming lazy. This serves as a hint to what will follow in Chapter 11. With the use of "lazy" here, Arthur bookends this warning passage with its earlier use in 5:11.[42] The next paragraph will function as a hinge between this paragraph and Section 3, which follows it. Before we get to that text, let's take a brief digression.

Digression: Caution Tape

How can Arthur so confidently declare that it is impossible to restore to repentance those with the descriptors that he listed? What does he see in these words that causes such a strong and terrifying assertion?

The answer is simple. He is still talking about the Exodus generation. This entire section, since introducing the comparison between Jesus and Moses, has been about the similarity of the Exodus generation and Christians. We covered that more closely in the prior digression, but he is still doing that comparison work here. All of the terms employed to describe those who cannot be restored are true of the Exodus generation[43] and they are also true of Christians. He chooses these specific terms because of the dual applicability and to further the warning he has been building throughout. Let's look at each item.

1. Seen the light: The Exodus generation saw the light when God led them with the pillar of smoke and fire. Christians have "seen the light" in the gospel message.[44]
2. Tasted the heavenly gift: The Exodus generation tasted the

heavenly gift of manna. Christians have tasted the bread of life.

3. Shared the Holy Spirit: The Exodus generation shared the Holy Spirit living within their camp and living within their anointed leaders. Christians have shared the Holy Spirit through the gift of the Spirit conveyed upon acceptance of the gospel message.[45]

4. Tasted how good God's Word is: The Exodus generation tasted the goodness of God's Word in the giving of the Torah. Christians have also tasted the goodness of God's Word in the teachings of Jesus and the apostles.

5. Experienced the miracles of the future universe: The Exodus generation experienced the miracles of the future universe in the ten plagues, the water from the rock, the manna from heaven, the preservation of their clothes, and the like. Christians have experienced the resurrection life of Jesus as well as God's continuing acts of miraculous provision and providence.

6. Fallen back: The Exodus generation "fell down dead" in distrust of God and failed to reach the promised destination. The same can be true for those who claim the name of Jesus yet do not stay the course until the end.

The Exodus generation is a powerful warning to alert everyone to the severity of turning away from God. Just like us, they received tremendous blessing from God, but it didn't profit them. They didn't make it to the finish line. Because this was true of them, Arthur surmises it also can be true of those who follow Jesus. Just like the Exodus generation, we have begun a journey with God and are on our way to final salvation. The Exodus generation didn't make it, and Arthur urges his audience (and us) not to make the same mistake.

The Christian life is like going up the down escalator. If you stand still, you are immediately going the wrong direction. If you stand still for long, you are back where you started very quickly. Arthur, by way of the Exodus generation, sees there is a point of no return. There is a distance backwards that one can drift where restoration becomes impossible. Arthur doesn't know where that line is, but he knows there is one. The Exodus generation crossed it, and he wants to ensure not even one of his friends makes the same mistake.

We don't know what specific happenings led Arthur to pen this letter, but it was something concerning enough that he had to confront it. If Arthur is confident in his friends' salvation, why does he use such strong language? He is confident . . . *for now*. They haven't done anything to question that, but they are sliding in the wrong direction. The heart of this letter is for them to realize the gravity of the situation and resolve to turn around and go the right direction.

Since Arthur will tell us that he doesn't believe that they have (or even that they will) cross the line, this whole warning remains only hypothetical. That is how we have to read this paragraph in its original context, but what about its doctrinal assertion? Can we use these verses to say some who have left the faith, can't come back? Can we fear that we or someone we care about has lost their salvation? Or is this all saying they were never saved to begin with?

These are fair questions to ask, but unfortunately, they are not answered by Arthur. Ultimately this passage is not about church discipline so it really isn't applicable in circumstances like that. These verses also can't be used to prove that one can or can't lose their salvation. These questions are simply beyond the scope of what Arthur was trying to say. It does stand as a stark warning nonetheless. There is a point of no return in one's faith journey. Once crossed, it cannot be re-crossed. Does this mean you can lose your salvation or does it imply that you were never truly saved at all? Humanly speaking, it doesn't matter. The point is that the end is not guaranteed in the beginning. Some who start the journey with us won't make it to the end. But we can't consign ourselves to this reality without a fight.

What does this tell us about today? As Christians, we have to make specific decisions in our relationship with God that believers of the past didn't have to make. As believers today we have to decide if our streaming subscriptions honor or dishonor God. We all agree there is plenty of content intentionally opposed to God and his Word. If we buy a slice, are we helping to make the whole pie? Now that we know many large corporations have unethical work practices, including slave labor, can we honestly purchase their products? Since research shows the damaging effects and addictive nature of social media upon young people (and all people really), can we maintain our accounts? I can't tell you the answers to these questions. You have to answer them for yourself.

I can tell you there was a way to avoid the rising persecution that confronted the audience. Christians could avoid the threat of persecution by not exclusively worshipping God and Jesus. As long as the idols were worshipped, the officials really didn't care who else you worshipped. If you didn't want to be persecuted, you could eat some meat sacrificed to idols, hang out at the ritual brothels, or be seen at the public festivals. A Christian could reason, "I am not really worshipping the idol—in my heart I only worship God." It is unclear that these actions were actually undertaken by the audience, but they would have been a daily threat to their faithfulness to God. A threat Arthur is unwilling to risk happening.

> Little children, guard yourselves against idols. (1 John 5:14)

THE FAITHFUL EXAMPLE: 6:13–20

> *6:13*Now given that God had no one greater to swear by when he made a promise to Abraham, he swore by himself *14*when he said, "I promise to bless you and give you many descendants." *15*As a result, Abraham obtained what was promised after he persevered.[46] *16*After all, people swear by someone greater than themselves and an oath is used to confirm the end of any dispute they have.[47] *17*So, because God really wanted to prove to the beneficiaries of the promise that his plan is irreversible, he guaranteed it with an oath. *18*God, who cannot lie, used two irreversible declarations so that we who rely on him could be strongly encouraged to hold on to the hope in front of us. *19*This hope

is an anchor for our soul, firmly secured behind the curtain. [20]This is where Jesus our forward scout[48] has entered; he has become high priest forever in the Melchizedek tradition.

For the entirety of Section 2, the discussion has been dominated by the unfaithful example of the Exodus generation. They received an initial demonstration of God's salvation and a promise of more to come. Due to their unfaithfulness, they didn't make it to the end and they missed out on God's promise. Arthur ends this section with a positive example. Just like he alluded to above, there is another example of someone in the Bible with a similar set of circumstances, yet who remained faithful to God and received what God promised. This is Abraham, of course. Like the Exodus generation, Abraham was invited by God on a journey away from his home to a place where he could live with God forever. Along the way, he received a promise that God would grant him a son. Unlike the Exodus generation, Abraham remained faithful to God throughout the many decades of his life and ultimately received Isaac as a fulfillment of that promise. Arthur ends this section, not with the negative warning to look away from the example of the Exodus generation, but with the positive encouragement to look towards the example of Abraham.[49] This is the backdrop that is painted with this paragraph and why it fits here at the end of Section 2. With that in mind, let's look at what Arthur has to say about God and Abraham.

The paragraph starts with the undeniable assumption that there is no authority or power over our God. For this reason, when he made a promise to Abraham, he swore by himself. God made promises to Abraham on several occasions, but Arthur is specifically referencing Genesis 22:17.[50] The fulfillment of this promise came with the birth of Isaac, which is why it can be said that Abraham obtained what was promised.

What are oaths and why did God swear one? In the ancient world, swearing an oath functioned as a regular part of society and created binding obligations between parties. Oaths were a part of business relationships that confirmed the intention of mutual benefit between the parties. Oath-taking is more or less identical to our modern-day use of contracts today. If we want to bind two parties together with mutual obligations, we sign a contract that specifies what each party must do, and what will happen if either party fails in its obligations, and we sign it to make it official. Signed contracts are governed by contract law. In the ancient world there was no contract law or governing bodies set to oversee contracts. Each party would call upon their god to exact punishment in the event of failure to live up to the terms. This served as confirmation of mutually beneficial intentions and set expectations in the case of failure.

That explains what oaths are and how they functioned in society, but why would God swear one? Arthur tells us the answer, "He really wanted to prove that his plan was irreversible." Why? Abraham received Isaac. Case closed. The reason is because God promised Abraham much more than just Isaac. Over the course of his lengthy life God made several promises to Abraham, some examples include:

1. I will make you a great nation. (Genesis 12:2)
2. I will give you this land to possess. (Genesis 15:7)
3. I will be God to your descendants. (Genesis 17:8)

Abraham persevered and received the initial fulfillment in the birth of Isaac, but there is so much more to come. It is these other aspects of the promise that we still wait for God to fulfill. Arthur will regularly refer to "the promise" throughout his letter and in each use, this is what he is referring to. We still await God's final salvation of a heavenly homeland where his people will dwell with him forever, and he will be our God. This is what God promised Abraham. It hasn't happened yet, but it will. God can't lie and he promised and swore that he will do it. The Old Testament narratives themselves refer to this event as a covenant (see Genesis 15:18), but Hebrews never chooses to use this term for this specific case. The main reason why is that both parties have relationship obligations within the structure of the agreement. (We'll talk more about covenants when Arthur progresses to that topic.) Arthur doesn't refer to this as a convent because God unilaterally obligates himself to do what he guaranteed to Abraham. There were no obligations placed on Abraham in order to earn its fulfillment. To

Arthur, this is better defined as a "promise" than a "covenant."[51] We'll talk more about the interplay between the promise to Abraham and the future covenants made later, but for now, what does this passage mean for us?

God made this promise to Abraham four thousand years ago, but that doesn't change that he will fulfill it. He will do what he promised to do. This being the case, we have every reason to cling desperately to this hope. Arthur offers the mental imagery of an anchor. The metaphor is not vividly developed, but it is powerful nonetheless. Due to this passage, the anchor was a popular iconograph among early Christians. This anchor secures us in God's presence. The anchor is beyond the curtain, imagery that will be discussed at length to follow. No matter what pain, persecution, or difficulty arises, no storm in life can dislodge us from the anchor of this hope.

Arthur concludes by telling us that Jesus is already in the presence of God on our behalf. He is further confirmation that God will fulfill his promise to Abraham, a promise we are the beneficiaries of. It says that Jesus is our forward scout. This is describing a military function. Jesus is the forward scout whose job is to go ahead of the troops and find the next camp for them. Jesus found our permanent home in the presence of God. His presence is a promise that we will soon follow him.

After his brief detour designed to deeply challenge his friends, Arthur is now ready to proceed to the topic of Melchizedek and the priesthood of Jesus.

PIECE OF MIND

1. Arthur identifies things as "heavenly" six times: the heavenly invitation (3:1), the heavenly gift (6:4), the heavenly version (8:5 and 9:23), the heavenly home (11:16), and heavenly Jerusalem (12:22).
2. "Invitation" is used rather than the traditional "calling" found in modern English versions. For this approach, see BDAG 549.
3. The literal Greek says, "he was faithful to the one who made him." This verse has been used to dispute the divinity of Christ and label him a created being. However, this is not a fair reading. The Greek word behind the term is far closer to the English word "did" than the English word "made." It is a generic verb whose meaning is entirely based on the context in which it occurs. If I said, "I did it" there would be no way to know what "did" means. But if I added, "I needed to buy a shirt, so I did it" the verb is

now assigned a meaning. The ambiguity of the Greek word is shown by its extensive treatment and range of meanings in BDAG, see 839–842. The meaning of "appoint" is made clear from the context due to the verbal parallel with 1 Samuel 12:6 LXX discussed below.

4. The reference to Moses being a "servant" is not intended to denigrate him. This is an honorable role in view of the one being served! Moses' honorific role as servant only serves to further highlight the exaltation due to Jesus in his role as Son, see Harris 72.

5. It is possible that Arthur also designates Jesus as apostle because by the time Hebrews was written nearly all of the original apostles were dead. Rather than see this role transition to a further line of New Testament believers, Arthur understands the role of apostle to transition back to Jesus himself, where he performs the role as our delegate while seated next to God.

6. The designation of Jesus as apostle and high priest further cements his connection to Moses. Moses operated in a similar capacity in representing the people to God and God to the people. Arthur may have found justification for the reference by the parallel with Moses being "sent" in Exodus 3:10, or it's possible his version of the LXX featured the word "apostle" in Exodus 23:20, see Lane 1:75–76.

7. The text of 1 Samuel 12:6 also goes on to say that the Lord "brought up your fathers from Egypt." This same word will be used in reference to God "bringing up" Jesus from the dead in 13:20.

8. "Members of his household" is drawn from 2 Samuel 7:25 and serves as the biblical basis for how Arthur can use the expression "his household."

9. Harris 84, "The author sees an analogous situation between the wilderness generation and his audience and urges them not to follow this example."

10. Acts 15:21 demonstrates that the reading of the Torah was a weekly feature of the Christian gathering. Today, Jewish readers follow a set annual reading cycle that goes from Genesis through Deuteronomy each year. A set reading cycle for all communities across the Jewish Diaspora likely did not exist at the time of Hebrews.

11. The pilgrim imagery is emphasized by Robert Jewett to the degree that he recommends renaming Hebrews to "To the Pilgrims."

12. The literal Greek says, "They constantly wander off *with reference to* their heart." Since it is customary in English for the heart to represent the person (like in the expression "the heart wants what the heart wants"), I chose to simplify it accordingly as, "Their hearts are constantly wandering off."

13. The identification of God's rest as a *place* of rest rather than a *state* of rest is further supported by its reference in the pseudepigraphic work of Joseph and Aseneth. It is found in 8:11 and is used in parallel with eternal life.

14. I choose to use the word "Messiah" throughout rather than the more traditional "Christ." They are synonymous terms, but Messiah conveys the deeply Jewish sense of the word. The concept of God having an anointed representative (remember Messiah means "anointed one") is exclusively Jewish. It is entirely based upon the Jewish Scriptures. I am convinced we could have avoided the New Age movement from hijacking the term into their teaching on "Christ consciousness," had we used the word Messiah instead.

15. Arthur shows here that his primary understanding of "sinned" is based upon the example of the Exodus generation. His concern is with the specific actions associated with spiritual adultery, as exampled in their unfaithful behavior.

16. Most translations use the more traditional "evil" rather than "corrupt." Corrupt works better than evil here since there is progression in mind. "Corrupt" is the result of that process that begins with being seduced by sin and led into unfaithful actions.

17. See Lane 1:82. I am not aware of any Hebrews commentator who supports the use of "plan," but this verse is specifically discussed in reference to this meaning in BDAG 1040–1041.

18. The literal Greek is "let us fear." Since the object of the fear in this context is not God, but members of the audience missing out on God's rest, the translation reflects this context of paying sincere and serious attention.

19. How does Arthur perceive the Holy Spirit to be the speaker of Genesis 2:2? He likely understands the Spirit to be the speaker of the entire creation narrative since God and humanity are spoken of in the third person throughout the account.

20. Arthur's connection of Psalm 95 and Genesis 2 in 4:3–4 are only possible when using the LXX. In the original Hebrew text, two different words are employed for "rest," but the same Greek word is used in both passages in the LXX.

21. How does Arthur conclude that "his works have been finished since the beginning of the world"? Arthur's entire argument hinges on the shared assumption between he and his audience that when it says God "rested on the seventh day" that he never stopped resting. This assumption was likely built on the fact that all prior days of the creation week end with "evening and morning, the first day" and so on. The seventh day features no such conclusory remark and would cause a close reader to assume the seventh day "rest" never stopped.

22. To produce a smooth translation, the clauses in 4:13 have been flipped to their logical order. In translation it is presented as, "Nothing created escapes his sight, quite the contrary, everything is naked and vulnerable in front of the one who will judge us." This is flipped from the ordering in the Greek text, "Nothing created escapes him, quite the contrary, everything is naked and vulnerable to the sight of the one who will judge us." Arthur purposely flips the natural association of "escaping his sight" and being "vulnerable in front of him" for rhetorical value.

23. Translators differ on how to present the final words. The literal Greek is, "to whom in reference to us is the word." The phrase is a shorthand expression which represents our requirement to give an account of ourselves at the Day of Judgment, see Attridge 136. I have chosen to represent this context more clearly with the translation.

24. The reference to God's Word being a "sword" is a further reference to the Numbers account of the Exodus generation's failings. Arthur pulled the word from Numbers 14:43. There it refers to the literal swords that will kill members of the Exodus generation who attempt to take the land after God had sworn to prevent their entry. Here Arthur uses it as the metaphorical "sword" of God's Word that truly cut the people out of the promised rest (Psalm 95).

25. This is a combination of the two different titles for the high priest position. In the New Testament the role is called the "high priest" and in the LXX it is called the "great priest." The combination here has the meaning of "the supreme priest."

26. Although this is the ideal reality taught by the Torah and evidenced in the Bible itself, it is not what actually took place in the New Testament period. The office was interconnected with Roman rule in the first century and the Hasmonean dynasty before that. As we will see in his description of the Tabernacle to follow, Arthur is more interested in what the Torah says than what was actually taking place in his time.

27. Hebrews 5:8 is the verse I alluded to earlier in which Arthur refers to Jesus being Son prior to his exaltation. Jesus was always "Son" in a trinitarian way, but enters into the eschatological role of "Son" at the enthronement.

28. To present the flow of thought effectively in English, verse 10 has been moved ahead of verse 9.

29. The interplay between Psalm 2 and Psalm 110 is stronger than just the use of "You." Psalm 110 further connects to Psalm 2 with the material in verses 2–3 (unquoted in Hebrews). Psalm 110:2 speaks of Jesus' "rod of power" which aligns with the "rod of iron" in Psalm 2:9. Psalm 110:3 speaks of Jesus being "begotten" just like Psalm 2:7.

30. The connection between learning and suffering is seen widely in ancient Greek literature due in large part to the two words rhyming. For this perspective and more on the connection, see Lane 121.

31. Arthur identifies things as "eternal" six times: eternal salvation (5:9), eternal judgment (6:2), eternal redemption (9:12), the eternal Spirit (9:13), the eternal possession (9:15), and the eternal covenant (13:22).

32. For the use of solid food and nursing infants in education contexts, see Attridge 159–163.

33. Righteousness is a "concept of relationship." This designation, and its further explanation is expertly covered by Kertelge in EDNT 326. In an early draft of the translation, I used "those in a right relationship with God" rather than "righteous" and "righteousness." I elected against this since the traditional terms are so ingrained in Christian usage.

34. The Greek word translated as "destination" in 6:1 is usually translated as "perfect" in modern English versions. Paul also uses the word as a reference to resurrection life and the world as it should be in 1 Corinthians 13:10 (ESV), "But when the perfect comes, the partial will pass away." Some have understood this verse as a reference to the completion of the New Testament canon, but that goes against Paul's earlier statement about the spiritual gifts, "So that you are not lacking in any gift, as you wait for the revealing of our Lord Jesus Christ" (1 Corinthians 1:7 ESV). When the "perfect comes" is shown to be equivalent to "the revealing of our Lord."

35. For the notion that the "dead works" in 6:1 refers to idolatry, see Whitlark 64–65.

36. The connection of laying on of hands with baptism in 6:2 is also found in Acts 8:16–17.

37. The translation understands 6:6 to be talking about "recrucifying the Son of God." The term can be understood as the simple "crucify" rather than "recrucify," but the latter is to be preferred based on its acceptance by the early church fathers, see Cockerill 274.

38. The Greek terms used in 6:7–8 to describe the two outcomes for the soil are pulled from Genesis 3:17–18, Deuteronomy 11:11, and Isaiah 5:1–5; showing once again how deeply entrenched Arthur is to the text of his Bible. The promise of this soil being set on fire is derived from Deuteronomy 32:22.

39. The literal translation would be "God is not unfair," but with the double negative creating a strong positive, thus yielding the translation "God is fair."

40. For this meaning, rather than "the full assurance of hope" in modern English versions, see Lane 144.

41. In English, "beloved" is a past participle, but the Greek is an adjective. This doesn't change that the meaning is describing the recipient of "love"—God's love in this case.

42. In 5:11, he calls the audience "lazy listeners." However, in 6:12, he says that his instruction is to prevent them from "becoming lazy." So, are they lazy or not? The point of the ambiguity is for the audience to respond defensively, "we are not lazy," and then live accordingly. In modern parlance we would call it reverse psychology. This is further evidenced by the fact that he says the message he wants to tell them is "hard to explain," yet he goes on to explain it anyway. "Hard to explain" likely doesn't mean it is too complicated for them—we already have seen he expects incredible biblical knowledge

to follow his letter so far. Rather, "it is hard to explain" because it is hard for them to hear. They are not living up to their high calling and Arthur feels forced to show this tough love to them.

43. Arthur's experiential vocabulary used in 6:4ff comes from Psalm 34 LXX, but compare the account found in Nehemiah 9:12–15 for similar vocabulary.

44. The translation above reflects "seen the light" rather than "enlightened" as is found in modern English versions for 6:4. This is done to facilitate the comparison between the shared experience of the Exodus generation and Christians, and to prevent the mystical view of "enlightenment" present in English today. The same Greek word occurs in reference to the Exodus generation in Psalm 105:39 and Nehemiah 9:12.

45. For the understanding that the Exodus generation "shared the Holy Spirit" as stated in 6:4, see Isaiah 63:11 (ESV), "Then he remembered the days of old, of Moses and his people. Where is he who brought them up out of the sea with the shepherds of his flock? Where is he who put in the midst of them his Holy Spirit."

46. "Persevered" is to be preferred over "patiently waited." The meaning is an active and prolonged demonstration of faithfulness rather than just passively waiting (the classic "long-suffering" gets the point across vividly).

47. Arthur adapts this language from Exodus 22:11.

48. The decision to use "forward scout" rather than "forerunner" as in modern English versions was to better emphasize the military imagery present in the word, see Harris 153.

49. The example of Abraham also serves as a hinge between Section 2 and Section 3 for two other reasons. The reference to God swearing an oath connects to Psalm 110:4, which Arthur will cover later on. Abraham is also the only biblical character to interact with the enigmatic Melchizedek, who will be a main focus in the next part of Hebrews. Abraham also serves as a great example for the audience in connection with repenting from "dead works" or idol worship. Joshua 24:2 tells us that Abraham was an idol worshipper at some point in his past. It is unclear if the "dead works" of the audience were a temptation or something they had actually partaken in, but it instills confidence to know that Abraham, the great man of faith, has this sin in his backstory. God doesn't call perfect people; he perfects called people.

50. It is ironic that Arthur uses Genesis 22:17 as the promise for Abraham's progeny in 6:14 when Isaac was already born and grown, and had just avoided sacrifice. The irony is intentional. The relationship of Abraham's faith to his willingness to sacrifice his son is further discussed in Hebrews 11.

51. Arthur's decision not to use the term "covenant" in relation to the relationship with God and Abraham is supported by the narrative of Genesis 15. The covenant initiating ritual is performed, but only by God. Abraham himself never enters into the formal covenant with God. Therefore, it is legally more accurate to call it a "promise" rather than a "covenant."

THE PRIEST (7:1–10:18)

TO BE CONTINUED...

CALVUS COULDN'T BELIEVE WHAT HE JUST HEARD. HIS HEART was racing and his insides were engulfed in fury. It felt like Fidelis was talking directly to him, but he knew it wasn't Fidelis. He may have had a hand in writing it, but this was definitely the work of Arthur. It was just like him not to sign his name at the start, he probably wouldn't even take credit for it. He would likely defer the compliment to something like "everyone pitched in."

His insides were still a raging fire, but it didn't take long for him to realize it wasn't Arthur he was angry at, or even Fidelis. He was angry at himself. These words wouldn't hurt if they weren't true. His anger melted into disappointment and shame. It had been a long time since he really took his relationship with God seriously. He thought he was coasting, going with the flow, but these words made it clear to him that he was rolling downhill. If his life was a garden for God, it had been a while since he had grown anything good to eat.

It hit him suddenly that his best friend tried to tell him this last year. Not only did he not listen, he tried to talk him out of doing what God wanted. At the time he considered his actions prudence, caution, wisdom, but now he saw them for what they really were: fear. He was afraid to share the fate of the faithful. His best friend had been in prison for nine months, just for doing the right thing, and he was too afraid to even go visit him.

An even more shameful thing, one he hadn't admitted to anyone, maybe not even himself, was that he had visited the temple of an idol, of a foreign god. He didn't go in or anything, but he went. He was so afraid of being locked up—or worse. He knew if the public officials just saw him in the area, they would be less likely to arrest him for being a Christian. He knew they were only interested in dedicated Christians, the kind that don't pollute their worship with other gods. A Christian like he used to be.

He couldn't believe that he had sunk to that level. To do something so faithless to a God that had been so faithful was unthinkable. Maybe he was the "worthless soil in danger of being cursed." That would certainly be fair considering his actions and inactions.

Even with all of this bouncing in his head, Calvus kept listening to every word from Fidelis' mouth. He almost couldn't believe it when he heard:

"Beloved, despite the fact that we are talking like this, we are certain of a better outcome for you, one that includes salvation."

He knew those words were also for him. A tear rolled down his cheek as he leaned in to listen.

INNER PIECE

Hebrews At A Glance
I. The Son (1:1–2:18)
II. The Word (3:1–6:20)
III. The Priest (7:1–10:18)
a. Meet Melchizedek
i. 7:1–3
ii. 7:4–10
b. High Priest Comparison
i. 7:11–19
ii. 7:20–25
iii. 7:26–28
c. The Covenant Comparison
i. 8:1–6
ii. 8:7–13
d. Holy Place Comparison
i. 9:1–5
ii. 9:6–10
iii. 9:11–15
iv. 9:16–22
v. 9:23–28
e. Covenant Sacrifice Comparison
i. 10:1–4
ii. 10:5–10
iii. 10:11–14
iv. 10:15–18
IV. The Faithful (10:19–12:29)
V. The End (13:1–13:25)

Two sections are now behind us with three more ahead of us. Hebrews is in full swing with many of the most famous passages now behind us, but so much more lies ahead. Let's review what we have covered before we proceed with unpuzzling Section 3.

Arthur used the first section to establish rapport with his audience as he invited them into the throne room coronation ceremony. Through a collection of Scripture citations he enabled us to be a fly on the wall looking on, as Jesus was being crowned as cosmic king. This jubilant presentation was interrupted with an associated warning at the beginning of chapter 2. Because Jesus is in a role superior to any other heavenly being, his message requires superior attention.

This spirit of warning continued in the second section as Arthur set up a comparison between the Exodus generation and Christians. We both experienced an initial demonstration of God's saving power. For the Exodus generation, it was the ten plagues and the splitting of the Red Sea. For Christians, it is the death and resurrection of Jesus. Both groups have been invited to enter into God's place of rest. The Exodus generation proved unfaithful and was barred from entry. This creates a dangerous precedent that Arthur reasons is true for Christians as well. All of Section 2 focused upon this risk and his encouragement for his friends to avoid it at all costs.

Arthur uses Section 3 to unpack the implications of Psalm 110 and its connection with the new covenant we have in Jesus. The comparison of the two covenants will feature heavily into this section as he explores the theological ramifications of the gospel story and what it means for his audience (and us) who live waiting for Jesus' enemies to be piled at his feet.

MEET MELCHIZEDEK: 7:1–3

*7:1*Now Melchizedek, who was king of Salem and priest of the Most High God, blessed Abraham whom he had met while Abraham was returning from defeating the kings. *2*Then Abraham gave him a tithe of everything. First and foremost, based on the meaning of his name, Melchizedek is the righteous king, but since he was king of Salem, he is also the peaceful king. *3*Since he has no record of a father, mother, lineage, birth, or death, he simulates the Son of God and remains a priest permanently.

Arthur begins Section 3 with a return to the discussion he started in 5:10 and to which he more subtly alluded in 2:17. I am referring to the high priestly role of Jesus as priest within the Melchizedek tradition.

Melchizedek is only mentioned in two places in the entire Old Testament: Genesis 14 and Psalm 110. Arthur uses the first paragraph to glean what we know of Melchizedek from his encounter with Abraham in Genesis before moving from the story to its theological implications. Let's look closely at what he tells us as he introduces this important topic.

The chapter begins by summarizing the unexpected meeting of Melchizedek and Abraham which takes place in Genesis 14:17–21. After narrating the events of Lot's kidnapping and subsequent rescue, Melchizedek appears in the story without warning.[1] We are told of his combined role of king and priest[2] and that Abraham offered him ten percent of the spoils from the battle. This fact will become more relevant in the next paragraph, but for now Arthur moves on to more gleanings from the Genesis encounter.

Arthur transitions to Melchizedek's name and what it tells us about him. Arthur translates the meaning of his name from the two Hebrew words that make up his name. He understands "Melchi" as "king" and "Zedek" as "righteous" and combines it as "righteous king." He then looks to the city we are told that Melchizedek was king of: Salem.[3] Arthur translated it as "peace" and interprets that Melchizedek is also the "peaceful king." The joint descriptors of righteousness and peacefulness in the kingly rule of Melchizedek are reminders of Jesus who also reigns with righteousness and peacefulness. We see both of these aspects displayed in the well-known prophesy from Isaiah.

> For to us a child is born, to us a son is given; and the government shall be upon his shoulder, and his name shall be called Wonderful Counselor, Mighty God, Everlasting Father, Prince of Peace. Of the increase of his government and of peace there will be no end, on the throne of David and over his kingdom, to establish it and to uphold it with justice and with righteousness from this time forth and forevermore. (Isaiah 9:6–7 ESV)

The next remark about Melchizedek is most peculiar. Arthur tells us that Melchizedek has no parents, date of birth, or date of death. How can he possibly make such a bold assertion for someone who appears completely human in his interaction with Abraham in Genesis? Arthur is not speaking literally of Melchizedek but *literaturely*. I am aware that *literaturely* is not a word, but it illustrates the point.The text of Genesis tells us that Melchizedek is a priest, but it doesn't name his ancestors confirming his priestly descent. Arthur reasons that Melchizedek's priesthood was not dependent on these features. Whereas with the priesthood of Aaron, priestly descent required records of a priestly father, mother, and lineage in order to be qualified to serve in the role of priest; this was not the case for Melchizedek. Furthermore, priests in the order of Aaron had a specific age in which they were qualified to serve so the record of birth had to be documented as well. Priests were expected to serve for life, so only death would remove a priest from duty.

The next remark continues the theme of peculiarity. We are told that Melchizedek "simulates the Son of God and remains a priest permanently." This reveals Arthur's interest in Melchizedek. Melchizedek is only useful in the discussion for what he teaches us about Jesus. When Psalm 110:4 tells us that Jesus is a priest "in the Melchizedek tradition," it means a priest with similar qualities as Melchizedek. Thus, Arthur's goal is to evaluate what kind of priest Melchizedek was in order to understand what kind of priest Jesus is.

With this in mind, Arthur can tell us that Melchizedek is a simulation of Jesus. This odd statement deserves more explanation. Melchizedek was a real person who really lived and really met Abraham. He was a real king and a real priest. But he did have a father and mother. He did have a genealogy. He did ultimately die. But the text of the Bible didn't record these details.[4] Arthur uses this "silence" to make a point.[5] Melchizedek was a priest for reasons other than his biological descent. In this way, he foreshadows the priesthood of Jesus who is also a priest for reasons other than biological descent.[6]

7:4–10

[7:4]Do you see how important this man is? Even Abraham, the father of the whole nation,[7] gave a tithe to him. [5]The descendants of Levi, who have the right to be priests, are commanded in the Torah to collect tithes from the people even though the people are their own family since they also came from Abraham. ⁶However, Abraham has given a tithe to someone who doesn't share their lineage and he is the one who blessed Abraham, the recipient of the promises. ⁷Now it is undeniable that someone ranked lower is blessed by someone who is ranked higher. ⁸So, in the one case, men who are destined to die receive tithes, but in the other case, someone received a tithe who is on record as still being alive. ⁹Considering that, you could almost say that Levi, who normally receives tithes, has paid a tithe to Melchizedek ¹⁰since he would have been inside of his great-grandfather's body when Melchizedek met him.

Arthur now draws more direct implications from the Genesis account. He turns his attention to the tithe given to him. Since Abraham was the father of the entire nation of Israel, the fact that he gives Melchizedek a ten percent offering is quite remarkable.[8] He now connects this thought to the priests in the order of Aaron, the descendants of Levi.

As part of their priesthood, the Levitical priests were commanded to collect tithes from the people of Israel, with whom they are related. Since all of the people of Israel are descended from Abraham then the Levitical priests are collecting tithes from their tribal siblings. The siblings are equal in rank. Arthur will now add another element from the Genesis story to prove that is not the case with Abraham and Melchizedek. Melchizedek pronounces a blessing over Abraham. In regard to this statement, he offers a truism. "Now it is undeniable that someone ranked lower is blessed by someone who is ranked higher."

These two factors work together to paint the whole picture. The tithing between the Levites and the Israelites is not indicative of their rank since they are collecting tithes from their siblings. Since Abraham and Melchizedek are not related, it must mean that Melchizedek outranks Abraham in spiritual hierarchy.[9] This is then proved by the fact that Melchizedek blessed Abraham. Abraham's willingness to tithe to Melchizedek and be blessed by him makes this outranking undeniable.

Arthur now adds another layer to the discussion. The Torah tells us that the Levitical priests die, but no death is recorded for Melchizedek.

This serves as a hint to where he is going in the discussion, but Arthur leaves it shrouded in subtly for now. He first proceeds with an illustration even he admits is perhaps too far. He introduces his thought with "you could almost say" to clarify he knows he is pushing a little too far, but he goes with it anyways. Since Levi is the great-grandson of Abraham, he puts forward that Levi is inside of Abraham genetically. He concludes from this that the priesthood of Aaron/Levi paid the tithe and therefore demonstrated that Melchizedek and his priesthood outranks theirs. The illustration may seem like a stretch, but it serves the same purpose as everything he has said so far in Section 3, the priesthood of Melchizedek is superior to the priesthood of Levi/Aaron.

Remember the twofold purpose of Hebrews:

1. to demonstrate that the new covenant is superior to the old and thus worthy of greater attention and faithfulness and
2. to showcase that the new covenant offers greater access to God to enable faithfulness in the midst of persecution and difficulties.

Arthur spent the bulk of Section 2 on the second aspect, so he is now spending Section 3 on the first aspect. The features of the new covenant are far superior to the old.

HIGH PRIEST COMPARISON: 7:11–19

*7:11*The Torah,[10] which governed the Levitical priesthood, was given to the people by God. However, if it was possible for that priesthood to reach the destination, why would we need a different type of priest to emerge[11] in the Melchizedek tradition? Why wouldn't he just be chosen from the order of Aaron? *12*So, when the priesthood is replaced, naturally an amendment is needed to the Torah as well, *13*because the person this is all about is part of[12] a different tribe—a tribe that has never served at the altar. *14*After all, it is a fact that our Lord sprung[13] from Judah, and Moses never said anything about priesthood for this tribe. *15*This is even more blatant when a priest like Melchizedek emerges. *16*He has become a priest because he has an unbreakable life and not because of a commandment governing his lineage.[14] [17]After all, God is on record as saying, "You are a priest forever in the Melchizedek tradition." [18]Now the prior commandment can be rescinded because of its limitations [19]so that a better hope can be commenced. This allows us to live in God's presence since the Torah didn't bring anything to this destination.

Arthur submits a rhetorical question for consideration. If the Levitical priesthood was capable of completing God's plan, why does Psalm 110:4 exist? There would have been no need for God to tell us that the Messiah would be a "priest within the Melchizedek tradition." Since God did prophesy a new type of priesthood for the Messiah, there must be a legal implication to its formation.

Arthur starts this paragraph by linking the Levitical priesthood to the Torah of Moses, which governed the minutest details of the priesthood. We see this primarily in the book of Leviticus, there are literally hundreds of laws that deal with the priests and their function. Arthur uses technical legal language to describe the problem this creates. If the priesthood is replaced, the Torah must be amended. This is contract language. Once a contract is signed it is binding. The Torah was a binding agreement between God and his people. Therefore, it must be formally amended to account for this change. Arthur doesn't dwell on this point yet though.

He defines the seeming disagreement further. Jesus' priesthood cannot be derived from the Torah as it presently exists because he is not from the tribe of Levi, neither is he a descendent of Aaron. Jesus is from the tribe of Judah and there is nothing in the Torah linking this tribe to priestly service.

How do we know Jesus is a priest then? If God's Word says that priests are descended from Levi and Jesus is not from Levi, why should we consider him a priest? Because of Psalm 110:4. God said that the Messiah will be a priest. Jesus is then revealed to be in this role because he shares the same priestly qualities as Melchizedek.

What is the main quality of Melchizedek that Arthur sees in Jesus? His resurrection life. Just like the Torah never narrates a death for Melchizedek, Jesus in his priestly role has an unbreakable life. A more literal rendering would be *unendable*. Jesus is shown to be a priest in the Melchizedek tradition because he can never die again. This is a superior claim to priestly status over the genealogical status that gave right to the Levitical priests.

This choice to describe Jesus as like Melchizedek (7:15) and Melchizedek as simulating Jesus (7:3) also helps us understand the meaning of Psalm 110. Verse 4 says, "You are a priest forever in the Melchizedek tradition." The word translated "tradition" can imply a succession of priests but it also can describe two things as similar. The succession of priests is accurate when talking about Aaron, but the latter meaning matches Arthur's understanding for the priesthood of Jesus. He doesn't visualize a succession of priesthood from Melchizedek to Jesus, but Jesus operating in a priesthood similar to what is described of Melchizedek in the text of Genesis—or rather what is *not* described in Genesis.[15] In Arthur's mind, not even Melchizedek is a priest in the tradition of Melchizedek. In view of Psalm 110, this is an honor reserved exclusively for Jesus.

Furthermore, the text of Psalm 110:4 demands an eternal priest. It says "You are a priest *forever*." Now that we see a man in heaven with an unbreakable life, we see a man (albeit more than a man) capable of fulfilling this role.

Arthur uses the second to last sentence to tie up the legal metaphor, "The prior commandment can be rescinded because of its limitations so that a better hope can be commenced." More than just being amended, Arthur now tells us the Levitical priesthood will be rescinded. It will lose its legal standing. The better hope is the priesthood of Jesus. This superior priesthood allows direct, unimpeded, and permanent access to God through him. Note how the verse says the prior commandment "can be rescinded" and the better hope "can be commenced." So, did it happen yet or are we still waiting for this legal transformation to take place? Yes! Yet again, Arthur breaks down the border between the present and the future; he invites us to ponder this question. He will address it more later on, but for now he is content to complete the thought he began in 7:11.

In the first sentence, Arthur established that the Levitical priesthood was not capable of reaching the destination. What destination? He now answers that question. It is the destination of God's people living in God's presence. The story of the Torah points to this destination, but it can't bring it to fulfillment. Each time the Torah story is read, it ends in the same place. The people are awaiting entry into God's place of rest. Then you reroll the scroll and restart the story. You see the Garden of God and relive humanity being banished from God's perfect presence. The Torah tells us of this promised destination, but it doesn't get us there. Only Jesus can do that.[16]

7:20–25

> [7:20]In all of this, God didn't fail to swear an oath. Now those who became priests were inducted without an oath being sworn, [21]but he was inducted with an oath by the one who told him, "The Lord has sworn and will not reconsider it, 'You are a priest forever.'" [22]This is why Jesus has become the cosigner to a better covenant. [23]In addition to that, there have been many priests because death prevented them from continuing in their service. [24]However, he holds his priesthood permanently because he lasts forever. [25]This being the case, he offers an unlimited salvation to those who approach God through him since he will stay alive forever to advocate for them.

Arthur now adds another facet to the conversation as he sets out to prove the absolute superiority of Jesus' priesthood compared to the Levitical priesthood. God swore an oath regarding Jesus' priesthood, but no such oath was sworn with the priests in the Aaronic tradition. This oath is recorded in Psalm 110:4, "The Lord has sworn and will not reconsider it, 'You are a priest forever.'"

Arthur now connects the concept of Jesus' priesthood with the new covenant. He will go on to spend a lot of time on this better covenant, but for now he alludes to one facet of Jesus' role within it. He cosigned for this new and better covenant. Arthur will leave the implications of this statement for discussion later on. For now, he continues the comparison of the two priesthoods.

The Levitical priests are unable to fulfill this type of oath even if one were to be given. They can't be priests forever, because they keep dying.

Josephus counted that there were eighty-three high priests from Aaron to the destruction of the Temple in A.D. 70—eighty-three men who couldn't not die.[17] But this is not the case with Jesus. He will remain a priest forever and live up to God's oath in Psalm 110. The next sentence is a crescendo to this paragraph, so let's look at it in depth.

He offers an unlimited salvation

The final sentence of this paragraph is introduced with "this being the case." Because Jesus remains a priest forever, he offers something greater than could ever be procured through the Levitical priesthood: unlimited salvation. This salvation is unlimited in scope and duration. The word translated as "unlimited" shares the same root as the word translated "destination" in 7:11 and 7:19, but with one important addition. It is prefixed with an additional word, "all" or "total," that completes the imagery. The idea is that the salvation Jesus offers brings us all the way to the destination. There are no layovers or delays. It brings us all the way into the heavenly world.

To those who approach God through him

This salvation is for those who approach God. Remember the judicial metaphor we saw in 4:16. God is the judge. Only those beckoned forward can pass the bar and enter his presence. Jesus invites us to partake of that invitation and come into God's presence. Since he is sitting next to God right now, we enjoy access to God through him while we await the direct access we will enjoy in the heavenly world.

Since he will stay alive forever

This unlimited salvation and direct access to God are only possible because Jesus can never die again. The permanent power of his life achieved through the resurrection enables the promise of this access. Since Jesus can't die, our link to God remains in place forever.

. . .

To advocate for them

What is Jesus doing with this access to God? He is advocating for us. He is allocating God's mercy and grace to our account. The enemy may be accusing us, but Jesus is advocating for us. He sits next to God and has his full attention as he mediates our relationship to him.

7:26–28

*7:26*A high priest like this is exactly what we need, so loyal, virtuous, and flawless. God has exalted him to heaven and separated him from sinners. *27*The other high priests have a daily requirement first to offer sacrifices for their own sins before they can offer sacrifices for the sins of the people. However, he has no need to do this because he sacrificed for their sins once and for all when he offered himself. *28*After all, the Torah appoints men with limitations to be high priests, but the oath which came after the Torah appoints a Son who is qualified forever.

Arthur will move on from the priestly comparison in the following paragraphs to other topics indirectly related to it, but he wraps up this conversation by summarizing the key truths he wants us to walk away with. First, he outlines the character of Jesus with a threefold description.

1. Loyal: This is often translated as "holy" in modern English versions, but it is a different Greek word. The sense is comparable to what was said of Jesus in 5:7. There the word "devotion" was used and here the synonym "loyal" is used to describe Jesus in his relationship to God.[18]
2. Virtuous: The literal translation of this word would be *unevil*. The double negative is reinforcing a strong positive. Jesus is absolutely free of anything wrong within his character.
3. Flawless: The same concept extends into this word as was found in "virtuous." Jesus possesses no flaw whatsoever. He is entirely perfect, fully qualified to perform his role as high priest.

Arthur further develops his description of Jesus to include his current location. He breaks this next item into a positive and negative feature.

1. Positive: God has exalted Jesus to heaven.
2. Negative: God has separated him from sinners.

These two work together to describe the utter transcendence of the position that Jesus now occupies. He is with God and he is not with sinners. In its use here, "sinners" doesn't mean "someone who sins" since that would include all of humanity. In this regard Jesus is a friend of sinners. Rather, Arthur is using "sinners" here as a synonym for "his enemies" from Psalm 110:1. Jesus is completely separated from his enemies as he awaits the time in which all of them will be piled dead at his feet.

These descriptions of Jesus bring to focus another element in which Jesus' priesthood is superior to the Levitical high priests. Because Aaron and his descendants were not completely loyal, virtuous, and flawless like Jesus is, they were required to deal with their own sins before they could deal with the sins of the people. Arthur already told us that Jesus was free of sin back in 4:15 so this exempts him from being required to make a sacrifice for his sins; his sacrifice is exclusively for the sins of others.

Arthur has another grand and theological statement packed into a succinct final sentence. Let's look at each component.

The Torah appoints men with limitations to be high priests

God's Word through Moses installs high priests who are incapable of being priests eternally. Because they all die, their role is limited to a lifetime and then transitions to another. They are further limited by their inability to not sin. Jesus is without sin, but they are not. The high priests' relationship with God and their ability to perform their services is mediated by the requirement to "first offer sacrifices for their own sins."

.   .   .

But the oath which came after the Torah

God's Word given in Psalm 110:4 came later than Moses. It is unclear if Arthur imagines the "after" as its original transmission through David or God speaking it to Jesus at the throne room coronation, but either meaning accomplishes the same result. The oath God swore installing Jesus as a permanent priest legally follows the priesthood described in the Torah. This serves to amend the priesthood into something viable for eternity.

Appoints a Son who is qualified forever

This oath from God installs Jesus, the Son of God, as a priest eternally. His sinless life and vicarious suffering prove that he is qualified for the job.

Is it interesting that Hebrews is the only place in the New Testament where the priesthood of Jesus is explored like this? It is certainly interesting, but why does he find it so important for his letter? Remember the situation of the audience. They are overwhelmed with the threat of persecution. They are gripped by fear as they see the cost to follow Jesus rising. It is harder and harder to be a Christian. This is all too similar to our world as well. The Western world is less hospitable to our faith than ever before. Arthur, guided by the Holy Spirit, knew exactly what encouragement to offer to those stuck in this situation.

The concept of Jesus as priest serves both goals Arthur has in mind for his letter:

1. to demonstrate that the new covenant is superior to the old and thus worthy of greater attention and faithfulness and
2. to showcase that the new covenant offers greater access to God to enable faithfulness in the midst of persecution and difficulties.

Arthur has offered a lengthy comparison on the two priesthoods showing conclusively that the priesthood of Jesus is superior to the priesthood of Aaron. The priesthood is ultimately a facet of the covenant, proving that the new covenant demands greater attention and faithfulness. But, the priesthood of Jesus also offers greater access to God. Through Jesus, we can approach God's throne and receive enabling grace to maintain faithfulness to God no matter what the world throws at us. Arthur is more than just an academic. He is more than a brilliant scholar. He is a desperate leader seeking to point his friends down the right path, and he knows this is exactly what they need to hear.

THE COVENANT COMPARISON: 8:1-6

[8:1]Now the main thing we are trying to get across is that we have a high priest who sat down next to the throne of the Majesty in heaven.[19] [2]He is a minister in the sanctuary, the original Tabernacle which God, not man, has built.[20] [3]After all, every high priest is appointed to offer sacrifices so it was necessary for him to have something to offer as well. [4]Now, if he were on earth, he wouldn't even be a priest since there are already priests here offering the sacrifices from the Torah. [5]They serve in a model of the heavenly version. This was proven to be the case when Moses was about to finish construction on the Tabernacle and God cautioned him, "Be sure you make everything exactly like the pattern you were shown on the mountain." [6]So, he has obtained a ministry more distinguished than theirs to the same degree that the covenant he mediates is better. The covenant is better because God instituted it on the basis of better promises.

Arthur now uses the concept of priesthood to launch into other facets of the overall covenant comparison conversation. He introduces the thought by identifying where Jesus serves as high priest. He reuses the name for God that was previously used in 1:3, Majesty and he reminds us that Jesus is operating his priesthood in heaven. He then goes on to use other biblical terminology to describe heaven.

Heaven is the original Tabernacle. Arthur will go on to explain from the text of his Bible how he knows that to be the case, but he uses a multitude of descriptors to pin down his view of the heavenly world. He also calls it the sanctuary, which describes the location in view of its unimaginable holiness. He also tells us this Tabernacle was not built by men; it was built by God himself. Despite its ornate appearance, the Tabernacle which stood from the days of Moses until Solomon was still just a manmade object. The original Tabernacle was supernaturally constructed by God himself.

Before unpacking this assessment further, Arthur introduces a new thought. He alludes to the sacrifice of Jesus when he hints that Jesus' role as a priest necessitates some kind of offering from him. He will pick this up further in chapters 9 and 10. For now he resumes the discussion of the priestly location of service with a surprising claim.

Arthur asserts, "If he were on earth, he wouldn't even be a priest since there are already priests here offering the sacrifices from the Torah." We can draw two important conclusions from what is said here. We'll address them in reverse order. He says that there are priests on earth "offering the sacrifices from the Torah." How can that be the case if Hebrews was written at least ten years after the Temple was destroyed? This problem is magnified by the fact that Arthur customarily refers to the sacrifices as though they are a present reality. This has been used to support an earlier date for Hebrews, but doing so ignores that later Jewish writers do the same thing.[21] Arthur never talks about the Temple, he only mentions the Tabernacle. For him, the operation of the Tabernacle is a present reality because of its presence in the Torah. The Torah constitutes its continuance, so Arthur perpetuates that reality by speaking of it in the present tense.

This leads to the the implication of the first part of the sentence, "if he were on earth, he wouldn't even be a priest." Arthur sets up a clear dichotomy. There cannot be two priesthoods operating in the world at the same time. So how can there be two priesthoods? Because there are two worlds. Our current world will be replaced by the heavenly world in the future, but for now they are two separate planes of existence.

Time/Space	Earth	Heaven
Present	Levitical priests	Jesus as priest
Future	Jesus as priest	Jesus as priest

Arthur continues the comparison between these two priesthoods.

He identifies that the Levitical priests serve in a model of the heavenly version. How does he know that? He proves it from his Bible. When the Tabernacle was being built, God told Moses to build it exactly like the pattern he was shown on Mount Sinai. Arthur understands that when Moses was on Mount Sinai, he was somehow present in the heavenly world. God showed Moses how to translate the heavenly reality into a metaphorical version for use on earth.

Using the fact of the priesthood's operating location, Arthur makes a thesis statement. Jesus' ministry is superior to the Levitical priesthood to the same degree that the new covenant is superior to the old. This superiority is shown to be infinite in degree since the location for the first covenant is earth and the operating location for the new covenant is heaven.

He adds a second thesis statement which leads into the lengthy quotation about the new covenant that follows in the next paragraph. He says, "The covenant is better because God instituted it on the basis of better promises." This will be drawn out further as the covenants are compared, but for now it is helpful to remember that the promises are those made to Abraham:

1. I will make you a great nation. (Genesis 12:2)
2. I will give you this land to possess. (Genesis 15:7)
3. I will be God to your descendants. (Genesis 17:8)

8:7–13

*8:7*Now if that first covenant had been without issue, there would have been no reason to expect a second one. *8*However, he identifies an issue with them when he says, "Pay attention; this is the Lord talking. The days are approaching when I will ratify[22] a new covenant with the nation of Israel and the nation of Judah. *9*This covenant will not be based on the covenant I made with their ancestors when I led them by the hand out of Egypt. This is because they refused to abide by the terms of my covenant so I disassociated myself from them. Pay attention; this is the Lord talking. *10*Since that was the case, this is what the new covenant will be like that I will make with the nation of Israel after those days. Pay attention; this is the Lord talking. I will install my instructions in their minds and engrave them on their hearts. I will be their God and they will be my people. *11*They will never have to teach any family member or fellow citizen to learn about the Lord because every single one of them will know me personally.[23] *12*This is because I will offer atonement for their wrongdoings, and I will never remind myself of their sins again." *13*Now right when he said, "New," he made the first one outdated and what has become outdated is about ready to expire.[24]

Previously Arthur reasoned that the Levitical priesthood was incapable of getting God's people to the destination since Psalm 110:4 said that there would be a new priest in the Melchizedek tradition. He now uses the same logic to assume there is an issue with the first covenant. If there wasn't a deficiency, why would we need a second covenant? Arthur detects the reason in the quotation of Jeremiah 31. This forms the longest quotation of the Old Testament found in the New Testament.

Before we turn our attention to the quotation itself, who is talking and when? We have been away from Arthur's quotation of Scripture for a little while, so let's refresh. Arthur looks for ambiguous dialogue in his Bible and then interprets who is talking, when, and why. Arthur tells us God is talking, but who is he talking to? When is he saying these things? We aren't told yet, but we will find out later in the letter. For now, we know God is speaking in order to identify a flaw in the first covenant. But hold on, who is "them"? It says he finds an issue with "them." Who is that? Following the context of the last paragraphs, the "them" is the Levitical priests. They have a flaw. They can't stop dying. Because of that they can't serve as eternal priests. God tells us now of a new covenant in which Levitical priests will no longer be required.[25]

As we did with the quotation of Psalm 95 back in Section 2, we are going to look at each line of this quotation since every facet of it will matter in Arthur's understanding of the new covenant and its superiority.

· · ·

Pay attention; this is the Lord talking.

The quotation opens identifying that the Lord is talking and urges the value of close attention to these words. The identification that God is talking, "thus saith the Lord," is repeated two more times throughout the quotation. For simplicity's sake we won't look at the two other instances, but know that they are there. Arthur finds value in the fact that God is saying these words, and God went so far as to tell us three times that he is the one who is talking.

The days are approaching when I will ratify a new covenant with the nation of Israel and the nation of Judah.

God used the first statement to note the importance of what he plans to say. He now says there is a time coming when he will ratify a new covenant. The new covenant will include the same parties as the first covenant: the nation of Israel and Judah. At the time that Jeremiah wrote these words Israel was two nations; the northern ten tribes were the nation of Israel, and the southern two tribes were the nation of Judah. Jeremiah includes both terms to make it explicit that the new covenant is with the people of Israel. We'll cover this and what it means for non-Jewish believers in the following digression.

This covenant will not be based on the covenant I made with their ancestors when I led them by the hand out of Egypt.

God proceeds to tell us that the covenant will not be based upon or similar to the covenant made with the Exodus generation. This is a legal statement. The old covenant, the legal relationship binding God to Israel, is not being amended. An entirely new legal relationship is being established. This further connection with the Exodus generation serves to interweave the argument that he has been building since Section 2.

This is because they refused to abide by the terms of my covenant so I disassociated myself from them.

God progresses to tell us why the new covenant will not be like the first covenant. God's people didn't obey it. The Exodus generation entered into a formal legal relationship with God and they failed to honor their side of the relationship. In Psalm 95, God says he swore they wouldn't enter his rest, and here it says he disassociated himself from them. This serves as another stark reminder about the fate of the Exodus generation.

Since that was the case, this is what the new covenant will be like that I will make with the nation of Israel after those days.

He said what the covenant will not be like, and now he will tell us what the covenant will be like. Before he progresses to that point, he tells us when he will make this covenant. He will make it "after those days." What does this enigmatic statement mean? When is "after those days"? We'll take up that question in the digression that follows the commentary for this paragraph.

I will install my instructions in their minds and engrave them on their hearts.

The first component of the new covenant that is described is the location of God's instructions. In the first covenant, God's instructions were engraved on stone. In the new covenant they will be engraved upon our hearts directly. We will do what God wants because we want to. There will be no outside compulsion; we will voluntarily choose to obey God's commands. The use of "their" when talking about God's people indicates that God is not talking to us. So who is he talking to? We'll find out later in the letter, but we do know who he is *not* talking to. He is not talking *to* us, but he is talking *about* us.

I will be their God and they will be my people.

Next, he tells us that he will be our God and we will be his people. This is a relational promise. God will be God to us, and we will be his people. Often God uses earthly metaphors to describe his relationship to us, like father, judge, or king; but here he uses the literal. We'll have a perfected relationship with God in which he alone is our God and we are his people. This is what God promised Abraham, and it is what he guarantees will take place within the context of the new covenant. Remember when Arthur told us in 8:6 that the new covenant is instituted on better promises? This is how he arrived at that conclusion. The new covenant is legally founded upon the promises made to Abraham, not the legal context established by the first covenant.

They will never have to teach any family member or fellow citizen to learn about the Lord because every single one of them will know me personally.

God goes on to tell us more of this new covenant which also serves to further explain what it means that God is our God and we are his people. In the new covenant, everyone will have a direct and personal relationship with God. No one will ever have to encourage anyone else to learn about God because every single person will know him directly.

This is because I will offer atonement for their wrongdoings, and I will never remind myself of their sins again.

The last description of what is different between the former covenant and the new covenant is the notion of definitive atonement. In the new covenant, God will offer an atonement with lasting effect. Previously we were told that the new covenant will install God's Word on our mind and enable us to never sin again, but now he tells us how the former sins will be dealt with. Some kind of complete atonement will be offered by God and he will never remind himself of our sins again.

As Christians, we sometimes have trouble thinking of God the Father as the source of our atonement. Our language usually places this on Jesus rather than the Father. Jesus died for our sins. Jesus paid our debt. This is certainly true, but remember, *God* gave his Son. He is the ultimate source for the atonement we have available to us in Messiah. God confirms that for us here. He offers the atonement.

What does it mean that he won't remind himself of our sins? It certainly intensifies the notion that the atonement is definitive, but Arthur will explain this further later on.

After presenting the longest quotation in the New Testament, Arthur offers only one line of commentary upon it. He will keep this quotation as the theological framework for the rest of this section, but he limits his immediate commentary to a single remark. The moment God called this covenant "new," the only possible term for the former covenant is "old." Arthur draws out the legal implications with a concise conclusion: outdated things eventually expire.

DIGRESSION: AFTER THESE DAYS

We talked before about how Hebrews is the only New Testament document to focus on Jesus as a priest, but Hebrews is also the only New Testament document that focuses on the new covenant. It is briefly alluded to elsewhere, but Arthur is the only New Testament author to quote Jeremiah 31, dwell upon it, and connect the Jesus story to it. Why is that the case?

This is again intimately connected to his purpose in writing:

1. to demonstrate that the new covenant is superior to the old and thus worthy of greater attention and faithfulness and
2. to showcase that the new covenant offers greater access to God to enable faithfulness in the midst of persecution and difficulties.

Arthur sets out to show that the new covenant is superior to the old as a primary goal for his letter. He has assessed that this topic is exactly what his audience needs to hear. They need to be reminded of the reason to keep going when things get tough and Arthur finds that motivation in the priesthood of Jesus and the new covenant he is the mediator of.

Before we go on, we need to define the word "covenant." The covenant is not the same as God's law or Torah.[26] The covenant is not the way that we get saved.[27] In the ancient world we could define a covenant as "a lifelong, legally-binding relationship of mutual benefit between two parties." This is intentionally technical so bear with me. Both the new and old covenants fit within this definition. This will become clearer within this digression and when we look at chapter 9.

When does the new covenant take effect? That was answered in the Jeremiah 31 quotation above, "This is what the new covenant will be like that I will make with the nation of Israel after those days." God will make the new covenant "after those days." Great! So, when is that? Arthur actually answered that question at the very beginning of Hebrews. In the very first sentence of his letter, he said, "God, who previously spoke in many different ways to our ancestors through the prophets, spoke to us at the end of these days through his Son." Arthur calls the present, "the end of these days." Great! But what does that mean? Let's look at the chart again:

Past	Present	Future
These days	The end of these days	After these days

There is a slight change from the words God used in Jeremiah compared to what Arthur says here. In Jeremiah God said, "after *those* days," but Arthur says, "at the end of *these* days." How did *those* become *these*? The words this, that, these, and those are demonstratives—their purpose is to *demonstrate* the nearness of an object. If I had a stack of Bibles on my desk and one in the kitchen; the Bibles on my desk would be *these* Bibles and the ones in the kitchen would be *those* Bibles. The only difference in the meaning of these and those is the proximity of a thing to me. Do you see what is happening here?

When Jeremiah originally recorded these words, the new covenant would be made after *those* days, but now Arthur can tell us we live at the end of *these* days. So, what does that mean? Just like Arthur has repeatedly talked about salvation being a future event, the new covenant has not yet started. With Jesus installed as cosmic king and covenantal priest in heaven, we do have access to some of the benefits of the new covenant, but we await its full implementation at the return of Jesus, after his enemies have been piled at his feet.

The future orientation of the new covenant is actually confirmed by the text of Jeremiah as well. Look at what God tells us the new covenant will be like:

- I will install my instructions in their minds and engrave them on their hearts.
- I will be their God and they will be my people.
- They will never have to teach any family member or fellow citizen to learn about the Lord because every single one of them will know me personally.
- I will offer atonement for their wrongdoings, and I will never remind myself of their sins again.

These are future realities that await us when the heavenly world overtakes our present world at the return of Jesus. Through the giving of the Holy Spirit, God has started to install his instructions on our hearts, but I still fall short regularly. I am betting you do too. We have the down payment towards the new covenant, but the full implementation is yet to come. The proof that the other three descriptors of the new covenant await us in the future are on full display every week in church. We constantly invite people to know God and to make him their God. We constantly remind people of their sins in order to evidence their need for atonement. This happens every week in churches all across the world. In Jesus, the new covenant benefits have spilled over into the present, but their final fulfillment awaits us in the future.

Arthur has consistently employed legal metaphors when talking about the covenant so it is helpful to look at a modern-day legal example. We live in a time after the new covenant has been executed, but before it has been made effective. It is like a modern-day contract. A contract is executed the moment that both parties sign the document, but it is not effective until the start date defined in the document. The new covenant was executed when Jesus went to the cross, rose from the dead, ascended to heaven, and sat down on God's throne. But it isn't effective until his return.

This is shown to be the case all throughout Hebrews; his focus is constantly on the future, a future he believes will become reality very soon:

- "Aren't the angels just ministering spirits sent to serve those who are about to receive salvation?" (1:14).
- "Now we are talking about the future world, which God did not subject to angels" (2:5).
- "We have become Messiah's partners but only if we stick closely to our original plan all the way to the end" (3:14).
- "We will enter the place of rest because of faithfulness" (4:3).
- "Then a Sabbath rest must be reserved for the people of God" (4:9).
- "We are certain of a better outcome for you, one that includes salvation" (6:9).
- "We who rely on him could be strongly encouraged to hold on to the hope in front of us" (6:18).
- "Now right when he said, 'New,' he made the first one outdated and what has become outdated is about ready to expire" (8:13).

Arthur is ultimately penning an eschatological letter. He believes that Jesus' return is soon and he doesn't want any of his friends to miss out on this great salvation. They have already come so far. They have not only gone from *those* days to *these* days, they are in fact at *the end of these days*. They already ran the race, all they have to do now is cross the finish line.

Does this change your perspective any? We live at the crossroads of history. We live in between the resurrection of Jesus and the general resurrection. We live when the old covenant is about to expire, and the new covenant is about to be implemented. We live in a time when the future is breaking into the present and heaven is starting to overlap with earth. This is what we have in Jesus now, yet we await so much more to come.

Before we return to the text and advance to chapter 9, we do have to ask the question about the covenanting parties. God explicitly said that the new covenant is being made with Israel. Most Christians today are not Jewish. Even Arthur's original audience was certainly not exclusively Jewish and maybe not even mostly Jewish. Is the new covenant for us too? Absolutely. Arthur's focus is on biblical language so it's a question he doesn't directly engage with, but his focus is on the biblical path of faithfulness. Anyone, Jewish or Gentile, "will enter the place of rest because of faithfulness" (4:3).[28]

With this overview of the covenant timeline behind us, let's look at how Arthur will expand this concept in the remaining chapters of his letter.

HOLY PLACE COMPARISON: 9:1–5

[9:1]So, even the first covenant has procedures for service to be used in the sanctuary on earth. [2]The first section[29] of the sanctuary was furnished with the lampstand and the table for the sacred bread, and it was named the Holy Place. [3]Past the curtain[30] was the second section which was named the Most Holy Place. [4]It included the golden incense altar and the ark of the covenant which was completely encased in gold. The ark contained the gold jar of manna, Aaron's staff that sprouted, and the stone tablets of the covenant. [5]The cherubim, which represent the presence of God, were above it and cast their shadow where atonement is made. Now is not the time to discuss these things in detail though.

Arthur continues the overall theme of covenant comparison by turning his attention to the covenantal holy spaces where priestly activities are performed. He begins with an overarching statement that the first covenant includes procedures for worshipping in the earthly sanctuary. He then goes on briefly to summarize the layout of the holy place as defined by the Torah.

Again, he is using the present tense in his description, but he is not referring to the Temple. His description remains aligned to the text of his Bible, not the Temple which would have previously stood in his lifetime.[31] His focus is on the covenantal order decreed by God in his Word, not its application in recent history. With that out of the way, let's look at his brief description of the Tabernacle's structure and furnishings.

He begins by defining the Tabernacle as a two-sectioned structure. The first section contained the lampstand and the table with the "bread of the presence" and it was named the "Holy Place." Arthur is drawing upon Exodus 25–26 for his description of the Tabernacle.

He then goes on to discuss the second section. Before outlining its contents, he tells us that it was separated from the first section by a curtain or, as some versions call it, a veil. He also tells us it was named the "Most Holy Place." Now he summarizes the contents of this section. He lists two pieces of furniture: the incense altar and the ark. He will go on to list the contents of the ark, but before we cover that, it's worthy of noting the incense altar was not in the Most Holy Place. Every other description we have of the Tabernacle or the Temple clearly defines the altar being in the first section. So should we assume Arthur got it wrong? We'll answer this question in a later paragraph, but let's first look at the ark and its contents.

Arthur lists three items as being inside the ark: the jar of manna, the rod of Aaron that budded, and the stone tablets. All three of these items continue the theme of the Exodus generation's shortcoming from Section 2.

1. The jar of manna reminds us of God's miraculous provision. This provision would ultimately be scorned by the people and lead to the end result of not entering God's place of rest. The manna is first described in Exodus 16 and the people's complaints about it are recorded in Numbers 11.

2. The staff of Aaron that budded reminds us of God's defense of Aaron when his role as high priest was challenged. The spirit of rebellion present in this event is also characteristic of the Exodus generation. This story is told in Numbers 16. The miraculous creation of life on the staff also showcases God's ability to resurrect the dead.

3. The stone tablets serve as reminders of the covenant and the associated expectations on both God and his people. However, these were not the original tablets. The first were broken when Moses saw the people worshipping the golden calf. This episode is narrated in Exodus 32.[32]

Before closing this section, he tells us of what stood above the ark. Most modern English versions translate it as the "cherubim of glory." He is referring to the angelic figures that adorned the top of the ark to cast a shadow on the "mercy seat." Remember in 1:3 when we saw that the word "glory" can refer to God's presence? That is the meaning here as well.[33] The angelic carvings are designed to represent or illustrate that God is present at the place where atonement is made. This is the location where blood is applied during the Day of Atonement which will feature notably in the discussion to come.

Arthur closes this section by telling us he doesn't plan to discuss the Tabernacle in greater detail. This remark indicates that Arthur saw allegorical detail in each of the items he mentioned, but he doesn't find value in covering it more than he has. He does have a point in mind with describing the Tabernacle but he leaves that for the next paragraph.

9:6–10

[9:6]Once all of the furniture was arranged like this, the priests were granted access to the first section regularly to perform their services. [7]However, only the high priest was granted access to the second section, but just once a year. He was required to take blood with him which he would offer for his mistakes and the mistakes[34] of the people. [8]The Holy Spirit uses this to show that the path into the Most Holy Place is not yet revealed as long as the first section is standing in the way, [9]which is a metaphor for the present time. This is when sacrifices are offered that only focus on food, drinks, and various purification rituals. [10]These external requirements can't rehabilitate[35] the conscience of the servant and are only imposed until the time of restoration.

Arthur begins to reveal his hand on why the Tabernacle imagery matters to his letter. Upon its completion, the first section was regularly entered by the priests to perform their various duties. But the second section was only entered once per year and only by the high priest.[36] Even he was forbidden from entering it without the blood of the sacrificial animals. This took place on the annual Day of Atonement described in Leviticus 16.

The Day of Atonement was the once-per-year event in which the sins of the people could be atoned for. The parallel between this onetime event and the sacrifice of Jesus are not lost on Arthur, and he leans heavily into that as his letter progresses.[37]

Arthur now advances to explain why he is telling us this. The Holy Spirit uses the God-ordained layout and activities of the Tabernacle to teach us something. There is no way to access the second section as long as the first section is standing in its way. That sounds like an obvious statement. What is Arthur, writing under the inspiration of the Holy Spirit, telling us?

The physical structure of the Tabernacle is a metaphor for time. Each part of the Tabernacle illustrates an era in God's timetable. Let's look at it:

Past	Present	Future
	The first section	The second section
	The Holy Place	Most Holy Place

Arthur tells us explicitly that the first section refers to the present time. This is the time when we await the final deliverance of God. Remember, for Arthur the new covenant, salvation, and rest are all future realities we are still waiting for God to provide in their fullest expression at the return of Jesus. Even though the Tabernacle is not still standing, the Torah testifies to its continuing validity as we await the consummation of history and full unmitigated access to God is granted in the future world, the heavenly world.

But wait, remember how Arthur placed the incense altar in the Most Holy Place? Theoretically he does it because the function of the incense altar was connected to the Most Holy Place, but could there be more to it?[38]

As he has constantly done, Arthur is blurring the lines between the present experience we have in Jesus and the heavenly world that still awaits us in the future. In Jesus, we have access to God, but greater access is still to come. In Jesus, we have atonement for our sins, but the full benefits of this forgiveness are still to come. In Jesus, the Holy Spirit has started transforming our hearts, but the full engraving of God's Word upon us is still to come. We live in the today of both Psalm 2 and Psalm 95. Today God has crowned Jesus king, but we also have to hear his voice to avoid the disaster of the Exodus generation. Arthur uses this blurring of time to showcase how Christians don't fit easily into either category. We live in the present world, but we are citizens of the future world.

Ultimately this connects to Arthur's understanding of the covenants as well. For his audience and for us two thousand years later, we are not exactly in "these days," but we aren't "after these days" either. We are at the end of these days. We are in a category where the lines between heaven and earth, the present and the future are blurred as we await the day when every single one of Jesus' enemies will be piled under his feet.[39] Maybe it would be better to visualize it this way:

Past	Today	Future
These days	The end of these days	After these days
The Holy Place	Incense altar	Most Holy Place

Arthur wraps this discussion with this final statement: "These external requirements can't rehabilitate the conscience of the servant and are only imposed until the time of restoration." He is talking about the present, not the past. Despite some of the new covenant's benefits being available to us now, we still await the rehabilitation of our conscience.[40] What does it mean to have our conscience rehabilitated? This is Arthur restating in his own words what God previously promised in the new covenant: "I will never remind myself of their sins again." There will be a day when sin is completely purged from our consciences.[41]

The science available now has proved to us more than maybe any other generation how damaging sin is to the mind. Studies have shown that pornography damages the brain the same as heroin.[42] That is one sin. The cumulative effect of a lifetime of sin upon the mind is absolutely devastating. The unhealthy urges, sinful desires, and tainted passions still haunt us—but not forever. There will be a day when God will wipe our very consciousness clean. He won't recall our sin and neither will we. We still await the day of restoration, but God has promised it's on the way.

9:11–15

> [9:11]Messiah appeared to enter the superior Tabernacle as high priest of the better future. This is the Tabernacle beyond the created universe not the manmade one. [12]He was granted access to the sanctuary once and for all to purchase an eternal redemption because of his own blood, not the blood of goats and calves. [13]After all, he offered himself spotless to God through the eternal Spirit. So, if it's true that the blood of goats and bulls and the sprinkled ashes of a heifer can externally purify the impure, [14]then isn't it certainly true that the blood of Messiah can purify your[43] conscience from dead works to serve the living God? [15]This is why he is the mediator of a new covenant so that those who have been invited can receive the promised eternal possession since he died to redeem them from the violations committed under the first covenant.

Arthur uses this paragraph to bring together the thoughts he has been building thus far in this section. He starts with a proposition:

"Messiah appeared to enter the superior Tabernacle as high priest of the better future." Jesus was born to die. He died to live. He lived to enter the heavenly world. He entered the heavenly world to be high priest within the Melchizedek tradition.

If you are comparing this translation with a modern English version, you will notice a clear difference. This translation says that Jesus is high priest of the "better future," but most modern versions say something to the effect of "the present good things." There are very few places in Hebrews with notable textual variants that affect translation. But this is the most significant of all of them. So, is Jesus the high priest of the present or the future? Yes! He is both, but the text itself can only be saying one. The manuscript support for the translation used here is much greater and this fits the eschatological context of Hebrews better.[44] Jesus is priest in the heavenly world today, but we await the day when that world becomes our world. Remember our graphic from before, it applies here too:

Time/Space	Earth	Heaven
Present	Levitical priests	Jesus as priest
Future	Jesus as priest	Jesus as priest

Arthur then proceeds to tell us how Jesus entered the heavenly Tabernacle, which he also calls the "sanctuary." He was granted access to this supreme holy place because of his own blood. This is like how Aaron and the Levitical high priests are granted access to the Most Holy Place because of the sacrificial blood of the Day of Atonement ritual. But Jesus' blood is infinitely more potent. It doesn't grant access to the manmade model of the heavenly reality; it grants access to the original itself.[45]

Why did he enter the celestial sanctuary? To purchase an eternal redemption. Redemption is not as notable a concept in Hebrews as it is elsewhere in the New Testament; it actually only occurs in this paragraph. While it may not be the primary category in which Arthur understands the salvation story, it is an image in his mind nonetheless. What does it mean to be redeemed? The word means to buy something back. What are God's people being bought back from? He leaves that answer for the last sentence of this paragraph, which we will explore in the following digression.

As the sacrificial animals were required to be spotless offerings, so Jesus offered himself to God without any blemish from sin. It says he offered himself "through the eternal Spirit." This remark reminds us that all three persons of the Trinity are involved in the redemption story. The Spirit is the person who brings the other two persons in the Trinity back together upon Jesus' completion of his earthly ministry. The Holy Spirit is envisioned as the resurrection force that brings Jesus back from the dead and the power that unites him with the Father in heaven.

Arthur submits a logical condition for how we can know the infinite power of Jesus' blood. He leans on the value of the Old Testament rituals to make his case. Arthur sets up his argument with an if statement: "If it's true that the blood of goats and bulls and the sprinkled ashes of a heifer can externally purify the impure." Before we can look at the next element in the conditional clause, we have to ask, is this true? Did animal blood really purify impure people?

Arthur, trusting in his Bible, submits to us a positive answer. It does purify the impure. All throughout the Old Testament, but particularly in the book of Leviticus, we are shown that animal blood is the medium through which God's people engage with God. It is the spiritual force that enables purification, forgiveness, and atonement to maintain the relationship with God. There are problems with this though. We'll cover more of them as Hebrews continues, but the one Arthur mentions now is, "externally."

The animal blood offered as a medium of cleansing can only purify the impure on the outside. It does allow the high priest to enter the manmade Tabernacle, but it doesn't effect inward transformation. Arthur uses this biblical imagery to submit that Jesus' blood can do that. His blood can effect inward transformation. It doesn't just purify the outside of a person; it disinfects the inside of a person too.

The exact terminology used is it "can purify your conscience from dead works to serve the living God." This hearkens back to the new covenant language that God spoke through Jeremiah 31, "This is because I will offer atonement for their wrongdoings, and I will never remind myself of their sins again." Jesus' blood is the force capable of enacting this bold promise. It can do what animal blood cannot. It can purify beyond just the outside of a person and eradicate the effect of sin upon the mind.

The goal of this eradication is not just to get sin out of the mind, but to get God into the mind. This then enables another aspect of Jeremiah 31 to be fulfilled: "They will never have to teach any family member or fellow citizen to learn about the Lord because every single one of them will know me personally." Remember, these are primarily future realities. We have the initial down payment, but we await the final fulfillment.

Why does Arthur say we are purified from dead works? And why does he specify God is living? "Dead works" is pulled from his earlier usage in 6:1. There we discussed how it is a reference to idol worship. The same context is true with the Living God. This term is used for God specifically when he is being compared to "dead idols." We can see that connection in these two other New Testament verses:

- We also are men, of like nature with you, and we bring you good news, that you should turn from these vain things to a living God. (Acts 14:15 ESV)
- What agreement has the temple of God with idols? For we are the temple of the living God. (2 Corinthians 6:16 ESV)

We don't know to what extent the audience was tempted to mix their worship with idols, but we know it was an ever-present threat in the reign of Emperor Domitian. Domitian was zealous for the gods of Rome and hated anyone who refused to worship them. He didn't care if you also worshipped others so long as you kept current on your worship of the Roman pantheon. As a Christian, it would be a constant temptation to worship the other gods a little bit. You know, show up at a festival. Take in some sacrificial meat. Hang out by the pagan brothels. Jesus can still be number one in your heart, right? Arthur's entire letter screams, "No!" God, through Jesus, demands exclusive worship. We can't have any involvement with the gods of this world. Jesus' blood can purify our mind from idols and enable us to be fully committed in our service to God.

Arthur submits a final point here which will open up a complex discussion on the relationship between the first covenant and the new covenant. Let's look at each part of it before we enter into another digression to outline this interrelationship.

He is the mediator of a new covenant

In 7:22, we were told that Jesus is the cosigner of the new covenant, and in 8:6 we were first told that he is the mediator of the new covenant. These two related pictures point to the same reality. Jesus cosigns for the new covenant to enact it and mediates the relationship to bind us to God in the context of an everlasting covenant.

So that those who have been invited

Who are the parties with God in this new covenant? Those who have been invited. Remember back in 3:1, when the audience was called, "recipients of a heavenly invitation"? The same idea is present here. We have been invited from heaven to heaven. We have been invited to salvation (1:14), nobility (2:10), and rest (4:3), all of which are benefits of the new covenant.

Can receive the promised eternal possession

What is it here that we are invited to? To receive the promised eternal possession. Remember "promise" always refers to the promise God gave to Abraham. God promised to give Abraham "this land to possess" (Genesis 15:7). Arthur expands the definition of "this land" beyond just the physical land of Israel into the heavenly counterpart, the eternal abode of God. The promised eternal possession that we have been invited to receive is none other than the future world, the heavenly world.[46]

. . .

Since he died to redeem them from the violations committed under the first covenant

Arthur wraps up his sentence with an introduction to the interrelationship between the promise to Abraham, the first covenant, and the new covenant. We'll cover the meaning of this line in depth in the digression.

DIGRESSION: THE DOUBLE-CROSS

In the last paragraph Arthur introduced the interrelationship between the promise made to Abraham, the first covenant, and the new covenant.[47] The interplay is extraordinary and connects with the message Jesus preached in his death, resurrection, ascension, and exaltation. Let's walk through covenant history to detail each of these elements before we look at what Arthur is saying.

Salvation history begins with the creation narrative. I guess technically the creation narrative is the beginning of all history. God's creation of the world and the subsequent sin of Adam and Eve plunges all of creation, the entire universe, into the grip of sin. Due to their disobedience, God banishes man from the garden and consigns him to death.[48] For man to dwell with God again, an atonement will be needed.[49]

God resumes salvation history in Genesis 12 with the call of Abraham. This invitation includes a promise which is developed into three aspects within the narratives that follow:

1. I will make you a great nation. (Genesis 12:2)
2. I will give you this land to possess. (Genesis 15:7)
3. I will be God to your descendants. (Genesis 17:8)

Keep in mind, God made a unilateral promise to Abraham. Abraham did not enter into a formal, binding covenant with God. God entered into a covenant with himself to do these things. Arthur said that

God backed up this promise with an oath. He has sworn he will fulfill these promises.

As God promised, Abraham's descendants did grow into a nation. But that nation was held in captivity in Egypt. With Moses as mediator, God extended his saving power, and rescued the people from the land of Egypt and the hand of Pharaoh. Upon leading the people to Mount Sinai, God meets the people and shows a full display of his awesome power. He enters into a formal legal relationship with the people right there on the mountain. This relationship is a binding covenant in the full sense of the ancient definition of the term. Remember the definition we used earlier? A covenant is "a lifelong, legally-binding relationship of mutual benefit between two parties." It is important to add one further element here: covenants have blessings and curses attached—blessings for obedience and curses for disobedience.

Do you see the problem this invites? God unilaterally and unconditionally promised Abraham. But he entered into a formal legal relationship with his descendants that is ultimately a relationship conditioned upon performance of certain commandments. There is no problem if the people obey the covenant, but we know this is not what happened.

Disobedience occurred almost immediately. The sin of the golden calf began this relationship with disobedience. It culminated in the unfaithfulness of the Exodus generation. It continued in the book of Joshua and Judges. It was still there in the age of the kings and beyond. This constant and continual relationship of disobedience is best summarized by Peter when he calls the Torah, "a yoke on the neck of the disciples that neither our fathers nor we have been able to bear" (Acts 15:10 ESV).

How do we reconcile this? God promised something unconditional to Abraham but now those conditions can't be upheld because they are behind the legal wall of a covenant that has been broken. God can't bless the people because of the covenant, but he can't curse the people because of the promise. Did God double-cross himself?

The best covenant illustration in our modern world is that of a mortgage.[50] Whenever I say that, someone tells me that the Bible says marriage is a covenant. While I agree that marriage is a covenant, it isn't upheld in our world. More marriages end than stay together. Mortgages make the best illustration in lieu of the astronomical rate of divorces. Most mortgages are thirty years which certainly fits the long-term theme of covenants. Mortgages are also binding relationships. I can't just say never mind after the paperwork is signed. Mortgages are intended for mutual benefit. But these benefits come with obligations. If I don't pay, I get foreclosed.

There is only one answer: someone has to pay the debt. Someone has to pay for the curses in order for the blessings to be rendered. There is an ancient Jewish teaching that if Israel would keep just one Sabbath day God would send the Messiah.[51] This is an accurate depiction of God in his promises, but it fails to take into account that there is an actual, formal, legal covenant in place. The covenant has curses that must be rendered. This is where Jesus comes in.

Arthur tells us that Jesus is the "cosigner" of the new covenant in 7:22. As a good cosigner, Jesus steps in to pay the debt when the people have defaulted on the agreement. It says that he "died to redeem them from the violations committed under the first covenant." Why did he do this? "So that those who have been invited can receive the promised eternal possession."

This is salvation in covenantal perspective. This is salvation for the people of God holistically. Corporate Israel (and those Gentiles attached) can receive the promise of Abraham since Jesus has paid the outstanding debt due, a debt incurred by the violations of the first covenant. Now a new covenant can be made. Foreclosure has been averted; a new agreement can be signed. Let's look at the time periods:

Time Period	Key Figure
Creation	None specified
The promise	Abraham
The first covenant	Moses
The cosigning (the cross)	Jesus
The new covenant	Jesus

We have one last thing we need to talk about before we move on to the commentary on 9:16–22. If you compare the following translation to one found in a modern English version, you will notice that other versions typically include the word "will" (with the meaning "last will and testament"). There is growing acknowledgement in scholarship that Arthur does not change topics but maintains his focus upon the first covenant. This makes the best sense of what we find in 9:16–22 and avoids the confusion of mismatching terms that comes with seeing "covenant" transform into "will."[52] Let's proceed to the text and see how it is conveyed there.

9:16–22

*9:16*Now[53] it is a requirement for the death penalty to be carried out against the party who broke the covenant since it is a binding covenant that has been broken. *17*After all, a broken covenant is proven valid when the death penalty is delivered to those who broke it since it isn't being enforced as long as the one who broke it is allowed to live. *18*This being the case, of course the first covenant was inaugurated with blood. *19*So, when Moses had told all of the people every commandment in the Torah, he mixed the blood of bulls and goats with water, scarlet wool, and hyssop. Then he sprinkled the mixture on the book and all of the people and *20*said, "This is the blood of the covenant which God established with you."[54] *21*Following that, he also sprinkled the Tabernacle and all of its utensils for ministry. *22*In fact, nearly everything is purified with blood in the Torah since there can be no pardon without the offering of blood.

The paragraph of 9:16–22 serves to explain the final sentence of the last paragraph, "Since he died to redeem them from the violations committed under the first covenant." Arthur proceeds to explain why the violations of the first covenant required the death of Jesus. Why was there not another way for the debt to be paid? Arthur begins by saying that the death penalty is required against the party who broke the covenant, which in this case is Israel.

Arthur tells us that the broken covenant is "proven valid" when the death penalty is delivered and that the covenant "isn't being enforced" if the death penalty is not delivered. What is he saying? Let's go back to our mortgage example. How do I really know that after making my payments the house will be mine at the end of the term? How can I be sure the agreement is valid? Until the obligations are fulfilled, there is trust in the faithfulness of the other party. But if I default on the mortgage the validity of the contract will be painfully proven. Foreclosure demonstrates the binding quality of the agreement. The power of the mortgage is seen when either I receive a house at the end of the term or I get foreclosed on due to breaking the terms.

If the covenant can remain broken without the curse of death being enforced, then it must mean that the covenant was not legitimate. God didn't enter into a real covenant with Israel. But he did enter into a real covenant! This is the very problem he is solving. In order to prove the covenant was real, God is forced to carry out the death penalty against Israel—unless someone can cosign for it.

Arthur doesn't progress to this point just yet; he dwells on the circumstances of the first covenant. He demonstrates that the death penalty was the planned punishment for disobedience when he recalls the inauguration ceremony for it. It was "inaugurated with blood." He describes the ceremony found in his Bible in Exodus 24 to demonstrate that the use of blood proves that death was the penalty for disobedience.[55] This may be somewhat of a stretch for us to connect, but it wasn't for Arthur's original audience or the Exodus generation. The sacrificial animals and the application of their blood is a known ancient practice for entering into a lifelong covenant. The animal is a way to symbolize your commitment to a lifelong, til-death-do-us-part, kind of relationship.

The severity of the situation is intensified since so many things are sprinkled with the blood. The Torah itself, the people, the Tabernacle, and all of the Tabernacle's utensils. Every facet of the agreement between God and Israel is sealed with blood. Everything bears the curse of death for noncompliance.

Arthur concludes this paragraph with another thesis statement, "Nearly everything is purified with blood in the Torah since there can be no pardon without the offering of blood." The use of blood as a medium of purification was not restricted to just the covenant inauguration ceremony. The use of blood occurred yearly, monthly, weekly, and daily. The book of Leviticus describes a complex cycle of sacrifices required to re-demonstrate this nature of the relationship. Every year there is another Passover and another Day of Atonement. Every month there is another new moon and more sacrifices. Every week there is another Sabbath and more sacrifices. Every day there are sacrifices. Pardon is intrinsically connected to bloodshed.

9:23–28

*9:23*So, it was required for the models of the things in heaven to be purified with sacrifices like these, but the heavenly versions themselves required better sacrifices.[56] *24*After all, Messiah entered heaven itself to represent us now in the presence of God, not the manmade sanctuary which is a counterpart to the originals. *25*He didn't offer himself over and over again like the high priest enters the sanctuary each year with animal blood *26*or else he would have had to suffer repeatedly since the beginning of the world. Quite the contrary, he has appeared once at the culmination of history to expunge sin by sacrificing himself. *27*In the same way that people are destined to die once and then face judgment, *28*Messiah was offered once to bear the sins of many, and then he will come a second time, not to bear sin, but to save those who are ready to welcome him.

Arthur now connects this curse of death for the broken covenant to the death of Jesus. He begins with a bold claim: "The heavenly versions themselves required better sacrifices." Animal sacrifices and the application of their blood performed in accordance with the Torah's commands were acceptable for the earthly Tabernacle. But they aren't sufficient for the heavenly originals. Something better is needed.

Arthur draws this out further and also reveals his hand on his perspective about these heavenly originals. Jesus entered heaven itself. Let's look at this fact before we proceed to the rest of the verse.

Perhaps when you have read Hebrews in the past you have imagined a heavenly Temple or Tabernacle in heaven. Perhaps you took it a step further and imagined Jesus offering his blood to the Father and applying it in the heavenly Most Holy Place. Would it surprise you that Arthur sees no such structure in heaven? Heaven itself is the Most Holy Place. Remember our table on the temporal aspect of the Tabernacle?

Past	Present	Future
The first section		The second section
The Holy Place		Most Holy Place

We can add a spatial understanding too. Arthur interprets the Tabernacle as a microcosm. It is a mini universe. It represents both time and space.[57] For now, we live in the Holy Place, but Jesus lives in the literal Most Holy Place: heaven itself, the resting place of God. We are separated from Jesus by space. He is in heaven, we are on earth. But we are also separated from Jesus by time. His present is our future. He is our forward scout. We will be where he is.

Time/Space	Earth	Heaven
Present	The Holy Place	Most Holy Place
Future	Most Holy Place	Most Holy Place

This aligns exactly with what we see in Revelation also. When everything is made right and heaven merges with earth and overtakes it, look at what is said: "I saw no temple in the city, for its temple is the Lord God the Almighty and the Lamb" (Revelation 21:22 ESV).

Let's return to our verse at hand to see how much Arthur is telling us with just one sentence. Jesus didn't just enter heaven, he entered to represent us. This was illustrated by the high priest's yearly entrance into the Tabernacle's Most Holy Place. But Jesus didn't enter and exit. He is still there now. He is crowned king and sits on God's throne. He is there on our behalf. He lives in the actual resting place of God, the literal Most Holy Place.

Arthur draws out that distinction between the annual Day of Atonement event and Jesus' death. There is much in common for him to work with as an illustration, but the metaphor breaks down if pressed too far. Jesus' death is not an annual event. It happened once and it will never happen again. One time is all it took to accomplish a permanent atonement.

Arthur finds a more suitable illustration to this single death of Jesus in the experience of humanity generally. We also die once. Jesus, in his full humanity, did the same. He didn't need to suffer and die repeatedly as the animals did on the Day of Atonement. He appeared once at the "culmination of history" and he "expunged sins" through his sacrifice. Sin's debt has been paid. The covenant violations have been covered. The new covenant can be signed. Arthur continues his illustration by acknowledging that death is not the end of the story for humanity or for Jesus. Humans face judgment after death. Jesus returns after his death.

Event	Humanity	Jesus
Death	Destined to die	Sacrificed himself
After death	Face judgment	Come a second time

Arthur pulls language from the famous Isaiah 53 passage and connects it to the sacrifice of Jesus by saying that he "was offered once to bear the sins of many" and that his return will not be to "bear sin."

> He poured out his soul to death and was numbered with the transgressors; yet he bore the sin of many, and makes intercession for the transgressors. (Isaiah 53:12 ESV)

Arthur ends his paragraph with another reminder that he reckons salvation as a future event. We may be "saved" now, but we'll know the true meaning of salvation when Jesus returns for those who can't wait to see him.

COVENANT SACRIFICE COMPARISON: 10:1–4

*10:1*Now the Torah foreshadows the better future but doesn't achieve its realization. The same sacrifices are offered each year indefinitely which can't qualify[58] those who approach. *2*Otherwise, wouldn't the sacrifices have been discontinued since the servants would have already been purified and had no awareness of sins? *3*However, there is a reminder of sins in the sacrifices every year *4*because the blood of bulls and goats can't eradicate sins.[59]

Arthur tells us plainly the Torah foreshadows this salvation but has no power to bring it about. The Torah establishes a continuous, never-ending, cycle of sacrifice. In order to have fellowship with God, the sacrifices must continue.[60] It offers no lasting solution to this problem. There is no way to have unmitigated access to God. There is no way for anyone other than the high priest to enter into the Most Holy Place. There isn't even a way for him to enter more than just once per year. This isn't what God promised Abraham. This isn't what the new covenant prophesied. The annual Day of Atonement foreshadowed it, but can't bring it about.

Note how Arthur uses "qualify" again. His focus has mostly been about how Jesus is qualified to serve as eschatological priest. He is capable of bringing us into permanent fellowship with God, but the Aaronic high priests are unable to accomplish this. They don't go into the Most Holy Place just once; they have to go in every year. They aren't qualified to offer permanent atonement. Arthur presents another rhetorical question to prove that is the case. If it would have been a permanent atonement, the high priest would have been completely purified in body and mind. These high priests would have received God's "atonement for their wrongdoings" and never been reminded "of their sins again" like Jeremiah 31 said. Because this was not the case, Arthur confidently concludes that the Day of Atonement can't accomplish a permanent atonement. It can't eradicate sins. It may be able to temporarily abate them, but it can't fully remove the impact of sins.

Did you notice what Arthur called this annual cycle of sacrifice? A reminder of sins every year. Every year the Day of Atonement event reminds everyone that sins have not been decisively dealt with. They have to be covered again year after year on repeat. But do you remember what Jeremiah said when Arthur quoted him in 8:12? "I will never remind myself of their sins again." Arthur interprets Jeremiah's words to tell us of a time when no further sacrifice will be necessary. Such is not the case in the Levitical priesthood, but this is exactly what the new covenant promises.

10:5–10

*10:5*This is why, when he came into the world, he said, "You didn't want a sacrifice or an offering, instead you prepared a body for me. *6*You didn't enjoy burnt offerings or sin offerings. *7*Then I said, 'It's written about me on the pages of the book,[61] I have come here to do what you want, God.'" *8*The reason why he says, "I have come to do what you want" is because of when he said, "You didn't want or enjoy sacrifices, offerings, burnt offerings, and sin offerings," even though these are offered from the Torah. *9*He repeals the first one so that he can establish the second one. *10*We are being made holy because Messiah Jesus offered his body once and for all since that is what God wanted.

Arthur now connects all of this to another passage from his Bible: Psalm 40. Just like before, he interprets the text as direct dialogue and explains who is talking, when, and why. Remember, he develops his perspective like a drama. He creatively imagines the persons of the Trinity in a dialogue with the Bible allowing us to eavesdrop in on the conversations. So, who is talking?

The question of who is easily answered. The "who" being addressed is actually stated in the text itself, God. Arthur tells us "who" is speaking as well. He tells us in verse 10 that it is "Messiah Jesus." So just like chapter 2, this is Jesus talking to God.[62] But when is Jesus saying the words of Psalm 40 to God?

Arthur actually tells us that too. He says it is "when he came into the world." The word for "world" is different here than in 1:6 (where it was translated as "heavenly world"). Here it must mean our world. This is

Jesus talking to God as he left the heavenly world and entered our world via the incarnation. Can we know why he said these words? We definitely can, but let's look at the actual text before we address that question. As with other lengthy quotations, let's look at each line clause by clause.

You didn't want a sacrifice or an offering

Jesus starts by telling God what he didn't want. He didn't want a sacrifice or offering. He draws attention to the word "want" because of its use later in the quotation. He also comments that God was getting sacrifices and offerings because they were commanded in the Torah. Psalm 40 is alluding to the same problem Arthur has made obvious in his letter so far. God didn't want things to be the way they are. He doesn't want a relationship with him to be mediated by annual applications of animal blood.[63]

Instead you prepared a body for me

Jesus, via Psalm 40, goes on to say that God prepared a body for him. Or does it? If you open your Bible to Psalm 40, you will probably find something similar to the ESV: "you have given me an open ear." How can Arthur's quotation of Psalm 40:6 be so different than the one in our Bible? Remember Arthur is using the Septuagint (LXX), the Greek translation of the Hebrew Old Testament. When the translator approached Psalm 40:6, a decision was made to translate less literally. Technically the Hebrew says that God "has dug ears for me." The imagery is that God opened the ears of the Psalmist to listen to and obey God's Word. The LXX translator chose to bring out the meaning rather than actual words in his translation. This yielded "you prepared a body for me" in the LXX.[64] This is the Bible that Arthur and his audience opened day after day. Ultimately the sense is the same, but the actual words used by the translator more clearly enable Arthur to interpret this Psalm as being spoken by Jesus. Upon Jesus' exit from heaven, God made a body for him. A human body just like ours.

· · ·

You didn't enjoy burnt offerings or sin offerings

This clause restates the idea present in the first clause and tells us that God didn't enjoy burnt offerings or sin offerings. Again, this is not what God wanted; he wants to offer a permanent atonement.

Then I said, 'It's written about me on the pages of the book

Jesus responds to God's displeasure with the current system. Jesus offers a solution. First, he identifies that this solution is already present in the Bible. It has already been prophesied. This is Jesus talking prior to the incarnation, but this statement is echoed numerous times in the Gospels:

- If you believed Moses, you would believe me; for he wrote of me. (John 5:46 ESV)
- These are my words that I spoke to you while I was still with you, that everything written about me in the Law of Moses and the Prophets and the Psalms must be fulfilled. (Luke 24:44 ESV)

I have come here to do what you want, God

What is it that the Bible tells us Jesus is going to do? The Psalm leaves it vague, but Arthur will go on to explain it further. Here it is defined as doing what God wants. God had two *wants*. The one he didn't want and the one he did want. The Torah's sacrificial system wasn't sufficient to enable permanent and lasting relations with God. The first want is repealed so that the second want can be established.

Arthur offers a summary statement of what he wants his audience (and us) to take home from his use of Psalm 40, "We are being made holy because Messiah Jesus offered his body once and for all since that is what God wanted." He uses similar language as 2:11. Although the sacrifice of Jesus is a single event, its application in our life is a process.[65] We are in process of becoming holy. How? The Psalm just told us. Jesus offered his body on the cross. Why? This is what God wanted.

Before we go on, what led Jesus to say this Psalm to God? Just like in chapter 2, Jesus is responding to God. Remember when we first talked about Jeremiah 31, we asked the questions, "who is God talking to?" He was talking to Jesus. God proclaimed his promise to establish a new covenant with Israel (and the Gentiles attached) and Jesus responds back to God confirming his complete willingness to do his part to make it a reality.

10:11–14

> *10:11*In addition to that, every priest must stand day in and day out as part of their ministry so that they can offer the same sacrifices repeatedly which can never eradicate sins. *12*However, he sat down next to God after he offered a single and permanently effective sacrifice for sins. *13*From now on, he is looking forward to when his enemies will be piled under his feet. *14*After all, he has permanently qualified those who are being made holy by a single sacrifice.

Arthur returns to interpreting his favorite Psalm, Psalm 110. There is a conundrum with what the psalm says in relation to how the Levitical priests performed their role. He tells us plainly that "every priest must stand." Their job is never done. Another year, more sacrifices. Another month, more sacrifices. Another week, more sacrifices. Another day, more sacrifices. Sin is never permanently dealt with by the Torah's sacrifices.

But the same is not true with Jesus. He sat down. In Psalm 110:1 God says, "Sit next to me until I pile your enemies under your feet." His posture proves his job is done. One sacrifice was sufficient. Now Jesus sits on the throne of God waiting for the day when the last enemy is laid dead at his feet.

Arthur pulls all of this language together into single thought. Jesus has permanently qualified us. We are in process of progressing in holiness. Both of these are due to a one-time event, a single sacrifice. Jesus' death has spread from past to present to future.

10:15–18

*10:15*Now the Holy Spirit testifies to us about this. After saying, *16*"This is what the new covenant will be like that I will make with them after those days. Pay attention; this is the Lord talking. I will install my instructions in their hearts and engrave them on their minds," *17*he goes on to say, "I will never remind myself of their sins or their defiance again." *18*Where these are pardoned, there is no longer a need for a sin offering.

Just like in chapter 3, Arthur now lets the Holy Spirit speak to us after we have overheard the conversation of God and Jesus. Just like before, the Holy Spirit talks directly to us. He restates the words of Jeremiah, previously spoken by God to Jesus, but now straight to us. The Holy Spirit wants us to walk away with two reminders from what God had said back in chapter 8.[66]

1. I will install my instructions in their hearts and engrave them on their minds.
2. I will never remind myself of their sins or their defiance again.

Arthur concludes this section with a promise. Once sin has been definitively dealt with, once it is permanently pardoned, there will never be another sin offering.

Many of us are familiar with the idea of progressive revelation, that theology unfolds within the Old Testament into the New Testament. I think Arthur would be surprised by such a notion. Everything he has told us about the death of Jesus, his resurrection, ascension, exaltation, the new covenant, and salvation has come from the Old Testament.

In fact, he has taught everything by merging the prophecies of Psalm 110 with other verses.[67]

Psalm 110	Corroborating Verse(s)	Comment
Sit next to me	Psalm 2: Today I have crowned you king. Jeremiah 31: I will offer atonement for their wrongdoings, and I will never remind myself of their sins again. Psalm 40: You didn't want a sacrifice or an offering.	Jesus is enthroned after offering a permanently effective sacrifice for atonement.
Until I pile your enemies under your feet	Psalm 8: You subjected everything under his feet. Jeremiah 31: I will make [a new covenant] with the nation of Israel after those days.	There is a period of time between Jesus' exaltation and everything being subjected to him in which we wait for God to make the new covenant.
The Lord has sworn and will not reconsider it	Genesis 22: I promise to bless you and give you many descendants.	In connection with God's promise to Abraham, he swears to install Jesus as priest.
You are a priest forever	Jeremiah 31: They will never have to teach any family member or fellow citizen to learn about the Lord because every single one of them will know me personally.	As a seated priest, Jesus will mediate personal relationships to God since no sacrifices will be required anymore.
In the Melchizedek tradition	Jeremiah 31: This covenant will not be based on the covenant I made with their ancestors when I led them by the hand out of Egypt.	Jesus' priesthood will be entirely different from that of Aaron just like the covenant is entirely superior.

Through all of these interpretative connections, only made possible by carefully reading his Bible, Arthur is working out the theology of the new covenant. He is answering the question of how we can have unmitigated access to God. How we can have a resurrected relationship with him in which no sacrifices will be needed anymore. How we won't need a Tabernacle or Temple or priesthood to mediate our access to him anymore. He will be our God and we will be his people. Just like John told us:

I heard a loud voice from the throne saying, "Behold, the dwelling place of God is with man. He will dwell with them, and they will be his people, and God himself will be with them as their God. He will wipe away every tear from their eyes, and death shall be no more, neither shall there be mourning, nor crying, nor pain anymore, for the former things have passed away." (Revelation 21:3–4 ESV)

PIECE OF MIND

1. A great resource for early views on Melchizedek is *Traditions of the Bible* by James Kugel see 275–291.
2. This combined role is also true of Jesus. The belief that the Messiah would occupy both a priestly and kingly position is drawn from the Messianic prophecy of Zechariah 6:13.
3. Salem is an early form of Jerusalem, which enhances the connection between Melchizedek and Jesus, see Kugel 278.
4. Madison Pierce has the best illustration for the difference between the historical Melchizedek and the Melchizedek presented in Hebrews. It is like Saint Nick and Santa Claus. The historical Melchizedek was a real person who really met Abraham like Saint Nick was a real person who was known for his generosity. The Melchizedek presented in Hebrews is more like Santa Claus. I encourage you to listen to her explain it in her YouTube discussion with Brennan Breed: https://www.youtube.com/watch?v=Fgrb-d6hDFRw
5. The exegetical interpretative method for using the silence of Scripture to make a point is called *quod non in Torah non in mundo* (Latin for "Not in the Torah not in the world"). For a discussion of this in relation to Melchizedek, see Bruce 159–160.
6. Some scholars have speculated that Melchizedek was a pre-incarnate appearance of Jesus or an angelic figure based on Arthur's description of him. These assessments miss the creative interpretive methods of Arthur and that his overall interest in Melchizedek is exclusively because of his appearance in Psalm 110:4. Melchizedek is used to teach us about Jesus and his priesthood since Psalm 110:4 tells us Jesus' priesthood will be like Melchizedek's priesthood.
7. Due to the present negativity in our culture associated with the word "patriarch," I opted not to use this word to describe Abraham in the translation of 7:4. I chose to use "the father of the whole nation" instead since this fits the context and is supported by BDAG 788.
8. Modern pastors often use the tithe of Abraham as justification for Christians tithing to their local church since it precedes the Torah's commands of the Levitical tithe. The story itself makes the teaching difficult to uphold though. Abraham was not tithing to a local congregation, but to a man he had never met before. Abraham was also not tithing off of normal income, but the spoils of war. The Levitical tithe shares the same problem in that it was not a tithe to a local gathering but for support of the Levites who had no land inheritance and for the operation of the Tabernacle/Temple. For the record, I think tithing is a biblical act and that these events point to a philosophy of

giving that Christians should honor. I do not think either event could be read as a clear commandment upon Christians though.

9. Most likely the historical Melchizedek is Shem, the oldest son of Noah, see Kugel 284. His life span was long enough to have lived before the flood and all the way into the life of the patriarchs. This would mean that technically Abraham is related to Melchizedek, but Arthur's implications are based on what the text actually says, not the purported history behind it.

10. I have opted to translate "law" as "Torah" throughout (except when plural, then it is "instructions"). This decision was made for several reasons. The first of which is that it is a proper noun, so I elected to reflect that in translation. Secondly, the Western world generally has a negative view of the word "law." As an individualist culture, the idea of an outside construct telling us what to do is typically viewed negatively. This couldn't be further from the approach of the biblical writers when talking about the Torah of Moses. David feels comfortable saying "I love your Torah" in Psalm 119. For a balanced approach to the subject of the Torah, I highly recommend the audio material of Dr. Dwight A. Pryor. For this topic, see "Jesus, Christians & the Law" and "Paul, the Law and the Church." Although Dr. Pryor passed away in 2011, his material is still available at www.jcstudies.com. I also recommend his book: *A Continuing Quest: The Dwight A. Pryor Legacy Collection*.

11. In 7:11 and 7:14, Arthur uses two odd words to describe the arrival of Jesus into the human sphere. The translation above uses "emerge" and "sprung" for these two words. Arthur pulled both of these words from the Messianic prophecy recorded in the oracle of Balaam in Numbers 24:17.

12. The Greek word translated "part of" is a form of the same word used in 2:14 to describe the incarnation, "*he took on* the same condition."

13. The use of "sprung" regarding Jesus' birth also serves to further highlight the differences between he and the Aaronic priests. Arthur describes the other priests as descending, meaning they are going down. But he uses "sprung" for Jesus indicating he is going up.

14. This commandment governing lineage in reference to the Levites is defined throughout the Torah. The priesthood begins with Aaron and his sons (Exodus 28:1–3). It would continue from there through Aaron's line (Exodus 40:14–15). Priests had strict requirements of who they could marry (Leviticus 21:7 & 21:13–14). Priestly duty started at age thirty (Numbers 4:30). The high priest served for life (Numbers 35:25).

15. For the understanding that "in the Melchizedek tradition" is a synonym for "like Melchizedek" in 7:15, see Ellingworth and Nida 97. This assessment led to the translation "in the Melchizedek tradition" rather than "in the order of Melchizedek" found in modern English versions. This word choice allows for both meanings present in the Greek word (as discussed in the commentary above): the succession of priests from Aaron until 70AD and the similitude in priesthood between Melchizedek and Jesus.

16. This "final stop" in salvation history is expertly described by David Moffitt (using the traditional English term "perfect"): "Perfection language is broader than resurrection and likely has to do with the ability of the human being to come into God's presence.... Perfection is therefore closely bound up with the purification of the human being such that humanity and God's presence can dwell together. Perfection has to do with making the human being fit to enter the world to come" Moffitt 262.

17. Josephus records this in *Jewish Antiquities*, Book 20 Chapter 10.

18. The description of Jesus as "loyal" is drawn from Psalm 16:10 and serves to connect Jesus' character to his resurrection: "For you will not abandon my soul to Sheol, or let your *holy one* see corruption" (Psalm 16:10 ESV, italics mine).

19. Throughout the commentary I have stressed that Jesus is sitting on the same throne as God. That seems to contradict what Arthur actually says here. Arthur is using the entire phrase "the throne of the Majesty in heaven" as a circumlocution, or round-about way of referring to God.

20. The reference to the heavenly Tabernacle being built (literally "pitched") by God uses terminology found in Numbers 24:6 LXX and serves as another connection to Balaam's oracle.

21. See Koester 53 and Attridge 8. Josephus is the most famous example of this practice.

22. This is another occasion in which Arthur has purposely misquoted the text. He again changes the verb (in this case he changes διαθήσομαι to συντελέσω). The new verb shares the same root as the word we have translated as "qualify" (2:10), "destination" (7:11), and "rehabilitate" (9:10) in Hebrews. This further reinforces the eschatological quality of the new covenant and its connection to the resurrection, definitive atonement, and the culmination of salvation history, see Pierce 79–81.

23. The literal Greek behind "every single one of them" is "from the least of them to the greatest." The imagery is that in God's kingdom every citizen, regardless of social status, will have the same privilege of direct access to him. Since it is not customary to describe citizenry as "least" and "great" in modern English, the translation did not seek to reproduce the words and instead used "every single one of them" to yield the intended imagery.

24. The decision to translate as "expire" rather than "vanish" is to reinforce the legal context found in the discussion of covenants. A legal arrangement doesn't "vanish," but it does "expire" or lose legal standing by becoming out of date.

25. For the approach that the "them" God finds fault with in 8:8 is the Levitical priests, see Pierce 89.

26. The covenant is also not the division of the books in the Bible. It's unfortunate this became the primary title for the two sections of the Bible. Throughout this book, I have used the customary terms "Old Testament" and "New Testament," but that is in conformity with tradition rather than accuracy in meaning.

27. The old covenant did not teach salvation by works (see Schnittjer 246). Salvation in the past and present is the same. It is also important to point out that the perspective that the new covenant hasn't technically started yet does not obligate us to perform the ritual commands in the Torah. Christians are obligated to follow the commands of Jesus and the apostles, which are cited from the Torah or based upon it.

28. A great verse that showcases the breadth of God's saving power in Jesus spreading beyond Israel to Gentiles is 1 John 2:2, "He is the atonement for our sins, but not just our sins, he is the atonement for the sins of the whole world." John is referring to how Jesus' death fully covers the sins of Israel and goes beyond to cover the whole world. This extends the salvation offered through Jesus to "whoever believes in him." Paul gets to the same end result but through a different approach. In Ephesians 2:19, he calls Gentile believers "equal citizens among the saints" and in Romans 11 he describes Gentiles as being "grafted in." Paul understands the saving power of God extending to Gentiles as they attach themselves to the God of Israel and his Messiah in faith.

29. The literal Greek speaks of the Tabernacle being comprised of two "tents" rather than two "sections" in 9:2–3.

30. The literal Greek is "after the curtain." In Greek the preposition "after" is used for time and not space. Arthur's word choice subtly hints at the temporal analogy he is going to make about the Tabernacle's structure in 9:8–9, see Harris 211.

31. Arthur's choice to use the Tabernacle in chapter 9 and throughout rather than the chronologically closer Temple could be to show that even in its perfect form it was still unfit for eternal communion with God. Had he used the Temple in his letter it could have been argued its issues were due to the problematic governance that took place in the decades prior to its destruction. By using the Tabernacle instead, Arthur precludes this line of thinking. Furthermore, Christians likely did not interpret the destruction of the Temple in A.D. 70 as final nor as a comment on its inadequacy until much later. Christian and Jewish thinkers at the time likely believed it would be rebuilt at some point in the (near) future like at its original destruction in 586 B.C. For this perspective, see Schenck2, or you can check out his summary of the temple and Paul on his YouTube channel: https://www.youtube.com/watch?v=rsl0DP9-0Zs. I disagree with Schenck that the theological ramifications of the temple's destruction led to the authoring of Hebrews, but I do think that its destruction intensified the challenges associated with worshiping the God of Israel under the reign of Domitian, see Whitlark 186–188.

32. The two tablets that contained the Ten Commandments did not feature the commands broken into two sets of five as is commonly supposed. Instead, the tablets were two copies that each contained the Ten Commandments. The tablets were then stored in a mutually accessible location by both God and Israel, the Most Holy Place. The idea is that the two tablets were copies of the agreement between God and Israel similarly to how copies of contracts are stored by both parties today.

33. It is possible that the word "glory" in "cherubim of glory" in 9:5 is meant to be understood as "ornate" or "gloriously designed" cherubim.

34. The translation of "mistakes" reflects that the word implies "sins committed in ignorance." This draws upon the dichotomy found in the Torah between sins of ignorance and sins committed "with a high hand." Later Rabbis would define high-handed sins as sins that were not repented of.

35. The word translated "rehabilitate" is the same word translated as "qualify" and "destination" elsewhere (typically perfect/perfected in modern English versions). This meaning is derived from the context since the object being "perfected" is the conscience and the sense is that the mind is being purified from the effect of sin upon it.

36. Technically the high priest does enter the Most Holy Place four times in order to perform the Day of Atonement ceremony. Arthur's point is that all of these entries occur on a single date in conjunction with a single event. The point of each entry is explained by the Temple Institute in their illustrated tour of the Holy of Holies: https://www.templeinstitute.org/illustrated-tour-the-holy-of-holies.

37. The origin of the Day of Atonement in Leviticus 16 is specifically stated to be "after the death of the two sons of Aaron." This connection between death and atonement probably assisted Arthur in drawing the connection between Jesus' death and the atonement available in him.

38. The functional connection between the incense altar and the Most Holy Places is discussed in Lancaster 767–769.

39. It is also possible that Arthur placed the altar of incense within the Most Holy Place because of how he understood Exodus 30:6, where the location of the altar is vaguely described there as "in front of the mercy seat." This verse doesn't definitively say which side of the curtain it is located on, but it is decisive in other places. It is possible that

this ambiguity led to Arthur locating it in the Most Holy Place. However, I am convinced the decision was intentional to represent its function and the current state in which the future is breaking into the present.

40. Personally, I am baffled at how some interpreters understand "the time of restoration" from 9:10 as the present age or the Christian age. Things haven't been restored yet! The promises of the new covenant are available in preview form, but so much more awaits us in the actual time of restoration.

41. The Greek word translated as "conscience" is broader than just the internal moral barometer we think of in English. It also includes the meaning "consciousness" and functions as a synonym for "mind," see BDAG 967–968.

42. Numerous researchers have shown the similarity in impact to the brain between heroin and internet pornography, but a good example is "Neuroscience of Internet Pornography Addiction: A Review and Update" by Todd Love from the National Institute of Health: https://www.ncbi.nlm.nih.gov/pmc/articles/PMC4600144.

43. Hebrews 9:14 features a textual variant that is detectable to readers even in translation. The manuscript difference is whether the conscience being purified is *your* conscience or *our* conscience. The translation above has opted to go with "your" following the textual decision of the Tyndale House Greek New Testament.

44. This textual variant is among the most challenging variants in Hebrews. The textual tradition is fairly evenly divided between γενομένων and μελλόντων. While γενομένων "the present good things" has early support, μελλόντων "the better future" has greater diversity of support. The textual decision adopted here has the support of several classic commentaries: Moffatt 120 and Montefiore 152. This same textual decision is used by the King James and New King James and follows the textual decision of the Tyndale House Greek New Testament.

45. For a great treatment on the religious symbology of blood and its power as a medium of purgation, see *Defilement and Purgation in the Book of Hebrews* by William Johnnson.

46. When referring to God's promise of "this land" to Abraham there is overlap in meaning between the geopolitical land of Israel and the heavenly world. Arthur's focus is upon the heavenly world as the permanent resting place of God and inheritance of the faithful, but this is not to exclude the meaning that present day Israel is the rightful possession of the Jewish people.

47. For the connection between the new covenant and the promise to Abraham, see Kaiser.

48. The imagery of the angels on the curtain that separates the Holy Place from the Most Holy Place (Exodus 26:31) is designed to break down the barrier separating man from God that was erected after Adam's sin in the Garden (Genesis 3:24). The barrier is only temporarily removed within the context of the Day of Atonement ritual. The permanent eradication of this barrier will be the full realization of the new covenant when everyone will know the Lord personally.

49. The literary point of Genesis 1–11 is to explain how the world as we know it could have been created by a perfect God. These chapters serve as a prologue to narrate how the world went from an idyllic place where man and God lived together to the broken, chaotic, and death-filled world we know today. It is ironic that so many Christians have sought to explain away these chapters rather than see that they are in fact explaining everything.

50. The mortgage illustration is best employed in the United States. Mortgage practice in other Western nations is less applicable for comparison with ancient covenants.

51. This teaching is from the Jerusalem Talmud in Ta'anit 1:1.

52. The decision to translate "covenant" as "will" in modern English versions is an attempt to resolve the difficulty posed by 9:16. The ESV captures the literal Greek, "For where a will is involved, the death of the one who made it must be established." The problem is that seeing this as a "will" is only resolved for a reader in modern contexts. We have ample evidence of inheritances in the ancient world transitioning ownership before the death of the testator (see Cockerill 405). The resolution is found in seeing the use of "covenant" in the specific context. Arthur is not talking about covenants in general, but the first covenant made between God and the Exodus generation.

53. The translation present for 9:15–22 is heavily indebted to the work of Scott Hahn. His work on this passage is the very finest example of Hebrews scholarship in the last twenty years (I literally cheered as I read it the first time). I highly recommend both of his articles which discuss his findings, see the bibliography for references to both of them.

54. Arthur has slightly modified Moses' speech from Exodus 24:8 to more closely resemble the words of Jesus at the last supper.

55. Arthur's description of the covenant inauguration ceremony in 9:18–21 contains details not found in the Exodus account (24:3–8). He could be drawing on tradition not found in the text or conflating details found elsewhere in the Torah for purposes of illustration, see Lane 2:244.

56. Notice the oddity that 9:23 talks of "better sacrifices" when speaking of the singular sacrifice of Jesus. This is merely to emphasize the "general principle" of the comparison, see Attridge 261.

57. Josephus has a similar view of the Tabernacle operating as a microcosm of the universe (see *Jewish Antiquities*, Book 3 Chapter 6). Arthur goes beyond this to describe the Tabernacle as a microcosm in the sense of both representing time and space. In 9:9, he describes the first section of the Tabernacle as representing the "present time," and in 9:24 he describes the second section of the Tabernacle as representing "heaven itself." This view contributed to his ability to assert that Jesus went "beyond the sky" in 4:14. He sees the sky/space as the material veil that separates our world from the heavenly world. The Tabernacle also functions as a miniature version of Mount Sinai. Similarly, to Arthur, this then yields a temporal and spatial analogy. The Tabernacle is pointing to a specific place (Mount Sinai) and a specific event in time (God descending on the mountain). For this view, see Schnittjer 309.

58. This is another notable textual variant. This time the variant is not as detectable in English since it relates to the grammatical form of the Greek words behind, "which can't qualify." Some manuscripts are connected to a singular object "The Torah" and some are connected to the plural "The same sacrifices." Grammatically, the verb should be in the singular, however the textual evidence is more strongly in favor of the plural. I am persuaded that the decision is intentional on Arthur's part. He purposely used less-than-perfect grammar to reinforce his point: The Torah is not the problem, but it is not *not* the problem either. It showcases the love of God and his desire to live with humanity, but it also institutes a cycle of sacrifice and priesthood that are not qualified for resurrection life. This textual decision is also supported by the Tyndale House Greek New Testament.

59. The terminology used by Arthur in 10:4 and 10:11 of "eradicating sins" is pulled from God's self-disclosure to Moses in Exodus 34:7. It also occurs in Isaiah 27:9.

60. Note that the sacrifices described in the Old Testament are not always sin offerings. Some are specific to sin, but many are relational in nature and serve to highlight the relationship between God and Israel, see Schnittjer 315–317.

61. The literal "roll of the scroll" is exchanged for the modern imagery "pages of the book" to facilitate ease of understanding. Early in church history scrolls were transitioned to the book format we are familiar with today.

62. Arthur detects the entry of another speaker in Psalm 40 due to the verbal shift taking place in verse 5. Verse 4 speaks in the third person and verse 5 shifts to first person. Arthur uses this to identify Jesus as the speaker of verses 6–8.

63. A similar theme of Psalm 40 is also found in Psalm 51. God is also said not to enjoy sacrifices or burnt offerings in 51:16. The same theme is found in the words of Hosea 6:6, quoted by Jesus in Matthew 9:13 (ESV), "I desire mercy, and not sacrifice."

64. For the best explanation of how "ears" became "body" in the Psalm 40 citation recorded in 10:5, see Lane 2:255.

65. Jesus' death is a sacrifice primarily in a metaphorical sense. The apostles understood the historical events of Jesus through the lens of the Torah. Jesus wasn't a sacrifice in the literal sense since the Bible strictly denounces human sacrifice. However, his death does have sacrificial merit. It accomplishes what no actual sacrifice could do: permanent atonement. For this reason, there is no need to envision a literal fulfillment of a heavenly Day of Atonement. This is the imagery present through which we understand the implications of Jesus' death, resurrection, ascension, and exaltation.

66. When Arthur quotes Jeremiah 31 in 10:17, he introduces additional text. In 8:12, he quotes it as, "I will never remind myself of their sins again." However in 10:17, he quotes it as, "I will never remind myself of their sins *or their defiance* again." He adds another item that God will not remind himself of. This additional text comes from Exodus 34:9, which is Moses' response to God's self-disclosure. Arthur previously referenced this in 10:4 and 10:11.

67. The interdependence of Psalm 110 with Arthur's holistic theology is taken up in *Psalm 110 and the Logic of Hebrews* by Jared Compton.

THE FAITHFUL
(10:19–12:29)

TIMES NEW ROMAN

FIDELIS WAS EXHAUSTED. HE HAD BEEN TALKING FOR OVER thirty minutes, and he was giving it everything he had. These priceless words had the power to rescue this entire community. This was possibly their last chance, the stop just before the point of no return. He didn't want to let them down by doing anything less than perfect. His legs felt like jelly as he strained to keep himself standing. As he shifted his balance, his eyes caught Florus.

Florus was just a boy the last time he had seen him, but now he was a young man, the spitting image of his father. Fidelis knew his father well; his faithfulness to God and boldness for Messiah were an inspiration. But it had cost him his life five years earlier. Florus hadn't taken it well. He hadn't smiled in years, or cried, or shouted, or anything. He was just there. The memory of his father had more life than he did at this point.

Florus diverted his attention to the ground; he didn't like to look anyone in the eyes, especially someone who knew him before it happened. He thought he was hiding his pain, but he wasn't fooling anyone but himself. That was one thing he was great at.

No one wanted to say anything about it, but they all knew he was deeply wounded. It was hard to say if he was madder at God or at his father. Everyone knew if his father went to that protest there were risks if people found out he was a Christian. There was no trial, or sentencing; he just never came home that day. In a way Florus died that day too. He barely ever came to service anymore; it was something of a miracle that he was here this night.

"You shouldn't throw away your confidence since it comes with a great reward."

Fidelis read with compassion and a sense of urgency. Something began to stir in Florus at these words. Florus fought hard to prevent the rush of emotions, but he couldn't push them down this time. He thought of his father. He felt angry and alone, but he also felt proud. His dad was a hero, his hero, but it was hard to accept that he was really gone. Fidelis kept reading:

"We are on the side of those who remain faithful and preserve their soul."

Florus knew all the right answers to say in church, but it never really dawned on him that his father would live again, at least it had not hit him in any personal way. Is that what motivated his father? Why God, why?

These questions ricocheted within his mind as Fidelis read on.

INNER PIECE

Hebrews At A Glance
I. The Son (1:1–2:18)
II. The Word (3:1–6:20)
III. The Priest (7:1–10:18)
IV. The Faithful (10:19–12:29)
a. The Great Reward
i. 10:19–25
ii. 10:26–31
iii. 10:32–34
iv. 10:35–39
b. In Faithfulness
i. 11:1–7
ii. 11:8–12
iii. 11:13–16
iv. 11:17–22
v. 11:23–28
vi. 11:29–31
vii. 11:32–38
viii. 11:39–40
c. The Great Crowd
i. 12:1–3
ii. 12:4–6
iii. 12:7–11
iv. 12:12–17
d. Two Mountains
i. 12:18–24
ii. 12:25–29
V. The End (13:1–13:25)

We have now covered three sections and only have two more ahead of us. Much of what Arthur intends to say has been said, but the most famous chapter remains. Let's review what we have learned so far before we advance.

The first section established rapport with Arthur's audience by inviting them into the throne room coronation ceremony. With a series of Scripture citations, he allowed us to eavesdrop as Jesus was crowned cosmic king. This paved the way to the first warning as Arthur challenged his audience to take the message of Jesus seriously.

Arthur picked up this spirit of warning throughout Section 2 as he levied a comparison between the Exodus generation and Christians. Both groups have been invited to God's place of rest. The Exodus generation proved unfaithful and were barred from entry. This creates a dangerous prerequisite that Arthur reasons is true for Christians as well. All of Section 2 focused upon this risk and his encouragement for the audience to avoid it at all costs.

Arthur used Section 3 to explore the implications present in Psalm 110, especially in its connection with Jeremiah 31. The prophesied new covenant is shown to be superior with Jesus as resurrected high priest enabling the most intimate of experience with God. He successfully cosigned for the first covenant violations through his death and mirrored the Day of Atonement through his single sacrifice. This theological development grants God the legal right to convey the promises made to Abraham upon his people and to implement the new covenant age upon Jesus' return.

Arthur transitions to Section 4 and with it picks back up on the spirit of warning from Section 2. He'll begin the section with strong warnings before adjusting his tone to narrate past examples of faithfulness. The "faith chapter" will get to the heart of what Arthur yearns to see his dear friends do in the midst of their difficulties. With that, let's proceed into unpuzzling Section 4.

THE GREAT REWARD: 10:19–25

10:19So, brothers and sisters, we have confidence to enter the sanctuary by the blood of Jesus. 20Because of his death we can use the new path he opened up for us through the curtain that leads to life. 21We also have him as a great priest over the family[1] of God. 22That is why we should approach God with genuine hearts in complete faithfulness since our hearts have been purified from a corrupt conscience and our bodies have been washed with pure water. 23We should maintain our commitment to hope without hesitation because the one who promised is faithful. *²⁴*Let's also think of ways to motivate one another to be supportive and *²⁵*not give up on gathering together² like some have the habit of doing. Quite the contrary, let's encourage each other even more as you see the day getting closer.

Arthur begins the section by directly addressing the audience again. He returns to a favorite term: brothers and sisters. He hasn't used the term in reference to his friends since 3:12. Remember that his ability to refer to his audience as siblings is based entirely on his Bible. We are siblings because Jesus called us his siblings in Psalm 22, quoted by Arthur in 2:12. Jesus' statement binds him to us and us to each other. We are one family under God, and this connection drives Arthur to protect his friends from the damage of drifting away.

What does Arthur want to tell his spiritual siblings now that he has their attention? "We have confidence to enter the sanctuary by the blood of Jesus." Arthur also pulls out another term we haven't seen in a while: "confidence." This term last occurred in 4:16 and 3:6. There we discussed how it has the sense of being "at home." We should enter the sanctuary, the heavenly world, the resting place of God, the same way we walk through our front door. We can have the confidence to be who we are, to be honest and open with God.

For now, we enter metaphorically through the medium of Jesus' blood to where Jesus is now. The cleansing power of Jesus' blood enables us to live in God's presence. Arthur restates the same basic thought in the next sentence, but this time it focuses less on the metaphorical access we have through Jesus today and more on the literal access we will have to God in the future. Jesus' blood, here stated as his death, opens a new path that goes right through the curtain. This path goes beyond the created order into the very dwelling place of God. The life this leads to is the resurrection life—the never-ending life that begins upon Jesus' return when we fully enter into God's place of rest.³

10:19	10:20
To enter	Use the new path he opened
The sanctuary	Through the curtain that leads to life
By the blood of Jesus	Because of his death

In explaining this wonderful reality that is partially present today and perfectly preserved for tomorrow, Arthur snaps back to his earlier discussion of the priesthood of Jesus. He reminds us that we have him as a great priest, the highest quality possible, over the family of God. Arthur consistently describes our relationship with God, Jesus, and each other with familial terms. This is the closest earthly approximation to the depth of intimacy God intends for us.

Arthur draws implications from this reality established. Since Jesus allows us to enter the sanctuary, since he opened up this path to God, since he is a great priest, and since we are united as a family, we should approach God! He is beckoning us to pass the bar and come to him.

He then defines the approach to God and how we are to do so. Let's look closely at each of these facets.

Genuine hearts

The first thing Arthur says should characterize our approach to God is genuine hearts. The literal Greek is "true hearts." The idea is that of honesty. There is no point in sending a fake version of myself down the path Jesus opened. We have to be honest with who we are and where we are in our walk and take the next step from there. This was true for Arthur's original audience as much as it is for us. As they saw the threat of persecution mounting, and became crushed under rising fear, they weren't honestly evaluating themselves. Arthur invites us to do the same. As our world changes, we need to assess what is really important to us. If the cost to follow Jesus goes up, are we willing to pay?

Complete faithfulness

The next descriptor is that of "complete faithfulness." Modern

English versions typically translate as "faith" rather than faithfulness, but Arthur is their commitment not their beliefs. They mentally assent to the truths of the Christian faith but they need to lock in their unwavering commitment to God in faithfulness as the world around them pressures their stand.

Purified hearts

How are we enabled to approach God with genuine hearts and complete faithfulness? It is because our hearts have been purified. The complete atonement made possible by the cross offers absolute purity in the inner person. Arthur has consistently used "hearts" to represent the inner life of people, and that is what the death of Jesus has purified. What are we purified from? A corrupt conscience. Our inner self, here pictured as our conscience or our mind, has been marred by the effect of sin upon it. The atonement Jesus offers is able to fully rehabilitate the damage caused and enable genuine and complete connection to God.

Washed bodies

But Jesus' blood did more than just purify our inner self. It also washed our physical bodies with pure water. Arthur certainly has the act of baptism in mind, but it goes beyond that. Too often we think of our relationship with God exclusively as a spiritual or immaterial reality, but it isn't. Our physical bodies matter. What we do in them affects our relationship with God as much as prayer does. We are physical and spiritual beings. Jesus' death purifies both.[4]

Arthur breaks the metaphorical approach to God and tells his friends what he wants to see them do. He includes himself when he says, "We should maintain our commitment to hope without hesitation because the one who promised is faithful." This statement mirrors his remark in 4:14, "We should maintain our commitment to Jesus the Son of God." Here he identifies our commitment to "hope." Keep in mind, hope is not wishful thinking or blind optimism. Hope is the certain expectation of what is coming. How do we know our hope is certain?

God made a promise. He never lies. He told it to Abraham, and it will come to pass.

With the approach to God behind him and the charge to remain faithful to the one who is faithful identified, Arthur now adds more practical advice. There is little in the way of practical commands in Hebrews before we get to chapter 13, but this is an example of specific behavior Arthur wants to see reinvigorated among his friends. So, what does he want them to do?

He wants his friends to "think of ways to motivate one another." His advice sounds odd, but it is exactly what is needed in times of persecution. We are a family, so we have to act like it. Arthur is geographically separated from the audience, so he likely doesn't know all of the needs present; he encourages them to sit and think about it. They need to support one another. Modern English versions typically preserve the literal Greek, "love and good works" but these aren't two things. These two words combine together to form one idea: take care of your church family.

There is a prerequisite command needed in order to do this properly. We have to actually gather together. There is no way to motivate one another to this type of care if we aren't together. Arthur plainly tells them that he knows some people have already abandoned this. The same is true for us. Far fewer people darken the door of the church now than several years ago. That can't be our habit.

What is causing members of the congregation to "give up on gathering"? This is almost certainly driven by the informants. Roman culture was filled with those loyal to the empire, always looking to rat out their fellow citizens for treason. Since Christians proclaimed "Jesus is Lord" rather than "Caesar is Lord," they were an easy target. The Roman government offered financial incentives to those who informed on this act of "sedition." This led to an environment where it was constantly a risk to be identified as a Christian or associating with Christians and would thus make gathering together a risky affair. Arthur leaves no room for this fear, gathering together is essential for the church.[5]

So, we are supposed to come together and motivate each other towards taking care of the local body, and what else? We have to encourage each other. This could also be translated as "challenge" each other. The Greek word possesses both the positive sense of encouraging someone and the opposite end of challenging someone to press on. For those who are struggling, we need to be an encouragement in their time of need. For those stagnating, we need to challenge them to move forward and not let the world push them back.

Arthur then expresses a sense of urgency. The day is getting closer. What day? He again shows his utter dependence on his Bible; there is only one good example in which the word "day" and "at hand" (translated "closer" above) appear together; it is from the same verse he will quote in the next paragraph: "The day of their calamity is at hand, and their doom comes swiftly" (Deuteronomy 32:35 ESV).[6] The Day of Judgment is coming. It is getting closer everyday. We can't waste any time. We must motivate each other.

10:26–31

> [10:26]Now if we continue sinning on purpose after we learned the truth, there is no longer a sacrifice for sins that can be made. [27]Quite the contrary, all that is left is a terrifying anticipation of judgment and a burning rage which will consume the opposition. [28]Anyone who violates the Torah of Moses is sentenced to death without mercy[7] based on the testimony of two or three witnesses. [29]If that is the case, don't you think a much more severe sentence is warranted for the one who disparages the Son of God, who thinks the blood of the covenant[8] that made him holy is ordinary blood, and who ridicules the Spirit of grace?[9] [30]After all, we know the one who said, "Justice is my job, and I will administer it," is also the one who said, "The Lord will avenge his people." [31]It is terrifying to fall into the hands of the living God.

Arthur ended the last paragraph by introducing the notion of a coming Day of Judgment and he proceeds in this paragraph to draw out the implications of it. Choosing to sin in view of a coming judgment would be completely illogical. Arthur is speaking specifically of intentional sin—specifically idolatry or apostasy. The grave concern he has for his friends is that they are on a path that leads to destruction. They are on a road that has a point of no return. He is confident they haven't crossed it . . . yet. As he did throughout Section 2, he offers a stern warning. The new covenant reality that we have tasted in Jesus is simply too serious to handle it flippantly. For those willing to throw away this intimate connection to God for the temporary security of worshipping idols, and thereby recanting their relationship with Jesus, are not worthy of it. Remember the persecution under Domitian is reserved for those who exclusively worship the God of Israel and his Messiah. Those who mix their worship with idols are not in danger. This is the threat facing his audience. Will they be singularly committed to the true God?

He then specifies that the sin to avoid occurs "after we learned the truth." There is certainly an education element present, but Arthur intends a relationship perspective too. We learned what is true and we learned who is true. This is shorthand for the entire experience of coming to know the one true God through Jesus. Knowing him is worth any price. At least it should be.

For those who forsake him, there is no reparation to be made. The same fate awaits them as the Exodus generation. Arthur continues to mine the danger of this past example and the risk that it represents for those who follow Jesus today. The Exodus generation proved there is a limit to God's patience—a point of no return. The fate that awaits them is judgment and fire. This fire will consume all of Jesus' enemies.

Arthur allows the tension to remain as he goes on to compare the situation to that of the Old Testament again. Since the message we have believed is more significant, disregarding it must be more serious. In the Torah, those who shunned its authority were sentenced to death if the matter was corroborated by two or three witnesses. This is similar to the rhetorical question of 2:2, "If the message God spoke through the angels became binding so that every violation received a rightful punishment, how will we escape punishment if we disregard such a great salvation?" Arthur proceeds with another question for his friends, "If that is the case, don't you think a much more severe sentence is warranted for the one who . . . ." Arthur expands his thought process in view of the discussion held up to this point to heighten the absolute incongruity that exists in abandoning faithfulness to God.

He starts by saying that such a person "disparages the Son of God."

This reminds the listener of the content in Section 1 of the letter. There Arthur invites us to witness Jesus being installed as cosmic king of the universe. Here he terrifies the audience with the power this position wields against one who belittles him. He progresses to the "blood of the covenant." Those who fall back in their relationship with God are counted as devaluing the blood of Jesus as something ordinary, the same as anyone else's blood. This pulls from the discussion of Section 3 regarding the new covenant and its implementation through Jesus' sacrifice on the cross. Finally, he comments that this person would be guilty of ridiculing the Holy Spirit. Arthur has previously associated the Holy Spirit with the sacrifice of Jesus and with direct communication with God's people. Those roles are flipped as the hypothetical person offends the Holy Spirit beyond repair.

Arthur supports his dreadful language with direct quotations from his Bible. He references two passages from Deuteronomy, 32:35 and 32:36. He already alluded to this passage in the last paragraph, but now he directly cites it. If the two quotations directly follow each other, why does he cite them as two separate verses? He is making two points. The first verse, "Justice is my job, and I will administer it" points to negative judgment. At the Day of Judgment those who are guilty of disparaging God's Son and his salvation will experience God's justice wrought against them. They will be piled at the feet of Jesus. A burning fire will consume them. But for God's people, the Day of Judgment is one of vindication. There we will receive the full reward of faithfulness, and God will avenge us from those who persecuted the church. This is blurred in some translations since the word translated "avenge" can also mean "judge." The meaning of "avenge" or "vindicate" is so clear in the original context of Deuteronomy that it is actually how the ESV translated it. "For the LORD will vindicate his people and have compassion on his servants" (Deuteronomy 32:36 ESV).[10]

All of humanity enters the Day of Judgment and there are only two possible outcomes, just like we saw with the two outcomes for the soil in 6:7–8.

The Day of Judgment	
Cursed soil destined for fire	Blessed soil
God pronounces judgment	God avenges his people

Arthur allows the tense tone to continue through this paragraph with a final remark: "It is terrifying to fall into the hands of the living God." Nothing could be truer. Remember that the name "Living God" is used specifically to distinguish God from idols. Not only does this remind us to stay away from all forms of idol worship, it reminds us only the true God can judge. Judgment is coming, and there are only two choices to make. Arthur develops this tension to urge his audience in the right direction.

10:32–34

*10:32*Let me remind you of the days gone by when you first saw the light; you endured a tough fight in your suffering. *33*Sometimes you were publicly degraded and persecuted, and other times you banded together with those who were being treated like that. *34*You were there for those in prison, and you joyfully accepted your possessions being seized since you realized you have a better possession that lasts longer.

As he did in 6:9, Arthur balances the scene of terror with one of confidence. He knows his dear friends have not crossed the point of no return and he uses this moment to remind them of all they have been through up to this point. This reminder serves to highlight how far they have already come and to prove how ridiculous it would be to slow down now. It is unclear how long ago the events presented here took place, but it must have been long enough that he needs to draw their minds back to it. It also had to be long enough that they should have made dramatic progress in their walk with the Lord.

Arthur starts by telling us this time was when they "first saw the light." He previously used this expression in 6:4 to define benefits of being in a relationship with God. He then summarizes their experiences from back then. "You endured a tough fight in your suffering." He connects this overarching statement to actual events that he goes on to name. Let's look at each one.

Sometimes you were publicly degraded

Arthur's summary of events begins with the audience being degraded. More than that, it was public. This is devastating in any culture but it is supremely defeating in the honor/shame cultures of the ancient world. This audience was willing to accept all manner of shame in connection with their relationship with God through Jesus. Jesus promised his blessing upon those who endure this kind of treatment in Matthew 5:11 (ESV), "Blessed are you when others revile you and persecute you and utter all kinds of evil against you falsely on my account."

And persecuted

Arthur continues his description of the past with "persecution." The word has the sense of "oppression." The audience was exposed to cultural and governmental pressure to relinquish their faithfulness to God, but they persevered.

And other times you banded together with those who were being treated like that

Arthur next comments that they willingly aligned themselves with those who were being degraded and persecuted. This is truly remarkable. Not only did they stand firm under pressure but they chose to stand with those under the same treatment. This places oneself in extreme risk of enduring greater oppression and trouble. The audience truly considered themselves as part of the family of God and shared in the affliction of persecution even when they weren't the object of it.

You were there for those in prison

Next, he mentions their support for members of their congregation who were imprisoned for their faithfulness. He'll note later that some members are still in prison. In the ancient world, very little attention was given to those in prison. Today we are used to prisoners receiving regular meals, water, and care items, but this was not the case in the ancient world. It was the duty of friends and family to care for prisoners and he praises their past willingness to do so. Similar to the prior statement, this also presented tremendous risk to those doing the caring. This could lead to public identification as a follower of Jesus and thus result in continued persecution.[11]

And you joyfully accepted your possessions being seized

Lastly, he mentions their attitude as their property was seized. They accepted it joyfully. They *enjoyed* having their stuff confiscated. It is unclear if the seizure was initiated by the government or looting of the populace, but either way their stuff was gone. "Possessions" is not defined, but it likely included items as notable as homes and businesses.

Why did the audience tolerate such horrid treatment? Because they were convinced they were rightful owners of a superior possession. Their earthly stuff didn't matter, it would all be gone someday anyway. Their heavenly "stuff" is what mattered. God made a promise and they were sure he would keep it.

10:35–39

> [10:35]So, you shouldn't throw away your confidence since it comes with a great reward. [36]This is why you need endurance so that you can receive what God promised once you have done what he wants. [37]After all, "in just a little while the one scheduled to arrive will get here and no longer delay. [38]My righteous one will live because of faithfulness. However, if he retreats, I will not accept him." [39]Now we are on the side of those who remain faithful and preserve their soul not those who retreat and end up destroyed.

The point of Arthur's reminiscing now comes to light. With so much of the race in the rearview mirror, they can't give up now. This confidence comes with a great reward. The Christian life is not a sprint, but a marathon. Better said, it's an ultra-marathon. It's a long and intense race and the skill needed is endurance. But the finish line comes with a great reward: the fulfillment of God's promise. After doing what God wants, meaning remaining faithful to him, the reward awaits. It is the gift of salvation, the resting place of God, the eternal inheritance, the better possession.

Arthur again diverts attention to his Bible. He doesn't identify the quotation as speech like he has before. In fact, he doesn't introduce it at all. He just starts quoting Habakkuk 2:3–4 but with a piece of Isaiah 26:20 added in. As we have before, let's look closely at each line of the quotation to see what Arthur sees.

In just a little while

Arthur attaches a piece of Isaiah 26:20 as an introduction to his quotation of Habakkuk 2:3–4. He does this to maintain the twofold aspect of the Day of Judgment he has been promoting since 10:25. Isaiah is prophesying of the coming "anger of the Lord." This continues the theme that there are only two possible destinies. Here Isaiah tells us of the unfavorable option, and Habakkuk is going to tell us of the better outcome.[12]

The one scheduled to arrive will get here and no longer delay

Arthur now switches over to Habakkuk and quotes a passage also referenced by Paul in both Galatians and Romans.[13] Arthur quotes more of the passage and focuses in on the future orientation of the words. He uses the LXX version of these words which are especially pertinent to the point he is making. Look at the differences in the text compared to the ESV.

Habakkuk 2:3 LXX	Habakkuk 2:3 ESV
The one scheduled to arrive will get here and no longer delay.	If [the vision] seems slow, wait for it; it will surely come; it will not delay.

In the Hebrew text, the thing that is "scheduled to arrive" and will "no longer delay" is the vision mentioned at the beginning of verse 3. The LXX understood the pronouns differently and read it as a person who was "scheduled to arrive." It was then easy for Arthur to pick this up and read it as a prophecy of Jesus' return and the judgment that commences upon that event.

My righteous one will live because of faithfulness.

The most important part of the quotation is now here. Arthur will spend all of chapter 11 interpreting the importance of this magnificent verse. It is only six words in the Greek text but it overwhelms with how much is being said. We'll cover more on it in the digression that follows this paragraph's commentary, but let's look at a few key points for now. "The righteous" is a relational word, emphasizing those in a right relationship with God. "Will live" is future tense, and Arthur understands this to be resurrection life. "Because of faithfulness" is the means by which a person attains to resurrection life. There is a lot to unpack here, and we'll look much more closely at it in just a minute.

However, if he retreats, I will not accept him

The Habakkuk prophecy ends with a warning that brings this quotation back to where it started. All roads converge into the Day of Judgment and then emerge on one of two paths. A happy path and an unhappy path. Either you "will live" or you "retreat." Either you are "faithful" or "not accepted."

Arthur comments upon the final line before diving into what we call the Faith Chapter. He confirms his confidence that his friends are a part of those who remain faithful and "will live" or "preserve their soul." Their current actions are a brief blip in their overall relationship with God and his Son, and he knows they will snap out of it and head in the right direction. The question can be equally posed to us. When the going gets tough, when the cost to follow Jesus goes up, will you retreat? Or will you remain faithful and preserve your soul?

DIGRESSION: AT FAITH VALUE

We are about to head into the Hall of Faith, the Faith Chapter. These forty verses recount biblical history with a palpable level of inspiration and excitement. Much of what Arthur has said up to this point has been singed with warning. But all of that is dissolved into hope and encouragement here. It is no surprise that this section is so beloved. Arthur intended for this part of the letter to stand out as truly special.

He masterfully introduces this portion of the letter with a bold claim introduced at the end of chapter 10. He asserts his dear friends "are on the side of those who remain faithful and preserve their soul not those who retreat and end up destroyed." He uses these words to set the tone for all of chapter eleven. Clearly Arthur chose the exact words he knows his audience needed to hear, words of hope found in real stories of real people. These real stories and real people bridge the gap of biblical history from the beginning of creation all the way to recent history for the audience. He wants them to see they have "such a great crowd of witnesses" cheering them on as they persevere in the arduous journey in front of them.

This chapter is designed to instill the audience (and us) with the strength of thousands of years of saints who came before. Arthur, like Habakkuk, believes that this one word, faithfulness, makes the difference between life and death. So, what does this word mean to him?

You have probably already noticed that this translation prefers the word "faithful" or "faithfulness" rather than simply "faith." Our English word "faith" is typically defined as trust, belief, confidence in God, or a set of religious doctrines apart from proof. This is definitely *part* of what faith means. But is there more than that?

I think an illustration is best to get to the core of the meaning. Our English word "faith" ultimately derives from the Latin *fide*. This sister word entered into English as fidelity. We typically think of fidelity in terms of the marriage relationship, so let's go with that example. For me to be faithful to my wife, for me to demonstrate fidelity, I certainly have to believe she is real. I also have to believe she is my wife. But there is so much more to it. I have to live in accordance with that reality. I have to love her, take care of her, and provide for her. Fidelity also assumes that our physical relationship is one of exclusivity. When we talk about being faithful in marriage, that is what we mean. It is also what the Greek word means. Biblical faith includes belief, but it is so much broader than that. It encompasses all the vastness of a healthy relationship. It's the value of loyalty, commitment, devotion, allegiance, and steadfastness. With this in mind, faithfulness is so much better than faith.[14] It's a relationship to God in sickness and in health, in freedom and in persecution.

Do you see why Hebrews is the book of the Bible to have a Faith Chapter? This has been the message of the entire book. Arthur is urging his dear friends to take their commitment to God seriously. He is watching them slide backward, and he is crying out for them to wake up and return to faithfulness. After so many chapters pushing them, he takes his hand off the wheel and lets the stories of the past speak to them. He carefully assembles a litany of examples that drive home the point of what he wants his audience to do.

I promised before that the Habakkuk quotation would factor into all of this. These words form the proof text for Arthur's understanding of the criticality of faithfulness in the life of the believer. "My righteous one will live because of faithfulness." This is a promise, but it's also a command. It's an encouragement but also a challenge. Arthur will use the following stories to prove its truth. Those in a right relationship to God *will live*. They will attain to the resurrection of the dead. How will they do it? Through faithfulness. Their steadfast and loyal commitment to God ensures it. They are being faithful to a God who was faithful first.[15]

Remember, Hebrews is not about how to be saved as we think about it. Arthur's audience have already been Christians for many years. He is challenging them to stay the course when life gets tough, to not give up as the cost to follow Jesus rises. He is urging them to remain faithful in the midst of persecution in confidence that when they reach the end of the journey, they will hear Jesus say, "Well done, good and faithful servant" (Matthew 25:23 ESV).

If you are a little confused right now, that's okay. This is a lot to take in, Arthur knows that. He is going to prove his thesis over the course of the entire next chapter, so it will come into perfect clarity as we progress. Fortunately, he starts the chapter with a definition for faithfulness. Or does he?

IN FAITHFULNESS: 11:1–7

*11:1*Now faithfulness is the deed to the things we hope for; it is the guarantee for the things we don't see yet. *2*It is because of faithfulness that God commended our ancestors. *3*In faithfulness, we recognize that the universe was created by the word of God,[16] meaning what we see originated from invisible things. *4*In faithfulness, Abel offered a better sacrifice to God than Cain. Because of his faithfulness, Abel was commended as being righteous since God approved of his sacrifices. Because of his faithfulness, he is still speaking even after death. *5*In faithfulness, Enoch was relocated to avoid death and no one could find him since God relocated him. Before he was relocated, he had been commended as having pleased God. *6*Now it is impossible to please God without faithfulness because the one who approaches God must believe that he is faithful and will reward those who pursue him. *7*In faithfulness, Noah built an ark to save his family as an act of devotion. He did this in response to being warned about what was not seen yet. Because of his faithfulness, he condemned the world and became the rightful owner of the righteousness that is based on faithfulness.

The first seven verses of chapter 11 are pregnant with perspective. They are virtually exploding with depth of content. Arthur picks up from his quotation of Habakkuk and flies off the launch pad as he examines the

concept of faithfulness. It will be helpful for us to look at each line individually to ensure we get the most out of what he means to say.

**Now faithfulness is the deed to the things we hope for; it is the
guarantee for the things we don't see yet.**

Arthur begins by telling us what faithfulness means. It would be
tempting for us to see 11:1 as a definition of faith/faithfulness, but it is
so much more. If you compare the above rendering to a modern English
version, you will notice considerable differences. Let's put them side by
side for review.

11:1	11:1 ESV
Now faithfulness is the deed to the things we hope for; it is the guarantee for the things we don't see yet.	Now faith is the assurance of things hoped for, the conviction of things not seen.

The differences in the translation boil down to two different
perspectives. Is the verse saying something subjective or something
objective? These are technical terms, but essentially, they boil down to
this:

1. Subjective — The verse is telling us what faithfulness is.
2. Objective — The verse is telling us what faithfulness does.

The subjective approach is tempting, and it is the one used by most
modern English versions, but there are many issues with it. The most
important of which is that the word translated as "assurance" in the
ESV has no record of a subjective meaning like this. It is only translated
this way to try to force a definition out of the verse.[17]

Far from being a definition of what the word faith or belief means,
Arthur tells his audience, in the midst of desperate times, what faithfulness yields. This verse is a promise of what is to come for those who
cling to God when life gets tough. Faithfulness is the title deed to the
things we hope for. It is the proof of ownership to the heavenly world

God has promised. Arthur draws this from Habakkuk, which already told him the reward for faithfulness, "My righteous one will live because of faithfulness." Here he restates that in a new and powerful way.

He adds a second line to draw out the meaning further—faithfulness "is the guarantee for the things we don't see yet." I am guessing none of you have seen the heavenly world God promised. None of us have entered into God's place of rest. Not yet at least. Faithfulness is the ticket. It is the certainty of arriving at this presently unseen place.

Do you see how powerful this start to the Faith Chapter is? Arthur is detailing the implications of Habakkuk's words for his audience as he urges them to press on in the midst of persecution. Faithfulness, loyalty, commitment—these are the values that matter most when life is at its hardest. Over the next 39 verses, he will prove that is the case with example after example.

It is because of faithfulness that God commended our ancestors.

Arthur hints at the direction this chapter will go with this remark in verse 2. Remember, we come to Hebrews 11 already knowing what it contains, but his original audience didn't. Arthur uses this line to set us on the road we'll be covering. He is going to navigate biblical history and prove that God commended those in the past for their great displays of faithfulness, just like Habakkuk promised.

In faithfulness, we recognize that the universe was created by the word of God, meaning what we see originated from invisible things.

Before getting to his first example of faithfulness, he starts with his audience. Let's first look at the refrain Arthur will come back to throughout this chapter, "in faithfulness." Modern English versions typically use "by faith." We have already talked about how faithfulness is closer to the heart of what Arthur is communicating, but why is "in" better than "by"? In the following examples of biblical figures, Arthur means to stress why they did what they did, not how did they do what they did. He is discussing the mode, not the means. Faithfulness is not primarily the power that performed the actions, it is the purpose of why they were performed. Although "by faithfulness" can also mean this, "in faithfulness" is much clearer on what is being described.[18]

The first thing Arthur says is done in faithfulness is the belief in God's creative power. Arthur is completely confident that his audience holds to the biblical creation account as a demonstration of God's unlimited power and complete authority. This is an act of faithfulness not faith. The world is literally filled with evidence that the God of the Bible created the world supernaturally in six days. That is actually what Arthur said too, "we *recognize* that the universe was created." Belief is not the point, faithfulness is. Just like today, the creation story was mocked by the world around first century Christians. We cling to what God said because it is what he said and because faithfulness to him comes with a great reward.[19]

In faithfulness, Abel offered a better sacrifice to God than Cain. Because of his faithfulness, Abel was commended as being right-eous since God approved of his sacrifices. Because of his faithful-ness, he is still speaking even after death.

Now we enter the Hall of Faith. Arthur will use the rest of the chapter to cover the Reader's Digest version of specific instances of faithfulness. Before we look at Abel, the first example offered, let's take a moment to ask why he picks the people he picks.

Arthur is using examples from his Bible to prove that "My righteous one will live because of faithfulness." He sets out to show that biblical history bears the truth of this sentiment. He'll show the interplay between the three components—righteousness, resurrection, and faith-fulness. We'll cover the interconnectedness as we look at each example, but is there more motivation behind his selections?

His list is not designed to be a list of the top heroes of the Bible. He has done a poor job if that is the case, because incredibly significant acts and memorable people are glossed over or omitted entirely while some entries on the list (I'm looking at you, Samson) could hardly be consid-ered as the highest caliber of faithfulness. Arthur selects people and describes events that break easily into one of two categories:

1. Those who experienced great suffering
2. Those who experienced great victory

Arthur reinforces a point of view he wants his audience to grab hold of. God does not treat his people evenly. Let that sink in. God feels no pressure to give you a life that is in any way a point of comparison to anyone else's. Everyone on this list demonstrated great faithfulness. Some of them win the battle, others do not. Some of them beat the odds, others do not. Arthur doesn't describe a God who gives us what is fair; he describes a God who is worthy of our praise no matter what hand we have been dealt. He gives us examples of saints who, instead of complaining, rose above the challenges and solidified their entry into the Hall of Faith. Arthur has a good reason for what he is doing, and we will see how he connects it all to Jesus before he is done. With that, let's turn our attention to Abel.

Arthur briefly summarizes the account of Cain and Abel.[20] Let's look at how the story fits into the Habakkuk mold:

- Righteousness: How do we know Abel was in a right relationship with God? Arthur tells us it is because God accepted his gift.
- Resurrection: Arthur sees the resurrection alluded to in the "speaking" Abel does after his death. This is a reference to Abel's blood crying from the ground in Genesis 4:10. This serves as a prefiguration or as a metaphor for the resurrection that awaits us in the future.
- Faithfulness: So, because Abel was righteous and because he will live, Arthur is able to apply the logic of "My righteous one will live because of faithfulness" to conclude that Abel must have been faithful.[21]

Arthur is demonstrating himself as a creative interpreter again, but do you see the power in what he is doing? He is looking at these Old Testament stories through a lens that enables them to speak directly to the world of his audience (and to us). They were crushed under the pressure of coming persecution. They were overwhelmed with fear at the thought of suffering or even dying for their faithfulness. Arthur is showing that it is worth it. Others faced this same threat and overcame, and God can do the same with them and us. Let's move on to Enoch and see another example of this exegesis.

In faithfulness, Enoch was relocated to avoid death and no one could find him since God relocated him. Before he was relocated, he had been commended as having pleased God.

- Righteousness: Enoch's right relationship with God is displayed in that he pleased God. This is from the LXX versions of Genesis 5:22. The Hebrew text says that Enoch "walked with God" but the LXX chose to translate the relational implication.

Genesis 5:22 LXX	Genesis 5:22 ESV
Enoch pleased God after he became the father of Methuselah	Enoch walked with God after he fathered Methuselah

- Resurrection: The resurrection is a little easier to see in Enoch's story. God literally relocated him to heaven. Enoch technically never died; he was transported to the heavenly world supernaturally by God.
- Faithfulness: So because Enoch was righteous and because he will live, Arthur is able to apply the logic of "My righteous one will live because of faithfulness" to conclude that Enoch must have been faithful. Let's keep going.

Now it is impossible to please God without faithfulness because the one who approaches God must believe that he is faithful and will reward those who pursue him.

Arthur interrupts his flow of thought to draw an implication from the Enoch story. He is so excited about what this tells us that he breaks the flow of his narrative to make sure we get the point he is making. But what is the point?

First, we have to look at what he actually says because the translation above is notably distinct from modern English versions.

Hebrews 11:6	Hebrews 11:6 ESV
Now it is impossible to please God without faithfulness because the one who approaches God must believe that he is faithful and will reward those who pursue him.	And without faith it is impossible to please him, for whoever would draw near to God must believe that he exists and that he rewards those who seek him.

Both translations tell us that it is impossible to please God without believing two things, but what are those two things? The first thing is that "he exists." At least that is how the verse has been understood since the church fathers, but what does the Greek text actually say? The literal Greek would be "It is necessary to believe that he is." Is what? Ancient readers guessed that the verb "is" without anything further must be saying something like "he is there" or more simply "he exists." There is a notable problem with this approach. We are eleven chapters into a letter that has assumed God's existence from the very first verse. More than that, the entire Bible assumes God's existence from the very first verse. It seems out of place to talk about the existence of God. It seems out of place because it is. Arthur is using a rhetorical technique. We should read the verse as "It is necessary to believe that he is _____." The missing word is intentional. He means for us to fill it in ourselves. The missing word is "faithful."[22]

The first thing we must believe in order to please God is that he is faithful. So, what is the second thing? There is less of a distinction between the two translations at this point. The difference is the tense. We have to believe that God *will* reward those who pursue him. We have to believe that God is presently faithful and that he will reward those faithful to him in the future.[23] This fits perfectly what Arthur has been trying to say throughout his entire letter. This also fits perfectly with what he said in verse 1.

11:1	11:6
Now faithfulness is the deed to the things we hope for	The one who approaches God must believe that he is faithful
It is the guarantee for the things we don't see yet	and will reward those who pursue him

The first clause of both focuses on the present reality. In 11:1 we have the deed and in 11:6 we believe that God is currently faithful. The second clause focuses on the future. In 11:1 it's the things we don't see yet, and in 11:6 it's that God will reward us. With that behind us, let's look at Noah.

In faithfulness, Noah built an ark to save his family as an act of devotion. He did this in response to being warned about what was not seen yet. Because of his faithfulness, he condemned the world and became the rightful owner of the righteousness that is based on faithfulness.

- Righteousness: We are explicitly told that Noah was righteous in Genesis 6:9 when we are introduced to him. Noah is actually the first person in the Bible to be described as righteous. This fact is how Arthur can tell us that Noah is the "rightful owner of righteousness."
- Resurrection: Noah's story is a dramatic illustration of God's authority to judge the world. The global scale of the flood points to the universal scope of the judgment of the future. Noah experienced something akin to salvation and resurrection in that he was spared the negative consequences of this judgment.
- Faithfulness: So because Noah was righteous and because he will live, Arthur is able to apply the logic of "My righteous one will live because of faithfulness" to conclude that Noah must have been faithful.

With that, Arthur progresses out of the early accounts of Genesis and shifts to the time period of the patriarchs. He will spend considerably longer talking about Abraham than he has spoken of the figures so far.

11:8–12

*11:8*In faithfulness, Abraham obeyed God and departed for a place he was going to become the rightful owner of. He did this in response to being invited even though he didn't know where he was going. *9*In faithfulness, he lived in the Promised Land as if he were a visitor in a foreign country. He lived there in tents with Isaac and Jacob who were co-owners of the same promise. *10*After all, he was looking forward to an established city, which was founded by God.[24] *11*In faithfulness, Sarah received the ability to conceive, even though she was past childbearing years since she considered the one who promised was faithful.[25] *12*This is how a large number of descendants came from one man[26] even though he was old enough to die.[27] There are as many as the stars in the sky; they are countless like the sand on the beach.

Arthur now transitions into the story of Abraham and will stay with him as the primary figure from verse 8 all the way though verse 19. Abraham has already factored into Hebrews as a positive example of faithfulness back in Section 2 and this time he takes centerstage in the Hall of Faith to show just how important Arthur considers him.

With the greater level of detail given to Abraham's story, the direct connections of the Habakkuk passage give way to more generalized aspects of the concept being played out. Arthur established the framework with the first biblical figures, and he expects you to work a little harder to visualize it in the stories of the patriarchs and beyond. We'll overview this paragraph and then apply the Habakkuk lens to it before we move on.

Arthur first narrates the "call of Abraham" from Genesis 12. He focuses on his obedience in the midst of the unknown. Abraham was invited by God to own a piece of land he had never been to before. Despite the fact that God promised Abraham this piece of land, he never actually formally owned it during his lifetime.[28] He lived like a nomad in temporary tents rather than in an established city. Arthur sees this as a great testimony of faithfulness. Abraham didn't make any place on earth his home. He was patiently waiting for the permanent place God would establish.

Arthur shifts the focus to include Sarah in the next verse, so let's connect these events of Abraham to the Habakkuk verse before we go on.

- Righteousness: We see Abraham's right relationship with God in full display in that God invited Abraham to live with him and offered him the Promised Land.
- Resurrection: This paragraph leaves Abraham's "resurrection" as a purely future reality. He was looking forward to the city God founded. This matches the situation that faces us too. We are still waiting for this city.
- Faithfulness: Arthur can conclude that Abraham is faithful since he was righteous and he will live.[29]

Next, we get to see the beginning of the promise being fulfilled. God swore to Abraham that he would be the father of a great nation and we see the down payment to that in the birth of Isaac. It is fitting that Sarah enters the picture since she gave birth to a son at the age of ninety. Let's look at Sarah's story through the same lens.

1. Righteousness: Sarah demonstrates her right relationship with God in that she considered God to be faithful.
2. Resurrection: Both Sarah and Abraham experienced life in the midst of death through the birth of Isaac. We are told Sarah was past childbearing age, and Abraham was old enough to die. God's supernatural ability to make life where there is only death is a foretaste of the resurrection.
3. Faithfulness: Arthur can conclude that both Abraham and Sarah must have been faithful then.

11:13–16

*11:13*Even though they were faithful they all died without having received what was promised. However, they perceived it a long way away despite the fact they were ready to usher it in. They even acknowledged that they were foreigners on the earth. *14*Now those who say things like this show that they are yearning for a hometown. *15*If they had reminisced about where they came from, they would have had a chance to return. *16*However, they wanted something better, a heavenly home. That is why God is not ashamed to call himself their God. After all, he prepared a city for them.

Arthur uses this paragraph as a brief interlude. An intermission in which he remarks on the outstanding quality of faithfulness found in Abraham and the patriarchs. As readers separated from these figures by thousands of years, we unfortunately tend to dwell on their failings more than their successes. We certainly can relate to them in their flaws, but it is hard to relate to their seemingly limitless ability to demonstrate faithfulness to God.

Arthur's supreme commentary on their faithfulness is that they died without receiving what God promised. Abraham, Isaac, and Jacob all received down payments of what God promised, but none of them received more than that. They exhibited lifelong faithfulness to God even though they didn't see fulfillment in their lifetimes. Arthur invites his audience to this reality. He can't promise that persecution won't come. I can't promise you that either. But I can promise you that what God promised will be fulfilled. Fulfillment was a long way away for them. They waved to it as though it was a distant traveler on the horizon, but it didn't arrive for any of them, at least not yet.

This is seen supremely in their willingness to identify themselves as foreigners on the earth. Arthur plays with the ambiguity of the word "earth." It can mean land or it can refer to the entire planet. Arthur draws this from Abraham's self-identification as a foreigner in Genesis 23:4. There it must mean "land," but Arthur reads into the text that Abraham really considered himself as a foreigner on the entire planet. They yearned for a hometown, but wouldn't settle for an earthly one.

This notion of Abraham and his direct descendants wanting something better than the earth offered speaks directly to his Roman audience of the first century and the present audience reading this book. Arthur's friends lived in the wealthiest society in history up to that point. They enjoyed benefits and comforts that would have been unimaginable in an earlier time. The same is true for most of those reading this book. But these places are not our home. The patriarchs knew that and they lived in tents. No matter where we live, we are subject to persecution, which is why we don't need to reminiscence about the past—we yearn for a glorious future.

Arthur caps off this interlude with a declaration about the patriarchs. God refers to himself as their God. This is a reference to when God met Moses at the burning bush. God introduces himself to Moses in Exodus 3:6 LXX as "I am the God of your ancestors. The God of Abraham, the God of Isaac, and the God of Jacob."[30] In some way God allows himself to be possessed by these three men in a relational way. Just like I might introduce myself as husband of, son of, or father of, God introduces himself as God of. Did you notice the use of double negatives again? God is *not* ashamed. This is a rhetorical technique to stress a strong positive. It means God is proud to call himself their God. Why does Arthur say it this way then? He wants the audience to search themselves. Would God say he is proud to be their God? Would he say that of us?

11:17–22

[11:17]In faithfulness, Abraham offered Isaac when he was put to the test. Abraham, the one who received the promises, was in the act of offering his one and only son. [18]He concluded that God could raise him from the dead since he told him, "Your descendants will come from Isaac." [19]Figuratively speaking, he essentially did get him back from the dead. [20]In faithfulness, Isaac blessed Jacob and Esau regarding the future. [21]In faithfulness, Jacob blessed both of Joseph's sons before he died and he worshipped God while leaning on his staff. [22]In faithfulness, Joseph referenced the Exodus of Israel's descendants and left instructions for his burial at the end of his life.

The last paragraph served to connect the Patriarchs to Moses, but Arthur has a little more to say about them before fully transitioning the stage to Moses. The most significant and famous of Abraham's trials hasn't been mentioned yet. Arthur saved this as the grand finale and he covers it perfectly now. This well-known story from Genesis 22 is told in miniature form here with all the key details mentioned.

This story is often used by skeptics to challenge the character of God or the obedience of Abraham in his willingness to undertake such a task. Arthur makes it unmistakable why neither point presents a problem. God promised Abraham that his line would proceed through Isaac. At this point in the story Isaac has not yet married Rebecca. He hasn't had Jacob or Esau. This can't be the end of the story for him. Abraham is completely convinced of God's faithfulness to fulfill his promise and thus reasons that God will raise Isaac from the dead should he actually die on the altar. This dramatic display reconnects us to Habakkuk's words.

- Righteousness: Abraham's right relationship is shown since he is the one "who received the promises."
- Resurrection: The resurrection is figuratively demonstrated in that Isaac was spared from death.
- Faithfulness: Since Abraham was righteous and will live, Arthur determines he must have been faithful.

Arthur now covers Isaac, Jacob, and Joseph in rapid succession. The events he chooses to cover overlook all of their memorable stories in Genesis and focus only on their deaths. This is a perfect fit for the Habakkuk illustration. Keep in mind his goal is not to illustrate the most faithful acts, he is out to prove that those who are in a right relationship with God and demonstrate faithfulness "will live." He is encouraging his friends that they can be confident in the resurrection and thus have no reason to fear any threat of persecution.

Isaac

- Righteousness: Isaac's right relationship with God is shown in that he had a blessing from God to pass on.
- Resurrection: The resurrection is alluded to with Isaac blessing his sons regarding "the future."
- Faithfulness: Since Isaac was righteous and will live he must have been faithful.

Jacob

- Righteousness: Jacob's righteousness is demonstrated with the blessing conferred to Joseph's sons (which serves to connect to Joseph covered next) and that he worshipped God.
- Resurrection: Several elements within this single-sentence commendation point to the resurrection. The blessing is said "before he died" and was made "while leaning on his staff." This reminds the reader of Jacob's words immediately prior to pronouncing the blessing on Ephraim and Manasseh. He made Joseph swear that he would not bury him in Egypt, but would bury him in the Promised Land. Jacob knows there is a resurrection and he wants to wake up from death in the land God gave him.
- Faithfulness: Jacob was righteous and will live so Arthur can assume he was faithful.

Before we move on to Joseph, where does Arthur pull the "leaning on his staff" from? This is another distinction between his LXX Bible and our Hebrew-based Old Testaments. Look at the LXX of Genesis 47:31 compared to the ESV. The LXX understood the Hebrew as referring to his staff whereas modern English versions understand it as his bed.[31]

Genesis 47:31 LXX	Genesis 47:31 ESV
Israel worshipped God while leaning on his staff.	Then Israel bowed himself upon the head of his bed.

Joseph

- Righteousness: Joseph is righteous because he trusted God to perform the Exodus.
- Resurrection: The resurrection is shown in his request for his body to be moved to the Promised Land.
- Faithfulness: Arthur is safe to conclude that Joseph was faithful since he was righteous and will live.

Following the patriarchs, Arthur advances with biblical history into the time of Moses and the Exodus generation.

11:23-28

[11:23]In faithfulness, Moses was hidden by his parents for three months after his birth because they knew their baby was special and because they weren't afraid of the king's rules. [24]In faithfulness, Moses refused to be called the son of Pharaoh's daughter after he grew up. [25]He picked to be mistreated along with God's people instead of indulging in the momentary pleasure of sin. [26]He considered being degraded for Messiah[32] more valuable than all of the riches in Egypt because he was fixated on the reward. [27]In faithfulness, he left Egypt because he was not afraid of the king's anger since he was focused on the one who is invisible. [28]In faithfulness, he kept Passover by applying the blood so that the Destroyer couldn't hurt them.

Arthur's treatment of Moses here mirrors his presentation of Abraham in 11:8–12. He surveys his life with several key events allowing for the broad treatment to align with the Habakkuk principle he has been demonstrating. Just like we did above, let's look closely at each of these events in Moses' life before we align it to this teaching.

The first "faithful" event in Moses' life was not even performed by him. The faith was demonstrated by his parents who hid him at birth instead of obeying Pharaoh's directive to kill all male children. The inclusion of both of Moses' parents in this episode is another instance in which the LXX text differs from the Hebrew text.

Exodus 2:2 LXX	Exodus 2:2 ESV
She conceived and gave birth to a son. They knew the child was special so they hid him for three months.	The woman conceived and bore a son, and when she saw that he was a fine child, she hid him three months.

Why did Moses' parents undertake this civil disobedience? We are told their decision was simply because they knew the child was special. The literal Hebrew and Greek here is "beautiful." We aren't told any more than that. The Exodus story will bring to bear the truth of this "specialness." Did his parents have a premonition from God on Moses' role in God's story? Maybe. But maybe they simply loved the baby God gave them and refused to see him perish no matter what destiny had in store for him.

The next event in Moses' life is his refusal to be identified as part of Pharaoh's family. Arthur draws this "refusal" from the time Moses killed the Egyptian. Look at the first verse of that story, "One day, when Moses had grown up, he went out to his people and looked on their burdens, and he saw an Egyptian beating a Hebrew, one of his people" (Exodus 2:11 ESV). Moses calls the Hebrew man one of *his* people. He didn't consider himself a son of Pharaoh. He didn't consider himself an Egyptian. He considered himself part of God's people.

This refusal included him being mistreated and degraded. Moses chose to forsake the privileges and wealth that could have been his as a member of Pharaoh's house. Why did he do this? We are given two reasons. He devalued the momentary pleasure of sin, and he valued God's reward more than all the money in Egypt. Remember what Arthur said back in 6:1 when he was describing the initial lessons, "repentance from dead works" and "faithfulness to God"? This is brilliantly illustrated when Moses turned from the idols of wealth and comfort and turned toward God even though that faithfulness meant being mistreated and degraded.[33]

The next event is a twofold description of the Exodus. Moses left Egypt and kept the Passover.[34] He was able to stand up to the most powerful ruler on earth because he committed himself to the invisible God. In doing so, he saved his people from the power of the tenth plague.

Let's look at these events through the Habakkuk lens and see how they cumulatively connect to the theme Arthur has been building.

- Righteousness: Moses' right relationship with God is shown in his "special" quality at birth and his willing identification with God's people.
- Resurrection: The resurrection is foreshadowed in Moses' rescue at birth and the salvation from the Destroyer.
- Faithfulness: Arthur can conclude that Moses was faithful because he was righteous and because he will live.[35]

Before we move from Moses, there is a lot in this short paragraph that would have been directly applicable to the first audience of Hebrews. Moses was the example supremely fit for their specific circumstances. Arthur's friends are overwhelmed with fear over the threat of rising persecution. The persecution is caused by their unwillingness to worship idols, the Roman pantheon. It is an expected civic duty for Romans to worship these gods. The audience's non-compliance with these social expectations leads to oppression, resulting in seizure of assets, imprisonment, and the threat of death. All they have to do to avoid such dreadful results is worship the other gods. Moses is a perfect example of someone who stood strong against such pressures.

Look at the events of his life through this theme. His parents "weren't afraid of the king." Moses "refused to be called the son of Pharaoh's daughter." He chose to be "mistreated along with God's people." He "considered being degraded for Messiah more valuable than" money. Arthur is calling his friends to deep introspection. Are they afraid of Emperor Domitian and his rules? Do they choose to identify with God's people and accept the mistreatment that comes along with that? Would they choose wealth over faithfulness?

I wish I could tell you these are just questions for ancient Christians. I wish I could tell you they have no bearing on our lives today. But I would be lying if I did. We have to ask these questions too. Our culture may not have literal stone or wood idols, but they are idolatrous, nonetheless. The message of Hebrews is to follow the example of Moses.[36] We have to consider "being degraded for Messiah more valuable than all the riches of Egypt." How do we do that? We stay "fixated on the reward" of faithfulness.[37]

11:29–31

[11:29]In faithfulness, they crossed the Red Sea like walking on dry ground but when the Egyptians tried to cross, they were drowned. [30]In faithfulness, the walls of Jericho collapsed after they walked around them for seven days. [31]In faithfulness, Rahab the prostitute didn't die with the disobedient because she welcomed the spies peacefully.

Arthur rounds out the time period of Moses and the conquest with a quick succession of events in the same way he narrated the events of Isaac, Jacob, and Joseph. The one notable distinction between the patriarchs and this paragraph is the general "they" in 11:29 and 11:30. Rahab is the only individual named in this section. This is because the Exodus generation was previously faulted for their lack of faithfulness in 3:19. The generalization of the conquest is also because Arthur commented that Joshua didn't offer them rest in 4:8. For these reasons, only Rahab is directly mentioned.

"They" of the Exodus

- Righteousness: The Exodus generation demonstrated a right relationship with God (at least at the time) when they stepped out into the parted Red Sea.

- Resurrection: The parting of the Red Sea which led to life for the Exodus generation and death for the Egyptians symbolizes the resurrection and eternal judgment.
- Faithfulness: Due to their righteousness at the time and because they survived the Red Sea, Arthur can conclude that the "they" of the Exodus generation demonstrated faithfulness (at least in that moment).

"They" of the Conquest

- Righteousness: The right relationship of the Conquest generation is shown in their willingness to walk around the walls of Jericho for seven days.
- Resurrection: Similarly to the Red Sea, Jericho is a symbol of the resurrection and eternal judgment.
- Faithfulness: The Conquest generation's right relationship with God and survival indicate that they were faithful.

Rahab

- Righteousness: Rahab is shown to be righteous (contrary to the expectation of her profession) since she assisted the Jewish spies and identified herself with the people of God.
- Resurrection: Rahab experienced a metaphorical resurrection in that she was spared from death at the destruction of Jericho.
- Faithfulness: Since Rahab was righteous and she will live, Arthur can determine that she was faithful.

11:32–38

*11:32*What else can I say? There isn't enough time for me to tell you about Gideon, Barak, Samson, Jephthah, David, Samuel, and the prophets. *33*Because of their faithfulness, they conquered kingdoms, enforced justice, and obtained promises. They shut lions' mouths, *34*extinguished powerful fires, and avoided being killed by the sword. They were strengthened despite limitations, became dominant in battle, and forced foreign armies to retreat. *35*Women received their family members back from the dead, yet others were tortured and refused to surrender so that they could obtain the better resurrection. *36*Others faced beatings, ridicule, and imprisonment. *37*Others were stoned to death, cut in half, and executed with the sword. Others were displaced and forced to wear sheepskin and goatskin, being destitute, persecuted, and mistreated. *38*They were forced to take shelter in deserts, hillsides, caves, and ditches. The world didn't deserve them.

Arthur breaks the flow of his narrative and abandons the structure he has been building so far. He also allows the Habakkuk theme to drop into the background as he identifies time as the enemy that prevents him from saying everything he wishes he could say. He limits himself to a summarization of other key biblical events disconnected from specific individuals. Why does he do this? He has a few reasons.

The first of these reasons for breaking his carefully crafted pattern is because he is now exiting the covenant time periods he has spent all prior sections of the letter establishing. Remember our chart from before? He now adds additional figures to each of the three Old Testament time periods.

Time Period	Key Figure
Creation	Abel
The promise	Abraham, Sarah, Isaac, Jacob, Joseph
The first covenant	Moses' parents, Moses, the Exodus generation, the Conquest generation, Rahab

Another reason is because he is shifting away from the theme "my righteous one will live because of faithfulness." This theme will remain in the background, but he will no longer develop it beyond identifying things that happened to unnamed (but largely guessable) members of the Hall of Faith. Remember the other theme I told you permeated this section? It has been in the background so far, but now it grabs the spotlight. It is the theme of incongruent result. Each of the events described by Arthur fits into one of two categories.

1. Those who experienced great suffering
2. Those who experienced great victory

Up until this point in the faith chapter, this has been in the background. We were left to ponder why Abel was killed, but Enoch was saved. There were no answers given as to why Joseph lived with the wealth of Egypt but Moses had to forfeit it. No answers are given now either. But this theme of incongruity is part of what Arthur wants his friends to walk away with. Arthur builds this final part of the faith chapter around it. The first half are those who experienced great victory, and the chapter redirects in 11:35 to those who experienced great suffering. Which group we are in is not for us to decide. Why does God give some a harder time than others? Why are things harder now than before? The limitation of the human experience doesn't allow these questions to be answered. What is up to us is faithfulness. Will we be found faithful when the going gets tough?

With that background in mind, let's turn our attention to the text. After blaming time for his inability to cover the following items in greater detail, he does list a few names. The names mentioned serve to help identify the unnamed participants in the exploits which follow. Rather than using the prior "in faithfulness," Arthur merely tells us that the following list is "because of their faithfulness." The events flow with similar items being grouped together so we will treat them all accordingly.

. . .

They conquered kingdoms, enforced justice, and obtained promises.

The first group Arthur shares is a threefold description of military victories true of a variety of individuals throughout biblical history. Due to their being mentioned, it would be hard not to think of the promises of victory told to Gideon in Judges 6:14 and the subsequent victory that took place in Judges 7:19–23. This also reminds the reader of the promise of victory given to Barak through Deborah in Judges 4:7 and the victory recorded in 4:12–24. Further examples could be cited for Joshua (Joshua 1:3), Samson (Judges 13:5), and David (1 Chronicles 14:10). These are all events that describe those who "experienced great victory."[38]

They shut lions' mouths, extinguished powerful fires, and avoided being killed by the sword.

The next group is those who were at the point of execution yet God miraculously intervened. The first event is that of Daniel in the lions' den told in Daniel 6. Arthur follows this with Daniel's friends, Meshach, Shadrach, and Abednego, who were preserved in the fiery furnace in Daniel 3.[39] The last item, those who weren't killed by the sword, is more generalized and refers to a few different events. Likely candidates include David (1 Samuel 17) and Elijah (1 Kings 19). These miraculous and providential events are for those who experienced great victory.

They were strengthened despite limitations, became dominant in battle, and forced foreign armies to retreat.

The next group of three continues the theme of military victory found in the first sentence. All of these also are more general in nature and could refer to several events. Those who were strong in the face of limitations could be a reference to the supernatural strength of Samson (Judges 16:28–30) or the courage of Gideon (Judges 7). Those who were dominant in battle could describe several of the judges and kings, but David is a good example (I Samuel 18:7). David is also likely a good candidate for one who forced armies to retreat, but the nearer reference would have been the military victories of the Maccabees that form the basis of the Hanukkah story from 1 Maccabees.[40]

Women received their family members back from the dead, yet others were tortured and refused to surrender so that they could obtain the better resurrection.

Arthur completes his list of great victories with the women who had family members returned to them after death. The examples of this from Arthur's Bible are Elijah raising the widow's son (1 Kings 17) and Elisha doing the same (2 Kings 4).[41] The pendulum now swings the other way into those who experienced great suffering. The first example actually serves to downplay the great victory just cited. Both of these widow's sons died again. They were resuscitated, a great demonstration of God's power over life and death, but it isn't the ultimate display. There is a better resurrection where one never dies again.

The first example of great suffering is from 2 Maccabees 7. The story describes seven brothers who are arrested along with their mother for their unwillingness to commit idolatrous acts. The text goes on to recount gruesome tortures that resulted in all of their deaths. They were willing to suffer such because they were completely confident in the resurrection.[42]

Others faced beatings, ridicule, and imprisonment.

The first grouping of those who experienced great suffering are those who were unjustly punished on earth. Punishments of this nature are also described in 2 Maccabees, but could also recall Jeremiah (Jeremiah 20:2).

Others were stoned to death, cut in half, and executed with the sword.

The next grouping is of those who were sentenced to death and not miraculously saved. Zechariah was stoned to death (2 Chronicles 24:21).

Tradition said that Isaiah was killed by being cut in half (this is recounted in the non-biblical work, Martyrdom of Isaiah 5:1). The prophet Uriah was executed by King Jehoiakim with a sword (Jeremiah 26:23). This is yet another group who experienced great suffering.

Others were displaced and forced to wear sheepskin and goatskin, being destitute, persecuted, and mistreated.

Not all of those who experienced great suffering were subject to physical pain or torture. Some were marginalized from society to the degree that they could not have any comforts of civilized life. The clothing references Elijah (2 Kings 1:8), but the rest are generalized to be suitable for most of the biblical prophets.

They were forced to take shelter in deserts, hillsides, caves, and ditches. The world didn't deserve them.

Arthur continues on with the notion that God's people are subject to being completely pushed out of society. He remarks that they are forced to take up habitations in nature because they are so dejected by the world around them. This also serves as a general remark fitting numerous prophets and those faithful to God in the midst of persecution. The final line of this paragraph serves to cap off this part of the Hall of Faith.

The world didn't deserve them. The society that possessed superficial capability to reject God's people were in fact the one's not worthy. We live in an upside-down world, but God promises to right all wrongs when the "time of restoration" comes.

What is it that Arthur hopes to accomplish with this gruesome and terrifying display of the horrors that God's faithful are faced with? He actually told us that in the way he structured the passage. The great victory examples are paired with the great suffering examples in reverse order.[43] Let's look at it displayed visually.

Great Victory	Great Suffering
There isn't enough time for me to tell you about Gideon, Barak, Samson, Jephthah, David, Samuel, and the prophets.	They were forced to take shelter in deserts, hillsides, caves, and ditches. The world didn't deserve them.
They conquered kingdoms, enforced justice, and obtained promises.	Others were displaced and forced to wear sheepskin and goatskin, being destitute, persecuted, and mistreated.
They shut lions' mouths, extinguished powerful fires, and avoided being killed by the sword.	Others were stoned to death, cut in half, and executed with the sword.
They were strengthened despite limitations, became dominant in battle, and forced foreign armies to retreat.	Others faced beatings, ridicule, and imprisonment.
Women received their family members back from the dead,	**yet others were tortured and refused to surrender so that they could obtain the better resurrection.**

The centerpiece of the whole paragraph is the resurrection. God has the power over life and death. Arthur urges his audience to rise against their fear and face persecution head on. They are equipped to do this, not because they are strong or powerful, but because God will raise them from the dead. There is no threat the world can throw at them that God cannot undo. The resurrection is worth any suffering. Paul encourages the Corinthians with the same line of thinking in 2 Corinthians 4:16–18 (ESV), "So we do not lose heart. Though our outer self is wasting away, our inner self is being renewed day by day. For this light momentary affliction is preparing for us an eternal weight of glory beyond all comparison, as we look not to the things that are seen but to the things that are unseen. For the things that are seen are transient, but the things that are unseen are eternal."

11:39–40

11:39 Although God commended all of them because of their faithfulness, they didn't receive what was promised. *40* He had something better in store, to include us so that we could all reach the destination together.

Arthur rounds out the faith chapter with a fitting conclusion. Everyone mentioned here received God's approval, but they didn't receive what God promised. This is true of both of those who experienced great suffering and those who experienced great victory. None of them entered God's place of rest or received the full benefits of the new covenant, at least not yet.

God has a better plan in mind, one in which all of God's people—those of the past and present and those who suffered and those who were victorious—everyone will cross the finish line at the same time. The resurrection is the great equalizer for God's people. At that time, we will all enter God's place of rest mentioned in Psalm 95, take up the nobility declared in Psalm 8, experience the full reality of the new covenant prophesied in Jeremiah 31, and see the cosmic king of Psalm 2. Don't give up now; there is so much to look forward to.

The Great Crowd: 12:1–3

*12:1*So, since we are surrounded by such a great crowd[44] of witnesses, we should remove every obstructive impediment and sin so we can run the race in front of us with endurance. *2*We should run with our focus on Jesus, the undisputed champion of faithfulness. He endured crucifixion for the joy that awaited him and disregarded the shame involved. He is now sitting next to the throne of God. *3*Concentrate on the one who endured this level of animosity at the hands of sinners so that you don't get exhausted and give up.

After recounting the incredible faithfulness found in chapter 11, we may be easily amazed at the great crowd of witnesses around us. "Great" is indicative of their quality and the size of the crowd. Arthur exits the faith chapter with a return to the call he has been pressing upon his audience. We have to keep going forward. This marathon race runs up the down escalator. If you stand still, you fall behind. This is a twofold expectation, just like in 6:1.

6:1	12:1
Repentance from dead works	We should remove every obstructive impediment and sin
Faithfulness to God	We can run the race in front of us with endurance

Arthur invites his audience into the footraces of the ancient amphitheaters and coliseums, where as many as fifty thousand people would pile in to watch these runners compete. The energy of the competition is the same energy found in arenas today, but with one important difference from what we are used to. In the ancient world, runners competed naked. In their mind, clothing was an encumbrance to one's best performance. Arthur captures that idea here. We have to get rid of anything that prevents our best performance in the race of faithfulness.[45] This is not a sprint that is over and done within a matter of seconds. The Christian life is a marathon that requires long-term endurance in order to reach the finish line.

In chapter 11, Arthur invited us to watch the performance of faithful generations of the past, but now he tells us that they surround us. So, are they watching us or are we watching them? Yes! Arthur intentionally blurs the metaphor beyond what the real image conveys because both ideas are true. As runners in the "faith race" in the modern era, we have the privilege of learning from so many prior runners. We can watch them "compete" through all of the challenges of the past and honor their legacy as we run our part of the race. However, Arthur also tells us that they surround us as we run. It's probably not intended to literally say that the past examples of faith watch us from heaven and cheer us on, but it is certainly an encouraging image!

More important than the great crowd is Jesus, whom we must focus on as we run. Arthur imagines Jesus occupying the seat of honor in the arena, visible to all of the runners. We can press through the pain and encounter the runner's high as we lock our eyes on the undisputed champion. This is an intentional departure from the more traditional "author and finisher" or "founder and perfecter" found in modern English versions. Arthur is continuing the race illustration with the terminology employed. He combines forms of the word for "starter" and "completer" to describe Jesus as the best runner off the starting block and the best runner at the finish line. Jesus is the undisputed champion of faithfulness.[46]

We may refer to Hebrews 11 as the hall of faith or the faith chapter, but it is not technically accurate. The most important entry is saved for chapter 12. Jesus is the supreme example of faithfulness for us to emulate. Remember how Arthur fit chapter 11 into the biblical time periods? Well, he has more to add to that. Biblical history doesn't end with the Old Testament. God has more to say and he says it through Jesus.

Time Period	Key Figure
Creation	Abel
The promise	Abraham, Sarah, Isaac, Jacob, Joseph
The first covenant	Moses' parents, Moses, the Exodus generation, the Conquest generation, Rahab
The cosigning (The cross)	Jesus
The new covenant	Jesus

Arthur wraps up these exemplars of faithfulness with the undisputed champion for our emulation. Jesus's journey of faithfulness is showcased with his willingness to endure crucifixion. How did he endure the cross? He disregarded the shame of the experience. Why did he endure the cross? For the joy that awaited him. This is the exact mindset that Arthur has been pushing his audience to take on for the prior eleven chapters. He is calling his friends to disregard, devalue, and dismiss their present suffering. His instruction is not because their suffering isn't that bad (although it is likely to get worse). They have to disregard the pain and shame because the joy that awaits them is worth it. The joy that awaits us is the same as what awaited Jesus. To enter into the heavenly world, come into nobility, and enter God's place of rest.

Do you see how this perfectly connects to what we saw in the Habakkuk theme?

1. Righteousness: Jesus' willingness to suffer crucifixion and shame proved his right relationship with God.
2. Resurrection: Jesus was literally raised from the dead as the first fruits of the resurrection.
3. Faithfulness: Arthur can conclude with complete confidence that since Jesus was righteous and, because he was raised, he must have been the undisputed champion of faithfulness. For Jesus, the "will live" has already occurred. Our future is his present.

Jesus is not just the perfect fulfillment of the Habakkuk theme he is also the perfect fulfillment of the incongruent results theme. Jesus is the best example of both categories. He experienced great suffering in his crucifixion, but he also experienced great victory in his resurrection, ascension, and exaltation. No wonder Arthur challenges us to run with our focus on Jesus. In him, we have everything we need to finish the race in front of us. No matter what befalls us, he is the source of strength to enable us to make it to the end.

How do we focus on Jesus? We concentrate on what he suffered. Jesus willingly suffered at the hands of sinners even though he had never sinned. Like Arthur said in 2:18, "He is able to help those in the midst of temptation because he was tempted when he suffered." Jesus sits on God's throne as our advocate, ready to help us keep going. Arthur urges his friends to look to Jesus to prevent exhaustion or worse, giving up.

12:4–6

*12:4*In your struggle against sin, you have not yet resisted to the point of bleeding for it. *5*Did you forget the encouraging words which address you as sons and daughters, "My son, don't underestimate the Lord's training[47] or give up when he corrects you. *6*After all, the Lord loves[48] those he trains and welcomes every son he disciplines"?

Arthur exchanges the race metaphor for a full contact sport. He has wrestling or boxing in mind when he says they have not yet "resisted to the point of bleeding for it." It is possible he means these words to say that they have not yet been persecuted to the point of death, but that is unlikely. Even if some members of the community had paid the ultimate price, those hearing these words for the first time hadn't. Arthur is continuing his athletic metaphor like our expression "blood, sweat, and tears." They haven't given it their all yet; they have more race to run, more match to fight.[49]

Arthur challenges them to keep going by quoting another passage from his Bible. He quotes Proverbs 3:11–12 which is perfectly suited to the athletic imagery he has been developing.[50]

Before we look at the quotation, Arthur first comments upon how it is addressed. It refers to them as God's children, his sons and daughters. This continues the family theme that has been building since Section 1. Jesus calls us his siblings which binds us to him as his younger siblings, and it binds us together as his brothers and sisters, members of the family of God. But this family connection also binds us all to God as his children. God is our father and treats us as his children.

In this passage, God's fatherhood is evidenced by his training of his children. Arthur invites his friends to interpret their challenging circumstances as God's fatherly training. This has been the subject of difficulty for many readers of Hebrews. How can we see the sinful actions of those who mean us harm as the heavenly discipline of a loving father?

For starters, it isn't meant literally. God is not actually inflicting persecution upon his children, but there is value in interpreting life's difficulties through this lens as we will see in the next paragraph. Secondly, God doesn't devalue pain in the lives of his children. As parents we often work hard, sometimes tirelessly to prevent our kids from experiencing pain, difficulties, and hardships. But such is not the case with God. He knows the value of challenging circumstances and what it can do to our faithfulness. God's love for us is perfectly demonstrated in the sacrifice of his Son, but our love for him can only be demonstrated when we sacrifice for him. Just like in Hebrews 11, we don't get to pick if we are those who experience great suffering or great victory. But we can choose to see whatever befalls us through the lens of a loving heavenly Father.[51] Let's continue on to see how Arthur applies this verse to the situation of his friends.

12:7–11

*12:7*You have to endure since God is training you like sons and daughters. After all, is there any child who doesn't receive training from his father? *8*So, if you haven't received training, which all of us have experienced, then it means you are illegitimate children not sons and daughters. *9*Besides we've had natural fathers who trained us and we respected them. If that is the case, shouldn't we accept the authority of our spiritual Father[52] to live? *10*Now they trained us briefly as they thought best, but he trains us for our benefit so that we receive his holiness. *11*Training doesn't seem enjoyable at the time, sometimes it even seems painful, but later on it yields the peaceful result of righteousness for those who complete their training.

Arthur calls for his audience to endure. Just like an athlete is willing to endure the pain of straining their muscles and the sacrifice of a rigid diet, so we need endurance in God's training. From this illustration, Arthur makes an odd assertion. "Is there any child who doesn't receive training from his father?" This rhetorical question implies a negative response. But this is contrary to how we innately think. Like the disciples who see the man born blind, when we see someone suffering, we often ask, "Who sinned, this man or his parents, that he was born blind?" (John 9:2 ESV). We instinctually associate suffering with sin just as Job's friends did. Arthur tells us the exact opposite is true. It is God's children who receive his training.

Arthur draws the illustration from the real world of parenting. Dedicated parents who care about the wellbeing of their children train them. This training necessitates unpleasantries. It is the duty of parents to prepare their children for life's responsibilities and challenges, and that process is rarely fun. But the reward is worth it, and most of us grow to understand and respect our parents for this upbringing.

Our earthly fathers were limited in their human condition from performing this role perfectly, but such is not the case with our spiritual Father. His training is not only for this life, but for the resurrection life. Our earthly fathers trained us to be like them, but God trains us to share his holiness. God can use the hardest parts of our life to make us more like him. It is through this lens that Arthur invites his friends to see their experience. They can choose to look at this persecution as the opportunity to prove their love for the Father who first loved them. It might be painful, and it definitely won't be enjoyable, but it will be worth it.

The reward for this perseverance is to live. This draws our minds back to the Habakkuk theme, "My righteous one will live because of faithfulness." It is our faithfulness in the midst of life's hardest moments that proves our deepest commitment to God. This process yields the "peaceful result of righteousness." Unfaithfulness yields a "heart corrupted by unfaithfulness," but faithfulness secures the exact opposite result. Peace with God and a right relationship with him. "You shouldn't throw away your confidence since it comes with a great reward."

12:12–17

*12:12*This is why, despite your arms and legs being worn out,[53] you have to keep going *13*and run straight towards the goal so that you get reinvigorated and don't get an injury. *14*Aim to be at peace with everyone,[54] and aim for holiness, because no one will see the Lord without it. *15*Be careful that no one misses out on God's grace and that no poisonous weed sprouts up to cause trouble and ends up contaminating many. *16*Also, be careful that no one is depraved[55] like Esau, who traded his birthright for a single meal. *17*After all, you're aware that later on, when he wanted to receive the blessing, he was denied because he didn't repent, even though he begged and cried for it.

Arthur resumes the race metaphor before shifting into the more practical implications he intends to draw from it. Every runner knows the part of the race he is talking about. There is part of the race when your limbs are deadweight and every part of your body screams in agony. Many runners give up. Some runners botch their form and twist an ankle or tear a muscle. Arthur urges his audience not to do the same. They need to run straight toward the goal. They need to focus on Jesus and be reinvigorated to finish the course. With that remark, he has completed his sports analogy and he transitions to practical expectations before offering another illustration from Scripture. Let's look at these closely to get the most out of them.

Aim to be at peace with everyone

The first thing Arthur challenges his friends to do is to aim for peace. In view of the persecution awaiting them outside, he means to be at peace as a church community. Both within the small church they are part of and the larger church throughout the Roman world. Christians need to be on the same team to weather the storm together. They can't allow their community to fall to infighting. As persecution mounts and members suffer losses of businesses and homes, as others are imprisoned or killed, they will need each other. They have to remain a family. As with all families, conflicts will arise. That is unavoidable. The lack of conflict is not the mark of strong relationship; the willingness to work through them is. I don't have any conflicts with people I don't know, but I have many conflicts with my family. But we work through all of them and find peace. This is the practical application of having the "peaceful fruit of righteousness."

Aim for holiness, because no one will see the Lord without it

The next thing we have to aim for holiness. Like peace, holiness is also a result of God's training. Holiness is a complex word with a meaning as impenetrable as God himself. Ultimately the word means "other than." It speaks of the completely different character and nature God has than what is present within sinful humanity. Holiness begins with the cross. Jesus' death is what makes us holy. But that is the beginning of a process. We progress in holiness as we slay the enemies that reside within us. As we overcome temptation and struggle against sin, we lay them at the feet of Jesus. This million-mile journey is composed of a billion tiny steps. But each step comes with a promise, "no one will see the Lord without it." Do you want others to see the Lord? Arthur invites his friends and us to take the next step.

. . .

Be careful that no one misses out on God's grace

The next three items are joined as something we have to be careful to avoid. The first is to be careful that no misses out on God's grace. This mirrors what he said in 4:1. "Since the promise to enter his place of rest remains open, we should take it seriously to prevent even one of you from missing out." There he had the Exodus generation in mind as an example of those who had the opportunity not to miss out on God's rest, but here he has in mind a different character, Esau. We'll cover Esau more when we get to him in the third "be careful." For now, it suffices to say that we have begun a journey, and it would be a tragedy not to make it to the end.

[Be careful] that no poisonous weed sprouts up to cause trouble and ends up contaminating many

The second item Arthur presses his audience to be careful of is the contagious nature of idolatry and sin. The warning comes from Deuteronomy 29:18 (ESV):

> Beware lest there be among you a man or woman or clan or tribe whose heart is turning away today from the LORD our God to go and serve the gods of those nations. Beware lest there be among you a root bearing poisonous and bitter fruit.

When I was in Bible college, my fellow students and I often talked about the big ministries we planned to start or the dangerous missions trips we wanted to take. I am content now when I learn these friends are still Christians at all. I know so many who threw in the towel and gave up on the race. That was especially true for Arthur's audience in the midst of difficulties. Unfortunately, it is contagious. Moses warned the people in the Old Testament, and Arthur renews that warning for the New Testament. We can't let the infection spread.

Also, be careful that no one is depraved like Esau

The last "be careful" is not to be like Esau. As we saw in the first "be careful," Esau is another example who mirrors the disastrous fate of the Exodus generation. He started his life as the son of Isaac with all of the rights and privileges of the firstborn. But he doesn't make it to the end of the race. Why? He traded it for a single meal. This exchange is recorded in Genesis 25:29–34, and his fate is sealed when Isaac blesses Jacob in Genesis 27. Esau valued the things of this world more than his birthright. He traded it for something as transitory as food. He crossed the point of no return. It didn't matter that he regretted it, the deed was done. Just like the Exodus generation, Esau serves as a serious warning not to give up.

TWO MOUNTAINS: 12:18–24

*12:18*Now you haven't approached something tangible, a raging fire, pitch blackness, a foreboding gloom, a violent storm, *19*a deafening trumpet sound, and a voice so intense it made those who heard beg for it to stop talking. *20*They couldn't handle the command that even if an animal touched the mountain it had to be stoned to death. *21*In fact, the phenomenon was terrifying to the degree that even Moses was so scared he was shaking. *22*Quite the contrary, you have approached Mount Zion, the city of the living God, heavenly Jerusalem, thousands of celebrating angels, *23*the firstborn community who are registered in heaven, God who is judge of everyone, the righteous spirits who have reached the destination, *24*Jesus the mediator of a new covenant, and the purifying blood that has something better to say than Abel.

The ominous tone of the first half of this paragraph is counterintuitive to the purpose of what Arthur means to say with these words. Arthur finished the last paragraph with the grave warning present in the example of Esau. Just as he has with all of the warnings after chapter 2, he uses this paragraph to encourage his audience. He does so by talking about two mountains. Why are mountains encouraging?

He narrates the palpable terror found in the Mount Sinai event and then compares it to the welcoming grace found on Mount Zion. This is encouraging because his friends haven't come to Mount Sinai—they have come to Mount Zion. The mountains are two different destinies, and he is completely confident that his friends are on their way to the better outcome. Remember our table from 6:7 and 10:31? We can add these two mountains to illustrate the two possible outcomes at the Day of Judgment.[56]

The Day of Judgment	
Cursed soil destined for fire	Blessed soil
God pronounces judgment	God avenges his people
Mount Sinai	Mount Zion

Just like the illustration of the two outcomes for the soil in chapter 6, it is either blessed by God or cursed by God, Arthur softens the warning found in Esau by expressing his certainty that his friends are on the right path, but he hopes this letter will spur them to run faster on the race. Let's look at the description of the two mountains to see how this unfolds.

Arthur is able to use the appearance of God on Mount Sinai, with all of its terrifying imagery, as a symbol of God's judgment. This is made even more possible because the Exodus generation doesn't make it to the place of God's rest. They don't get to Mount Zion; they arrive at Mount Sinai.

Arthur potently describes the palpable terror that Mount Sinai exhibits.[57] The scene is pure terror. The top of the mountain was engulfed in flame yet somehow wrapped in darkness (Deuteronomy 4:11). A storm raged with wind like a tornado (Deuteronomy 5:22 LXX). A sound like a blasting trumpet pierced their ears (Exodus 19:16). The horror was so overwhelming the people begged for it to be over (Deuteronomy 5:24–27). The situation is so terrifying that even Moses, the man who talked to God face to face, admitted his fear. Or did he? This is not found in any description of the Mount Sinai event. Arthur knows his Bible so well. How could he make a blunder like that?

Moses does admit his feeling of terror in the Torah, but it's not at this event. It is when he feels God's anger towards the people due to their idolatry in the Golden Calf event (Deuteronomy 9:19). Arthur uses this misplacement to make his use of Mount Sinai clear. This mountain is reserved for the depraved. It is the destiny of the cursed soil. It is the inheritance of the unfaithful. The faithful get a different mountain.[58]

Arthur rapidly shifts gears from ominous to welcoming as he tells his friends what they have come to. Mount Sinai was not named, but Mount Zion is explicitly identified. It's more than a mountain though; it's a city for the people of God to live in. It's the heavenly version of the earthly city of Jerusalem. The angels who worshipped the Son at his coronation are now celebrating the final victory of God.

Who is in this glorious city? The firstborn community. Arthur used the word firstborn to describe Jesus in 1:6, but now he uses it as a name for all of his siblings. We are made equal heirs with Messiah (Romans 8:16). Remember this city is our future but its Jesus' present. We will be equal heirs with him in the future, but in the present our names are already registered there. Who else is there? God, the universal judge. Remember the word "judge" also means "avenger." The God who righted every wrong and avenged every enemy lives in this city. His heavenly home merges with the earthly sphere at this coming event.

Arthur progresses to further describe the citizens. Not only are they the "firstborn community"[59] and "registered in heaven,"[60] they are the righteous spirits[61] that have reached the destination. The goal of God's resting place has been reached. Who else is there? Jesus. He is the mediator, the middle-man, in the agreement that unites us to God. His blood purified our sins and enabled an intimate and permanent relationship with God.

There are only two possible futures for every person who has ever lived. Mount Sinai and Mount Zion. All of humanity enters the Day of Judgment and every judgment results in one mountain or the other. Arthur expresses confidence about which mountain his friends are heading toward. Will you join them on this path?

We are told in conclusion that this blood is better than Abel. Why? How does Abel fit into the picture? Abel serves as an example of a faithful martyr and shows that Jesus is more than a martyr.[62] He is the Savior! But is there more to the Abel reference? Notice that Abel is not the only figure who appears seemingly at random in this chapter. The reference to Esau in 12:16 is entirely unexpected as well. But maybe they are not as unexpected as they seem.[63]

Both figures appear in conjunction with the comparison of the two mountains. Esau appears right before it, and Abel appears at the end of it. When we looked at the text, we saw how the two mountains vividly describe the horror of God's judgment that fell upon the Exodus generation.

What do Abel, Esau, and the Exodus generation have in common? First they each appear in one of the key Old Testament timelines we have already seen Arthur being fond of.

Time Period	Key Figure
Creation	Abel
The promise	Esau
The first covenant	The Exodus generation

Each of these characters also share another important feature. They are all given a choice. All three of them serve as examples of the importance of making the right choice with your life. Abel chose to give God a righteous gift. Esau chose to forfeit his birthright to Jacob. The Exodus generation chose the path of unfaithfulness. Arthur uses Abel and Esau to bookend the Exodus generation. Esau appears on the Mount Sinai side as a warning of what happens to someone who goes down the wrong path. Abel stands on the Mount Zion side as a positive example of choosing to follow God even in the face of a high price to pay. These brief mentions serve to reinforce the entire point that Arthur has been making throughout his letter. God said it best in Deuteronomy 30:19 (ESV), "I have set before you life and death, blessing and curse. Therefore choose life."

12:25–29

[12:25]Make sure you don't refuse to listen to the one speaking! After all, if they didn't escape punishment when they refused to listen to him when he warned them on earth, we have no chance of escaping punishment if we reject him when he warns from heaven. [26]His voice shook the earth then, but now he has promised, "Next time I will not just shake the earth, I will also shake the sky." [27]This quotation reveals that the earth and the sky are shakable things and will be replaced so that what is unshakable can prevail. [28]We should be grateful because we are being welcomed into an unshakable kingdom. To show our gratitude, we should serve God in a way that pleases him with constant devotion [29]considering that our God is a consuming fire.[64]

Arthur brings home the point of the two mountains. How did the Exodus generation get to the wrong mountain? They refused to listen to the one speaking. This is the same warning we saw Arthur present in Section 1. God previously spoke to our ancestors, but he has spoken to us through his Son. This better messenger requires better attention. The former message was given through angels, through a human mediator, and on the earthly plane. This message was given by God through his heavenly Son. We can't risk rejecting it!

Arthur brings the severity of attention to its head by quoting once again from his Bible, "Next time I will not just shake the earth, I will also shake the sky" (Haggai 2:6 LXX).[65] The text of Haggai plainly tells us that God is talking immediately prior to this verse so what does he mean to tell us?

At Mount Sinai God shook the earth with a violent earthquake (Exodus 19:18), but in the future more will shake than just the earth. God will shake the entire created order. Arthur told us that the Son is the origin of the earth and the sky in 1:10, and both will be shaken as part of the coming judgment. Nothing in creation will be exempted. Anything that can be shaken will be shaken. And all of the shakeable things will be replaced with unshakable versions. Arthur told us in 1:12, "You will wad them up like an old shirt, and just like clothes, they will be replaced with something new." This aligns perfectly with what John sees in Revelation 21:1–4 (ESV):

Then I saw a new heaven and a new earth, for the first heaven and the first earth had passed away, and the sea was no more. And I saw the holy city, new Jerusalem, coming down out of heaven from God, prepared as a bride adorned for her husband. And I heard a loud voice from the throne saying, "Behold, the dwelling place of God is with man. He will dwell with them, and they will be his people, and God himself will be with them as their God. He will wipe away every tear from their eyes, and death shall be no more, neither shall there be mourning, nor crying, nor pain anymore, for the former things have passed away.

The only rational response to this unshakeable kingdom is gratitude. There is nothing else we can do for a God who can literally rewrite the universe. How do we show our gratitude? We serve him. Starting now and continuing forever. He deserves our constant devotion. After all, he is a consuming fire. That doesn't sound safe. There is nothing safe about him. We must admit along with Mr. Beaver in *The Chronicles of Narnia*, "Safe? . . . Who said anything about safe? 'Course he isn't safe. But he's good. He's the King, I tell you."[66]

PIECE OF MIND

1. "Family" is the same Greek word translated as "house" and "household" in 3:2–6. The English word "family" better captures the sense of the Greek word and is thus translated that way here. Unfortunately, it could not be used in chapter 3 due to the comparison made between the builder of a "house" and the "household" that resides within it.
2. "Gathering together" is a form of the word "synagogue." The word also has eschatological overtones as the "ingathering of Israel" at the resurrection when God unites all of his people together. It carries this meaning in 2 Maccabees 2:7 and 2 Thessalonians 2:1.
3. Hebrews 10:20 is notoriously difficult to interpret. The literal Greek text says, "through the curtain, that is his flesh." Many early interpreters understood this to mean that Jesus' flesh "veiled" his divine spirit in the same way that the Tabernacle curtain veiled the Holy Spirit in the Most Holy Place. There is nothing wrong with this in concept; it is doctrinally accurate to conclude, but it is difficult to construe such a meaning in the specific context of Hebrews. Although it is the more complex answer grammatically, since it requires the preposition "through" to be understood in two different senses (this is reflected as "because of" and "through" in the translation above), the context essentially demands to take "through his flesh" in parallel with "by the blood of Jesus" from 10:19. For support of this position, see Harris 273–274.
4. The notion that Jesus' sacrifice also purifies our bodies, "washed with pure water," is not often contemplated by Christians today since we typically focus on the spiritual aspect of Jesus' work. The goal of the cross is to prepare us for the resurrection and a

physical experience with God. While it is accurate that the resurrection will be a fully renewed form of our body, I think it is still appropriate to draw from this verse the importance of caring for our bodies to the same degree that we care for our souls. Christians should eat healthy and exercise. We should avoid vices that damage our bodies and habits that wreck our health. This is a way to honor God as the creator of our bodies and Jesus as the one who purified them.

5. For more background on informants and informant culture, see Whitlark 37–43.

6. For the understanding that "the day" in 10:25 refers to "the day" from Deuteronomy 32:35, see *Deuteronomy and Exhortation in Hebrews* by David M. Allen. This is yet another occasion in which Arthur references the Song of Moses showing how intrinsic it is to his theological framework. I highly recommend this book for those interested in seeing even more connections between Hebrews and Deuteronomy.

7. "Without mercy" is another reference to Deuteronomy. This comes from 13:8, and the context is also about idolatry just like Hebrews. The reference to "two or three witnesses" in the same verse is yet another reference to Deuteronomy (this time 17:16) and the context there is also idolatry. This further demonstrates the critical nature that Deuteronomy played in Arthur's theology but also showcases that the sinning on purpose from 10:26 is a specific reference to worshipping idols and/or apostasy, see David M. Allen 75–77.

8. "The blood of the covenant" is drawn from Exodus 24:8 and was previously quoted by Arthur in 9:20.

9. The warning passage of 10:28–31 again shifts to the third person just like in 6:4–8. This serves to distance the audience from the claims being made in the warning from their direct situation. Arthur wants them to live by faithfulness but doesn't think they have retreated past the point of no return. The severe tone of all of the warning passages is designed to scare them straight.

10. For the understanding presented above that the two quotations in 10:30 are designed to make two different points and thus describe the two different results of the Day of Judgment, see Cockerill 492–493.

11. For the assessment of ancient prison conditions, see Witherington 355.

12. Arthur has previously inserted other texts into his quotations (like when he embedded Isaiah 34:4 into Psalm 102 in Hebrews 1:12), but the insertion of Isaiah 26:20 into Habakkuk 2:3–4 in Hebrews 10:37–28 is more notable. The shared context of the coming of the Messiah, resurrection, and judgment contributed to his ability to combine these texts into a single message. These verses also share contextual overlap with Psalm 40 cited in 10:5–7. The Habakkuk reference to Jesus as the "one scheduled to arrive" (literally "the coming one will come") serves as the biblical basis for Jesus being called such in Revelation 1:4.

13. In addition to Hebrews, Habakkuk 2:4 is quoted in Romans and Galatians. Each of its occurrences emphasized a different element. Its occurrence in Romans 1:17 focuses on "the righteous." Galatians 3:11 focuses on "because of faith" and Hebrews focuses on "will live."

14. The very first definition of "faith" in BDAG (818) is faithfulness, reliability, fidelity, and commitment. This is not to say that it can't mean "faith" elsewhere in the New Testament, it most certainly does. The context of Hebrews demands the meaning of faithfulness, especially the context of Hebrews 11, where Arthur is specifically illustrating the faithful actions of past exemplars.

15. For the connection between Habakkuk and the faith chapter, see Cockerill 509–514.

16. Arthur's reference that "the universe was created by the word of God" is from Psalm 33:6 (ESV), "By the word of the LORD the heavens were made."

17. There are numerous challenges with the attempt to translate Hebrews 11:1 subjectively. The primary problem mentioned above is that there is no recorded instance in which ὑπόστασις (translated as "deed") has the meaning "assurance." This is pointed out by Lane 325–326 (although I disagree with the meaning chosen by him there). The meaning "deed" is from BDAG 1041 and is found in ancient Greek documents. The larger problem with the subjective meaning is its sense in the context. The definition of "faith" as "assurance" or "confidence" defies the immediate sense found in the Habakkuk quotation and the examples established in the rest of Hebrews 11. The objective view is found in the King James and New King James versions (albeit in a different interpretation than the one supported in this translation).

18. The refrain "by faith" being understood as "in faithfulness" is due to my conviction that it is a Dative of Manner, see Wallace 161. The purpose of Hebrews 11 is to spur the audience on to "emulate those who inherit what is promised because they persevered faithfully" (6:12). Therefore, it makes the most sense contextually that Arthur is telling them the mode by which these figures persevered rather than the means.

19. I would be remiss not to mention the incredible work of Answers in Genesis in supporting biblical creationism. I highly recommend their ministry for methods on understanding the evidence in favor of a six-day creation rather than evolution. You can visit their website at www.answersingenesis.org. If you haven't been, plan a trip to the Creation Museum and Ark Encounter in Northern Kentucky.

20. It is not apparent in the LXX version of Genesis so it is unlikely Arthur was aware of this detail, but the story of Abel contains an amazing allusion to Jesus. The ESV translates Genesis 4:4 as "Abel also brought of the firstborn of his flock and of their fat portions. And the LORD had regard for Abel and his offering." However, the word for "had regard" in the Hebrew text is the same root as the Hebrew name of Jesus. A literal rendering would be, "God *Jesused* Abel and his offering," or "God *salvationed* Abel and his offering." I learned this from Dr. Golan Broshi on the One for Israel Podcast available at this link: https://www.youtube.com/watch?v=hi_Etq3T0ak.

21. Many believers are troubled by the seeming lack of fairness in the story of Cain and Abel. Both Cain and Abel bring offerings to God but only Abel's is accepted. Many attempts have been made to explain God's reasoning, but I think the text of Genesis does the best job, "The LORD said to Cain, 'Why are you angry, and why has your face fallen? If you do well, will you not be accepted? And if you do not do well, sin is crouching at the door. Its desire is contrary to you, but you must rule over it.'" (Genesis 4:6–7 ESV). The gift was secondary to their character, represented by their deeds.

22. For the understanding that "faithfulness" is the missing word, I recommend the research of Donald Hartley, see his article "Hebrews 11:6—A Reassessment of the Translation 'God Exists,'" in *Trinity Journal NS*. It can be troubling to think Arthur used a missing word to make his point looking at how notably this changes the meaning of the verse. However, biblical writers do this all the time. Arthur did it earlier in his letter with the same word in 3:2 and modern English versions correctly add it in there. Are there any other times that translators miss it? Yes, the most important one being Matthew 22:21. The ESV translates it as, "Therefore render to Caesar the things that are Caesar's, and to God the things that are God's." However, it should be read as, "Render to Caesar the ___ of Caesar and render to God the ___ of God." The missing word, drawn from the context, is "image." This produces the reading, "Render to Caesar what is made in the image of Caesar and render to God what is made in the image of God." Jesus is challenging them that they are in possession of a coin with a graven image of an idol and urges them to give themselves (since people are made in the image of God) back to God in repentance.

23. Technically the second part of 11:6 is not in the future tense. The literal rendering would be "The one who approaches God must believe that he is faithful and *becomes a rewarder* of those who pursue him." The tense of "becomes" is technically present but has the meaning of what God will be in the future, rather than what he is now in the present (faithful). For this reason, the future tense is used in translation.

24. This is a reference to Psalm 87:1 (ESV), "On the holy mount stands the city he founded."

25. Hebrews 11:11 is notoriously difficult to interpret. The ambiguity and challenges associated with it yield two possible perspectives (summarized in Harris 314–315). The verse can be read as commending the faithfulness of either Abraham or Sarah. Both have challenges but Sarah is to be preferred. If Abraham were to be read, it would be rendered as (with Abraham being the implied subject from the prior verse), "In faithfulness, *Abraham, with* Sarah, received the ability to conceive, even though she was past childbearing years, since *he* considered the one who promised was faithful." The biggest problem is that Abraham's name has to be assumed with no other example of that occurring in chapter 11. Furthermore, seeing Abraham as the subject is not consistent with the text of Genesis. We know from the birth of Ishmael that Abraham didn't need supernatural power to do his part in conception, but Sarah did. The natural reading of the text implies Sarah as the subject of "faithfulness." So, what are the problems with that then? The literal Greek behind "received the ability to conceive" is "received power to deposit seed." This certainly implies the male role in procreation. It's not easy to make sense of the wording, but Arthur probably means to imply that Sarah "received the ability for the deposition of seed *to produce a child*."

26. This explicitly refers to Abraham as "one man" (Greek "from one") which confirms the same meaning in 2:11. Arthur drew the identification of Abraham as "the one" from Isaiah 51:2. This chapter of Isaiah also goes on to connect the promise given to Abraham and its eschatological fulfillment yet to come.

27. A similar statement is made by Paul in Romans 4:19 (ESV), "He did not weaken in faith when he considered his own body, which was as good as dead (since he was about a hundred years old)." Both statements are probably dependent on the Jewish proverb recorded in the Mishnah (Avot 5:24).

28. Technically, Abraham was the legal owner of a small plot of land within the Promised Land. He was the legal owner of the Cave of Machpelah. This story is recorded in Genesis 23, and the cave served as the burial plot for both Sarah and Abraham. It is a great foreshadowing of the resurrection that the first plot of land Abraham buys is a burial plot. The implications are true for us too. Right when we commit ourselves to Jesus, God buys our burial plot. He metaphorically claims ownership of that piece of land to guarantee that we will be raised from the dead.

29. Abraham's call from God in Genesis 12 mirrors the incarnation of Jesus. Abraham was invited by God to leave his home, where he was notably wealthy, and live as a foreigner in the place God called him to go. Similarly, Jesus leaves his heavenly home, where he was wealthy in glory, and lived as a man on the earth.

30. When God self-identifies himself to Moses at the burning bush he calls himself, "The God of Abraham, the God of Isaac, and the God of Jacob" (Exodus 3:6). Why does he repeat the word "God" three times? Why doesn't he just say, "The God of Abraham, Isaac, and Jacob"? Early Jewish commentators interpreted this peculiarity as confirmation that every generation must undertake the task of knowing God for itself, they cannot rely on their parents' relationship with God, they must make one for themselves.

31. The reference to Jacob's staff in Hebrews 11:21 is more complicated than just a differing translation in the LXX. Ancient Hebrew was written without vowels. This creates occasions in which the same consonant combination can create more than one word. This can be exampled in English with "BRD." These consonants can make numerous words by adding different vowels in between. It could be bread, bird, bride, or beard. This different interpretation of the consonants is what led to it being Jacob's bed in our version of Genesis 47:31 and his staff in the LXX.

32. "Degraded for Messiah" is drawn from Psalm 89:50–51. He previously referenced this Psalm in Hebrews 1:6.

33. That Moses considered this degradation "more valuable than all of the riches in Egypt" serves to further illustrate the theme of incongruent result. Moses' journey of faithfulness required him to forsake the riches of Egypt, but this is the opposite of Joseph's journey which required him to accept the riches of Egypt. This is brilliantly addressed by the early church commentator Ephraim, "The people took the riches of the Egyptians, while Moses took Joseph's bones." For this quotation and more ancient assessments, see Kugel 602.

34. Some interpreters consider the event "in faithfulness, he left Egypt" in Hebrews 11:27 as Moses' exit from Egypt after killing the Egyptian man recorded in Exodus 2:11–15 rather than the actual event of the Exodus. This is possible since this would yield a better chronological reading, but is ultimately unlikely since we are explicitly told in that story that Moses was afraid of Pharaoh in Exodus 2:14–15. This is further confirmed since a few ancient manuscripts add this as an additional line in 11:23, confirming they didn't interpret 11:27 to be the same story. The chronological argument is not notable since Arthur goes out of order in the Abraham story as well (Abraham lived in tents with Isaac and Jacob in 11:9 before Isaac's birth is narrated in 11:11).

35. Arthur arranges the events of Abraham (11:8–11) and Moses (11:23–28) to function as a mirror. The mirror reverses the image so the first "in faithfulness" of Abraham mirrors the third "in faithfulness" of Moses. In 11:8 "Abraham departed," and in 11:27 "Moses left." In 11:9 Abraham lived "as if he were a visitor," and in 11:24 Moses "refused to be called the son of Pharaoh's daughter." Abraham's recounting of "in faithfulness" in 11:11 is of Sarah, and Moses' "in faithfulness" in 11:23 is of his parents.

36. For the understanding that the description of Moses in 11:23–28 was especially relevant for the audience of Hebrews, see Whitlark 70–74.

37. An unwillingness to worship idols would be costly even from a monetary standpoint. The audience, living in or around Rome, would have been expected to swear oaths and make sacrifices to the Roman gods as a part of business partnerships. This is what Paul means when he tells believers not to be "unequally yoked" in 2 Corinthians 6:14 (although its customary application to romantic relations is equally valid). This would make business transactions a challenging endeavor since any purchase could reveal your Christian faith or cause you to compromise it with "dead works." As Christians today, we should hold the same perspective and ask if the companies we do business with are actively opposing our values. Many large corporations are. Arthur expected his audience to find creative solutions that didn't result in compromise. He also realized this may mean having to consider "being degraded for Messiah" as more valuable than riches.

38. The reference to "obtained promises" is the one instance in Hebrews in which "promise" is not a reference to the specific promise God made to Abraham, although these promises of military victory are certainly based upon it.

39. When discussing Daniel's friends, I used the more familiar Shadrach, Meshach and Abednego. These are actually the names given to them by the Babylonians, their Hebrew names were Hananiah, Mishael, and Azariah (see Daniel 1:6–7). The king's remark in 3:25 that he sees a fourth man in the fire is worth considering. It is certainly indicative that Jesus is with us in times of persecution and hardship, but it's worth noting that the king is the one who saw him. Nothing in the text tells us that the three Hebrew men were aware of this "fourth man." We may not always sense God's presence when going through hard times, but those around us will see him even if we don't.

40. Due to the proximity of events, Arthur recounts many faithful examples from the Maccabees. For convenience of reference, I include the references to 1 and 2 Maccabees for those curious to look at the original stories Arthur references. Arthur's use of these stories does not mean he considered them Scripture, only that he considered them historically accurate accounts.

41. The "women who received their family members back from the dead" could include the miracles of Jesus too. Arthur may have been familiar with the stories of those raised by Jesus (Matthew 9, Luke 7, and John 11).

42. The martyrdom of the seven sons in 2 Maccabees 7 also includes references to the Song of Moses, which Arthur has referenced numerous times in his letter. This story is expanded greatly in its retelling within 4 Maccabees.

43. The technique of connecting items in reverse order (discussed above in 11:32–38) is called chiasm. This is a reference to the Greek letter X (Chi). This method is used elsewhere in Hebrews, but this is the most important place for understanding the intent of the passage. For more examples on chiasm and other rhetorical features in Hebrews, see Attridge 20–21.

44. Literally "a great *cloud* of witnesses" rather than "a great *crowd* of witnesses." It is accurate that this word can mean a cloud, but it is also used to represent a large grouping of people. The literal image of a cloud was not intended by Arthur, see Lane 398, and compare with BDAG 670.

45. For the notion that ancient runners competed naked, see Witherington 326. It is tempting to see the "every obstructive impediment" and "sin" which Arthur advises his friends to remove as two different things. The impediment could be distinguished from sin as the things that shift our attention away from God or distract us yet which are not technically sin (work, friends, hobbies, etc.) This is unlikely though. Arthur is defining what the metaphor means. Just like a runner removes impediments in a physical race, so should we remove sin in our spiritual race.

46. The translation of Jesus' title is difficult to render in English. The incredibly terse and compact form used in Greek is pregnant with meaning and the translator must choose whether to translate the words or the imagery. I opted to go with the race imagery being conveyed by translating as "Jesus, the undisputed champion of faithfulness." The literal Greek would be "of faithfulness, the beginner and finisher." For those curious on the translation process, a single article connects beginner and finisher together indicating a single image is in mind, not two. "Of faithfulness" being in front showcases its importance in the thought (modern English versions often add "our" but it is not present in Greek). For the meaning of champion, see Lane 397. "The undisputed champion of faithfulness" captures the meaning and recreates the original imagery of Jesus being hailed as the supreme member of the "Hall of Faith."

47. The above translation reflects "the Lord's training" rather than "the discipline of the Lord" found in modern English versions. This choice was made to further the athletic imagery began in 12:1 and broaden the notion beyond that of just "correction." This is

a subset of training (found in 12:6), but God's training has more in scope than just fixing what is wrong, it also includes making good things great. This passage envisions God in his fatherly role performing the function of a coach.

48. The quotation of Proverbs 3, "the Lord loves those he trains" serves as the biblical basis to how Arthur was able to refer to his friends as "beloved" in 6:9.

49. Further indication that 12:4 is not talking about martyrdom is the terminology employed. "In your struggle against *sin*, you have not yet resisted to the point of bleeding for it." It is a struggle against *sin*, not *sinners*. Arthur is urging his friends to war against the temptation of sin; namely idolatry, and is acknowledging here that they have not yet given it their all for this battle.

50. The quotation of Proverbs 3 in Hebrews 12:5–6 is a further connection with Deuteronomy. In fact, the author of Proverbs is writing his text as a commentary on Deuteronomy 8:5. This further solidifies Arthur's consistent approach regarding the similarity of circumstances for the Exodus generation and his audience, see Theissen2.

51. The notion of God's fatherhood towards his people was not unique to Jesus. For its use in Rabbinic Judaism, see Cohen 20–22. This does not mean Jesus' teaching on the fatherhood of God is not distinctive. This is seen most clearly in Jesus' identification of God as "my Father" in Luke 2:49 as opposed to "our Father." This personal and intimate relationship between God and his Son is extended to us through Jesus. For more on the Fatherhood of God, I highly recommend Dr. Pryor's work, *Our Father, Our King*.

52. The literal Greek is "Father of spirits." This serves to balance our "natural fathers" from earlier in the verse. The literal Greek there is "fathers of our flesh." This showcases our earthly parents as the origin of our biological life and God as the origin of spiritual life. The title also connects to Numbers 27:16 where God is called, "God of spirits."

53. The reference to "arms and legs being worn out" alludes to Job 4:3–4, Isaiah 35:3, and the apocryphal Sirach 25:23.

54. "Aim to be at peace" is based on Psalm 34:14.

55. The literal Greek is two terms, "sexually immoral" and "profane." The context demands the sense of "depraved" or even "unfaithful." Esau's specific sins are not in view, except for his disregard for his birthright as something not worth sacrificing for. Although it is relevant to point out that many Jewish interpreters did understand Esau as sexually immoral based upon his taking of two wives recorded in Genesis 26:34–35. For this perspective, see Lane 454–456.

56. For the perspective that the two mountains of 12:18–24 are symbolic for the two possible outcomes at the Day of Judgment, see Cockerill 642–645.

57. The description of the two mountains in 12:18–24 would have created a near sensory overload for the audience. Prior to the invention of visual entertainment like television and movies, people possessed far greater imaginative power. The colorful description of the mountains would have been virtually overwhelming to the original hearers and conjured the exact intent of Arthur—a palpable experience of terror that collapses into comfort. For this perspective, see Mackie.

58. For the connection between the Mount Sinai event and the Golden Calf episode in 12:21, see *Godly Fear or Ungodly Failure* by Michael Kibbe (see pages 211–212 for his summary on this topic).

59. The title "firstborn community" in 12:23 receives biblical support from the citations in Section 1. In 2:12 Jesus refers to his faithful followers as the "family gathering" which is the same Greek word translated as "community." In 1:6, Jesus is called the "Firstborn," but now that honorific title is extended to his "brothers and sisters."

60. The idea of names being registered in a heavenly book is also recorded by Luke (Luke 10:20), Paul (Philippians 4:30), and John (Revelation 20:15). The notion of such a book is first mentioned in Exodus 32:31–32. This is another reference to the Golden Calf episode as Moses prays that God "blot me out of your book" rather than see his people be blotted out. This is an unbelievable demonstration of Moses' faithfulness to represent the people as mediator. He is willing to take on eternal consequences for their sin. This is also a foreshadowing of Jesus who would pay for our sins and procure an eternal redemption.

61. Some interpreters see the "righteous spirits" as distinct from "the firstborn community." The idea of "spirits" is understood to imply disembodied saints not yet resurrected. It is not necessary to see this division though. Both terms are describing the same gathering of redeemed humanity upon completion of the Day of Judgment. The term "spirit" is used not because they don't have a body, but because the work of being brought to "the destination" was spiritual in nature.

62. In 12:24, Jesus' blood is said to have something better to say than Abel. This is likely a reference (as before in 11:4) to Abel's blood crying out from the ground in Genesis 4:10. Technically Arthur compares Jesus' blood to Abel himself, not just Abel's blood. This is similar to 1:4 where Jesus' role (literally "name") is compared with the angels themselves rather than the angels' role. This is designed to heighten the celebration of Jesus. Just one aspect of Jesus (either his role or his blood) is superior to whole categories (prior faithful martyrs or angels).

63. The reference to Esau was probably not as unexpected to the original audience as it is to us. For more on how Arthur subtly hinted at the Jacob and Esau narratives throughout chapter 12, see Asumang2.

64. "A consuming fire" is from Deuteronomy 4:24. This is yet another reference to Deuteronomy and again it is within a context regarding idolatry.

65. Arthur's discussion of the shaking of the earth and sky at the Day of Judgment is not just from Haggai 2:6. This is also drawn from Psalm 96:9–10 LXX, "Worship the Lord in his holy court. All of the earth must be shaken from his presence. Proclaim among the Gentiles 'The Lord is King, and he has established the heavenly world which will not be shaken.'"

66. *The Chronicles of Narnia* quotation is from *The Lion, the Witch and the Wardrobe* by C.S. Lewis. HarperCollins Publishers, 1994, page 86.

THE END (13:1–25)

STORY TIME

FIDELIS WAS WRAPPING UP NOW. THE LETTER WAS ALMOST done, and it would be up to God for its powerful words to take root and renew this group to their former passion. Fidelis prayed that it would. He cared deeply for these friends. It wasn't fair that it was so much harder for them to be Christians than those who lived elsewhere, but that was beyond his control to fix. Rulers come and go, policies change, but "Jesus is the same yesterday, today, and forever."

Those words were a comfort to him as much as he hoped they would be a comfort to this group. Especially Camilla. He tried not to look at her; she had already been crying for some time, and he knew if he looked at her for too long, he would start crying as well.

Camilla and her husband Salvius were the rock of this church. They may be young, but they personified faithfulness. Their marriage was a love story that inspired everyone. They have the kind of deep and abiding love reserved for fairy tales. At the center of that love was their God. Only because of their passion for God could this unbelievable love could flow back and forth between them. They seemed to be in some kind of rhythm, always in a balance of who was supporting whom.

She was devastated when he was sentenced to prison. The officials didn't care what lives they broke, only that their gods remained honored. It was just a matter of time before someone as bold as Salvius was locked up. Camilla remained strong through it all—she even risked her own safety visiting him almost every day. Camilla squeezed the hand of Livia as she intently listened, wondering through her tears, what her husband would think of this letter. It seemed like just the thing they had been praying for.

Just as he feared, Fidelis looked too long at Camilla and shed a single tear. It was impossible to hold back, but he hoped it was the only one, at least until he finished reading. This letter was too important for anything to diminish its message. He summoned the last bit of strength that he had and set out to read the last few paragraphs.

He continued on,

"Take care of those in prison as you would if it were you in prison and those who are being mistreated as if it were you being hurt."

INNER PIECE

Hebrews At A Glance
I.   The Son (1:1–2:18)
II.   The Word (3:1–6:20)
III.   The Priest (7:1–10:18)
IV.   The Faithful (10:19–12:29)
V.   The End (13:1–13:25)
a.   Pleasing Service
i.   13:1–6
ii.   13:7–17
b.   Closing Remarks
i.   13:18–19
ii.   13:20–21
iii.   13:22–25

Four sections are now complete with the last one being all that remains ahead. Arthur's letter is essentially complete now, and he leaves only conclusory remarks for the final chapter. Let's review where we have been before we press on to the final chapter of unpuzzling Hebrews.

Arthur used the first section to gain rapport with his audience by inviting them into the cosmic king coronation ceremony. His creative handling of the Scriptures enabled the audience to experience this heavenly event. This gave way to the first warning where Arthur challenged his audience to take seriously the message of Jesus.

Section 2 made much of this warning as he compared the situation of his audience with that of the Exodus generation. Since the Exodus generation failed to reach the destination Arthur warns his friends not to repeat the same mistake.

The third section was used to explore Psalm 110 and its connection to Jeremiah 31 and Psalm 40. Psalm 110 paved the way for understanding the new covenant with its seated priest, and Arthur demonstrates that reality through the section. He ultimately connects the legal background of the new covenant with the Abrahamic promise and the Mosaic covenant.

Arthur forms Section 4 around the word "faithfulness." He begins by introducing his key text from Habakkuk before applying it through a series of biblical examples to demonstrate the value of being faithful to God through persecution and hardships. He caps off the Hall of Faith with its supreme member, Jesus, before urging the audience to run the race in front of them. He wraps this section by comparing the two possible outcomes at the Day of Judgment with the two covenantal mountains of the Bible.

Arthur ended section 4 with the call to be grateful in view of this future awaiting us and "to serve God in a way that pleases him with constant devotion." Arthur starts Section 5 with a practical guide to doing this as well as a final summarization of his core points throughout the letter. He ends his letter with a prayer and brief personal remarks.

Pleasing Service: 13:1–6

13:1Continue to love each other like family. 2Don't stop showing hospitality, because this is how some people hosted angels without realizing it. 3Take care of those in prison as you would if it were you in prison and those who are being mistreated as if it were you being hurt. 4Everyone should respect marriage and prevent the marriage relationship[1] from being compromised, because God will judge those who sin sexually. 5Live without loving money; instead be satisfied with what you have. After all, God has told us, "I will never abandon you and I will never give up on you," 6which is why we can confidently respond, "The Lord supports me, so I won't worry; what can anyone do to me?"

Arthur concluded Section 4 by urging his friends to "serve God in a way that pleases him." He now uses the first part of Section 5 to offer practical ways to accomplish this.[2] Hebrews as a whole has not focused upon much in the way of practical guidance. Arthur's instructions for his audience have focused upon resolving to stay committed in the midst of hardships. He told them to really pay attention (2:1), contemplate Jesus (3:1), take it seriously (4:1), give it all we've got (4:11), maintain our commitment (4:14), and so on. As he concludes his letter, he adds advice of a much more practical sort. Let's look at each point closely.

Continue to love each other like family

He begins with love. His wording implies the community already loves each other, but he urges them to continue to do so. He means for love to be demonstrated in a very practical way. As he said earlier when he mentioned their "loving support" for the saints in 6:10 he means for them to express their love by taking care of one another. This is a serious risk to take on in the midst of persecution. As members of the community are outed as Christians and suffer social pressure to compromise or are ostracized into a weakened financial state, taking care of each other is all the more important, but also more dangerous. Arthur urges them to disregard these fears and to take care of each other like a family.

Don't stop showing hospitality

The next item is a specific way the community can support each other. He asks them to show hospitality to each other. His wording shows again that this is already a practice in the community, but his encouragement is for them to keep it up. Hospitality was an important value in the ancient world, especially critical for Christians in the midst of persecution. Public inns were often associated with idolatry and sexual immorality and thus traveling Christians avoided them. The willingness on the part of ancient Christians to open their homes to traveling preachers and leaders was vital in order to ensure the continuing mission of the gospel.

Arthur grounds his request for hospitality with the reminder that some who showed hospitality in the past were actually hosting angels without knowing it. The most popular example of such an account is that of Abraham and Sarah who hosted God and two angels in Genesis 18.[3] Arthur doesn't mean to imply this is likely to happen, but only to undergird the critical nature of continuing to show hospitality.

. . .

Take care of those in prison

Arthur then progresses to another way they can love each other like family. He tells them to take care of those in prison. We know from 10:34 that the community's past included members in prison for their Christian convictions and now we know that its present does as well. Arthur encourages them to take care of their imprisoned members just like they would want someone else to take care of them if they were in prison. This is a practical outworking of the very words of Jesus, "Love your neighbor to the same degree you would love yourself" (Mark 12:31). As stated in the commentary on 10:34, ancient prisons didn't care for their inmates and it was up to the friends and family to ensure those in prison had food, water, and daily necessities. Arthur urges them to take on this task.

And those who are being mistreated

The next item closely aligns with the prior. Arthur tells his friends to take care of those being mistreated. This is another indication that the threat of persecution has started to give way to actual physical harm in the community. The Greek text is nonspecific to the exact circumstances, but identifying with Jesus has brought some form of beatings to the church. This is either officially as part of governmental punishment or unofficially as part of the audience's marginalization by the society around them. Either way some of their members had physical injuries inflicted because of their identification with God and his Son. Arthur enjoins them to take care of these members "as if it were you being hurt." He again connects this request to the "love commandment" of Jesus.[4] They should take care of those suffering the physical pain of persecution the same way they would want someone to take care of them if they were in pain.

Everyone should respect marriage

Furthermore, Arthur challenges the entire community to respect the institution of marriage. This is a job for everyone, and not just those who are married. How does he envision this respect? They should not allow the marriage relationship to be compromised with adultery. This may seem at first like a significant departure from the matters he has been discussing. However, keeping the marriage relationship undefiled fits perfectly into the larger theme when looking at it from an ancient perspective. Sexual immorality was connected to idolatry. The temples of the Roman gods featured cultic prostitutes and use of these services was considered a civic duty for men.[5] Christians who used these immoral services, or were associated with them would be seen as supporting the worship of the Roman pantheon and, thus, less likely to incur persecution. But here, Arthur completely eliminates this as a viable option for his friends. Ultimately, this command is grounded in the Day of Judgment. God's judgment will find out those who betray his institution of marriage and compromise their faithfulness to him with idols.[6]

Live without loving money

Arthur rounds out the first paragraph with a call to avoid greed. He tells his friends to live without loving money. This appears disconnected from what preceded, but it follows the theme of idolatry as well.[7] Business partnership with the unbelieving world often required sacrifices or oaths being made to the Roman gods. Arthur encourages his audience to "be satisfied with what you have." This is perhaps even more relevant within our culture of consumerism.[8] We face an onslaught of advertisements daily. It's estimated that the average American sees up to ten thousand ads per day.[9] Ten thousand! Every one of these advertisements shares the same philosophy—you don't have enough, but if you buy my product then you'll be satisfied. Friends, true satisfaction is found in our relationship with God.[10]

For Arthur's audience, the inability to make business partnerships could prevent them from making enough money to survive. Arthur totally discounts this possibility by quoting Deuteronomy 31:6, "I will never abandon you and I will never give up on you."[11] It is fitting that this final occasion of overhearing God through the Scripture is directly spoken to us. We aren't eavesdropping anymore. God has something to say and he wants us to hear it directly from him. He confirms his trustworthiness to take care of his people. Next, Arthur will allow us to reply back to God with a Scripture quotation of our own.

Arthur puts within our mouths the words of Psalm 118:6.[12] Would it surprise you to learn that these words were penned by the psalmist when he was also in the midst of persecution? These words become especially fitting for the audience to cling to as they run the race in front of them. They don't need to worry about their daily provisions—that is God's job. He will never abandon them, or us for that matter. We can be confident when we rely on him for our daily bread.

13:7–17

13:7Remember your leaders who taught you the word of God. Reflect on the results of their lifestyle and emulate their faithfulness. 8Messiah Jesus is the same yesterday, today, and forever. 9Don't be led astray into any unfamiliar teachings because it is better for you to be nourished by grace than by food which hasn't benefited those who live by it. 10We have an altar that those who serve in the Tabernacle aren't permitted to eat from. 11After all, the high priest takes the animals' blood into the sanctuary as a sin offering but their bodies are burned outside the camp. 12In fact, this is why Jesus suffered outside the city walls so that he could make the people holy with his own blood. 13So then, we should go to him outside the camp and accept being degraded like he was 14because we don't have a lasting city here. Quite the contrary, we yearn for the future city. 15Because of Jesus, we should always swear allegiance to God's name which is like offering him a sacrifice of praise. 16Don't stop supporting each other, because sacrifices like this please God. 17Be influenced by your leaders and follow their guidance because they guard your souls knowing that they will be judged. Please let them enjoy doing this and don't make it difficult since that wouldn't be in your best interest.

This long and complicated paragraph is bookended with two instructions regarding the community's leaders. Hebrews 13:7 focuses on the leaders of the past, and 13:17 focuses on the leaders of the present. This paragraph is notably complex in its contents which seem to bounce around all over the place. Knowing Arthur, we will find this not to be the case, but it will require a close inspection of each line. Let's begin with his first sentence.

Remember your leaders who taught you the Word of God. Reflect on the results of their lifestyle and emulate their faithfulness.

Arthur begins this complex thought with very simple advice. They are to remember their leaders. These are the original leaders of the community who have since died. We aren't told how they died or when, but this gives further indication that the time in between when they "first saw the light" (10:32) and the present is notable. All of the original leaders are gone. Two things are told to us in connection with these leaders.

The first is that they taught the audience the Word of God. They didn't use their position to get famous or rich or to push a platform or an agenda. They used their position to teach God's Word. This is the humble job God calls leaders to. They aren't there to give us their own word, but to teach God's Word. These men of their past had committed themselves to know the Word and to make it known. And for that, they should be remembered.

The second thing we are told about the leaders is to "Reflect on the results of their lifestyle and emulate their faithfulness." This is even more telling on the character of these men. Not only did they teach the Word, they lived it. They walked the talk to the degree their lives could be held up as an example for those in the community's present. What are the results of their lifestyle? Arthur means things like confidence in God (3:6), hope in the future (6:11), perseverance (6:12), righteousness (12:11), peace and holiness (12:14). These men honored God's Word in what they said and did, and Arthur calls his audience to emulate their faithfulness.

Messiah Jesus is the same yesterday, today, and forever.

Arthur still has this subject of leadership in mind when he writes my favorite verse of the book. This declaration is a one sentence summary of the message he has been trying to get across for the entire letter. The person of Jesus, in his role as Messiah, is always the same.[13] He never changes. His character of love, mercy, and grace is enduring. He was the same before the incarnation when he agreed to enter into the world in the body prepared for him. He was the same in the past when he learned obedience from what he suffered. He was the same at the cross and at the resurrection. He is the same "today" when he is seated on God's throne as cosmic king. And he will be the same forever as he advocates to the Father on our behalf.[14]

This is a beautiful piece of theology that speaks deeply to the human heart, but what does it have to do with the leadership? Leaders come and go, but Jesus doesn't. The former leaders are gone, and new leaders are in place for the community. This is an experience we are all too familiar with. Pastors, preachers, leaders of all kinds will change; but Jesus never changes. From this foundation, Arthur will offer a final bit of summarizing teaching.

Don't be led astray into any unfamiliar teachings

Arthur urges his audience not to fall prey to unfamiliar teachings. This comes immediately after he challenged them to remember their former leaders and focus upon the timelessness of Jesus. The message that was "confirmed for us by those who had heard him" will always be the message. This is the living gospel Jesus preached through his sinless life (4:15), atoning death (2:17), victorious resurrection and exaltation (8:1), representative priesthood (10:21), and coming return (9:28). What are the unfamiliar teachings? The literal Greek is "foreign teachings," and it has the same meaning as the "dead works" of idolatry that have constituted the warnings throughout his letter.[15] His friends cannot compromise their faithfulness to God and his Son with the worship of foreign gods. They must remain completely committed to the Word of God, which was originally preached by the community's first leaders.

· · ·

It is better for you to be nourished by grace than by food

Arthur seemingly makes a startling shift to the topic of food. How can he go from "unfamiliar teaching" to grace being better than food? Rather than introducing a new topic, Arthur is justifying his prior statement and building toward another comparison between Jesus and the Day of Atonement sacrifices.

His point will be reserved for verse 13, "We should go to him outside the camp and accept being degraded like he was because we don't have a lasting city here." Arthur is continuing the same topic of idolatry. The connection is somewhat easier to make in the ancient world where gods are often served with food. These sacrificial meals were the subject of debate in the early Christian world.[16] Similar to his approach elsewhere, he urges his friends to avoid any contamination from idolatry. They can't participate in the festivals that surround them. They aren't a part of that world.

Arthur's initial statement begins this topic merely by pointing out the spiritual value of grace over the physical value of food. The notion of food strengthening or nourishing the body is drawn from Psalm 104:15. The grace found in the teaching of the original leaders possesses value beyond what any physical food can provide. Let's progress to see how Arthur connects all the dots from this point to his ultimate theme of abstaining from idolatry.

We have an altar that those who serve in the Tabernacle aren't permitted to eat from.

Arthur begins with a thesis statement. He draws from his prior comparisons of the Levitical priesthood and the Day of Atonement to establish the point that he will make in verse 13. In the Levitical priesthood, some sacrifices were able to be eaten by the offeror, others could only be eaten by a priest, but some were so holy that no one could eat them. The Day of Atonement sacrifice is in this most holy category. This sacrifice can't be eaten. Remember he isn't talking about the Temple; it has already been destroyed. He is illustrating the utter sanctity of the sacrifice of Jesus by comparing it to the holiest sacrifice in the

Levitical system. Arthur is using this final part of his letter to summarize the points he has already made, not introducing new material.[17]

The high priest takes the animals' blood into the sanctuary as a sin offering but their bodies are burned outside the camp.

We are now told why the Day of Atonement sacrifice could not be eaten. The blood of the sacrifice was taken into the Most Holy Place but the bodies were burned. This detail about the complete and total burning of the animal's body is from Leviticus 16:27. Remember Arthur is continuing his theme of comparing Jesus' sacrifice to the Day of Atonement. Arthur sees this once per year solemn occasion as sharing similarity which he uses to highlight the complete transcendence of Jesus' sacrifice compared to the Levitical offerings. This transcendence demands our closest attention.

In fact, this is why Jesus suffered outside the city walls so that he could make the people holy with his own blood.

Arthur now demonstrates the points of comparison he has been building. Just like the animals sacrificed for the Day of Atonement are burned outside the camp, so Jesus suffered outside the city. All four gospel writers describe Jesus being led out of the city to Golgotha (Matthew 27:32–33, Mark 15:21–22, Luke 23:26–33, John 19:16–17). Crucifixions were customarily conducted right outside the city wall like this so that the execution was public and served as a deterrent not to defy Rome. Arthur once again assigns Jesus' blood the power to make the people holy. The animal sacrifices on the Day of Atonement offered limited atonement, but Jesus offers "an unlimited salvation" (7:25).

We should go to him outside the camp and accept being degraded like he was because we don't have a lasting city here. Quite the contrary, we yearn for the future city.

As we found above, the goal of this comparison between the sacrifice of Jesus and the Day of Atonement that was introduced in the remark about food and grace is mentioned here. Arthur doesn't want his point to be missed so he states it clearly here. Remember the two goals Arthur has in mind for his letter? We see them on display in this paragraph:

1. to demonstrate that the new covenant is superior to the old and thus worthy of greater attention and faithfulness and
2. to showcase that the new covenant offers greater access to God to enable faithfulness in the midst of persecution and difficulties.

The second goal is on display first in the total supremacy of Jesus' sacrifice when compared to even the holiest sacrifice made by the Levitical priests. The first goal is then demonstrated when Arthur urges his friends to make sacrifices of their own. They can't conform to the sinful and idolatrous world around them. They have to be willing to metaphorically leave their culture and pay the price that entails. They will be degraded for Jesus, and they will be degraded like Jesus. But it is worth it. They have to forfeit even the simple things like meat sacrificed to foreign gods. The grace of knowing him is worth all the food in the world.

Why is this price worth paying? We give up something temporary to gain something permanent. Although it is fair to say that no city on earth is lasting, the one he has in mind is Rome.[18] The audience is constantly buffeted with the notion that Rome is an eternal city. It isn't. It will fall. It will be replaced by "the city that has foundations which was established by God."

Because of Jesus, we should always swear allegiance to God's name which is like offering him a sacrifice of praise.

The sacrifice of Jesus enables us to enjoy a permanent relationship with God. For this reason, we should continually promise our faithfulness to him. He is worthy of undying loyalty. This act is like offering him a sacrifice of praise. This phrase is drawn from Arthur's Bible in Psalm 50:14.[19] While the idea of praising God in song is certainly an aspect of this "sacrifice of praise," the context speaks of another primary intent. The "sacrifice of praise" is offered when we express our faithfulness and allegiance to God in the face of opposition. When we stand for God when everyone calls for us to backdown, that is the sacrifice he is looking for. Arthur calls for his friends to remain committed even when it could cost them everything. After all, it isn't a sacrifice if it doesn't cost you anything.[20]

Don't stop supporting each other, because sacrifices like this please God.

While on the topic of sacrifices that delight God, Arthur shifts to another concept that he has employed elsewhere. We also honor God when we support each other like a church family should. When we bear one another's financial hardships we showcase our devotion to God. Just like at the beginning of this chapter, Arthur's wording assumes this is taking place, but he reiterates it here as something that should continue.

Be influenced by your leaders and follow their guidance because they guard your souls knowing that they will be judged. Please let them enjoy doing this and don't make it difficult since that wouldn't be in your best interest.

Arthur concludes this long and complex paragraph with a return to where it began. He started with the topic of leadership and he ends with it as well. Before he encouraged his friends to remember their former leaders, and now he asks them to be influenced by their present leaders. These community leaders are likely the ones who reached out to Arthur to craft this letter, and it is by their prayers that it is being received well. Arthur comments that these leaders guard their souls. The Greek word for "guard" is literally "lose sleep." It implies the long hours and thankless work of looking out for this community. The job comes with a heavy responsibility; the leaders will be judged for their work. They will have to give an account of the stewardship of leading God's people. This is a grave duty, one that demands full sincerity. It is not to be undertaken lightly.

There is no sense that these leaders are anything but the fitting continuation of the ministry of those original leaders. Arthur tells his friends to "be influenced" by them. The Greek word can have the stronger meaning of "obey," but in this context, it has the sense of "allow yourself to be persuaded by."[21] In reminding his friends of the difficult task leadership represents, he commends them to make it easy for their leaders. Don't be the person the pastors don't like. There is no benefit in that since these men are tasked to "guard your souls."

With the conclusion of this paragraph, Arthur advances to some final remarks as he brings his letter to its end. Let's move on and finish our journey together.

CLOSING REMARKS: 13:18–19

13:18Pray for us, because we believe our motives are sincere since we are trying to be helpful in all that we do. 19I specifically encourage you to pray that I can return to you sooner.

Arthur now transitions into a few personal remarks to close out the letter. He begins by requesting prayer for "us." He is requesting prayer for the entire community that supported this letter and its delivery, that is the sister church rooting for the audience to "run the race" and "focus on Jesus." He doesn't offer any clarity on what he wants them to pray for, but he does tell them why this group is worthy of their prayer time. Their "motives are sincere" and they "are trying to be helpful in all" that they do. This line reveals the worst-case-scenario in Arthur's mind, that his friends would misinterpret this letter as anything other than an honest attempt to help them.

Arthur then provides a specific prayer request. He asks that they pray specifically for him so that he can return to them sooner. We don't know what circumstances prevent his visit, but we hear in his prayer request that he wants to get to his friends as soon as he can. They have been geographically separated, and this letter is an attempt to temporarily replace his ability to be present with them. His prayer is that this will be remedied, and he will be reunited with his friends face to face. With his brief request for prayer, Arthur now transitions to a prayer of his own.

13:20–21

> *13:20*May the God of peace—who brought our Lord Jesus, the great shepherd of the flock, back from the dead by the blood of the eternal covenant—*21*may he equip you with everything helpful to do what he wants and to make us into something that pleases him through Messiah Jesus. May all glory go to him forever and ever. Amen.

Arthur offers a prayer for his friends as he concludes his magnificent letter. The long and complex prayer is spread out over two verses. The first half of the prayer is entirely consumed with describing the God he is praying to. Arthur is overwhelmed with the character of God and the salvation he has demonstrated in his Son, so he dramatically defines God as an act of worship before proceeding to the prayer request. The second half serves as the actual request that he prays for his friends and for his own community. The New Testament is filled with beautiful benedictions, but this may be the most beautiful of them all. If you have never used this in your own prayer time, I highly encourage you to take time with God and pray these words as an act of worship. To ensure we get the most out of this prayer, let's look closely at each line.

May the God of peace

Arthur begins the prayer by calling God "the God of peace." This appears to have been a set expression in the early church since it is found numerous other places in the New Testament.[22] Why does Arthur pray to the God of peace? Peace has not been a primary concept within his letter. He only uses the word five times, including this occasion.[23] His purpose here is to identify God as being characterized by peace. With the threat of persecution growing, he is not a God of conflict, but of peace. More than just being characterized by peace, God offers peace to his people. Even more than that, God will institute a time where peace is permanent. When we enter into his resting place, heaven and earth will unite, and peace will reign. After all, Jesus is the peaceful king.

This remark is also a direct affront to Rome. The empire promised its people *Pax Romana*, the peace of Rome. Their promise was to be so dominant in military might that no force dare oppose them. Their promise was to squash any act of rebellion and execute any who challenged their authority. Rome may have promised to rule with peace, but they only ruled with fear. True peace is found in the God of peace, a fitting beginning to this final benediction.

Who brought our Lord Jesus

God is the "God of peace," but who else is he? He is the one who brought Jesus back from the dead. Arthur takes an aside to tell us about this Jesus. We'll focus on God's act of bringing him back from the dead in a later line. Arthur uses the expression for his Savior "our Lord Jesus."

Jesus is first *our* Lord. He is in a relationship united to us so that we can refer to him as *ours*. He is our *Lord*. As Lord, Jesus is the master of our lives, and he is cosmic king. He reigns supreme, but we have to choose him to act as Lord of our lives. He rightfully has this rule through his saving sacrifice, but we surrender to his authority when we allow him to lead our lives. This is also another subtle jab at Rome. The Roman world was used to hearing "Caesar is Lord," but for Christians "Jesus is Lord."

Secondly, he is called by his name, Jesus. The cosmic king is not an anonymous figure. He is the historical Jesus of Nazareth. He is a man, yet more than a man. His name means "salvation," so it is no wonder that "there is no other name under heaven given among men by which we must be saved" (Acts 4:12 ESV).

The great shepherd of the flock

Arthur gives us more about Jesus than just his title and his name. He is also the great shepherd. This is another comparison to Moses, as we saw in 3:2–6. In Isaiah 63:11, Moses is called a "shepherd of his flock."[24] But Jesus "deserves more glory than Moses" so he is the *great* shepherd. Moses led the flock out of Egypt to Mount Sinai, but Jesus leads the flock out of death and to Mount Zion. The shepherd imagery recalls Jesus' own words as well, "I am the good shepherd. The good shepherd lays down his life for the flock" (John 10:11).

Back from the dead

Arthur returns to God by telling us from where he brought Jesus back. Arthur's word recalls another part of Isaiah 63:11 LXX. Let's look at the whole verse, "The one who brought back from the land, the shepherd of the flock." Arthur employs similar language used of God for the Exodus and applies it to Jesus in the greater Exodus. This "great salvation" comes with a warning label though. The Exodus generation didn't make it to the destination, so don't repeat their example of unfaithfulness.

By the blood of the eternal covenant

Arthur grounds God's saving work in Jesus with an encapsulation of all that he said in Section 3 of his letter. God brought Jesus back from the dead "by the blood of the eternal covenant."[25] The first covenant had issues (8:7), so a new covenant was promised in Jeremiah 31. No issues will be found in this covenant, it is eternal. It is never ending. It has been sealed with the blood of the spotless Savior, Jesus our Lord. By this blood, "we have confidence to enter the sanctuary" and "to live in God's presence."

May he equip you with everything helpful to do what he wants

After this dramatic description of the God we pray to, Arthur now tells us what he is praying for. He prays that God would equip them. The word has a rather plain vanilla sound, but its meaning is what counts. The Greek word has a broad context of uses and can have the sense of fixing something damaged, making something new, or furnishing something to completion.[26] Does it resonate how important it is that the author chose to use this word as the key verb, the main thing he is asking? The prayer is for God to take us where we are and make us usable. I love that the word can mean to fix something that is broken, it can mean to improve something that is sluggish, and it can mean to make something better than it is. In essence, the prayer is for God to meet us wherever we are and make us into all that we can be.

But what does Arthur pray God equip his friends with? "With everything helpful." That sounds overly broad, but it is qualified by "to do what he wants." God equips us with what we need in order to do what pleases him. Just like we are told in 10:7 that Jesus came to do what God wanted, so does Arthur desire for his friends to take on that mission. Their lives cannot be about idols, or fear, or anything less than the pursuit of God and his Son. This prayer request is broad enough to meet the audience where they are, but also to stay with them wherever they go. They need to be equipped with everything helpful to overcome the persecution they face, but this prayer still applies even if the persecution goes away. They (and we) will always find value in praying that God equip us to do what he wants.

And to make us into something that pleases him

Arthur expands the scope of doing what God wants to the essence of our identity. It isn't enough that we do what God wants—we have to become something that pleases him. Arthur transitions from "you" to "us" as he advances into this second aspect. He includes himself and those on his side of the letter along with the audience to show this is the goal for all Christians. The ultimate goal for every follower is to bring a smile to God's face.

Through Messiah Jesus

Arthur's prayer has been a tall order. He yearns for his friends to be equipped to do what God wants and to become something that pleases him. How can they (or we) ever live up to such a daunting task? It is through Messiah Jesus. He is the power that makes that mission possible. His life, death, resurrection, ascension, and exaltation are the sole means by which such a powerful result can be produced.

Previously in the prayer, Jesus was called our Lord, but he is also Messiah. He is anointed with the Holy Spirit as the eschatological king, priest, and prophet. He is the fulfillment of all that the former prophets hoped for. But his role is not yet complete. He is sitting on God's throne as cosmic king, but he sits "looking forward to when his enemies will be piled under his feet" (10:13). He is the Messiah, but his job as Messiah is not done yet. There is more work to be done. "He will come a second time, not to bear sin, but to save those who are ready to welcome him" (9:28).

May all glory go to him forever and ever. Amen.

The prayer ends the only place it could, with all glory going to God. His unlimited power displayed in the eternal salvation through Jesus earns him never-ending praise. The prayer ends here because the story of humanity ends here as well. God is inviting us into his resting place so that we can participate for all eternity in giving him glory. Resurrection life makes this possible and it awaits those who maintain their "commitment to Jesus the Son of God" (4:14).

13:22–25

[13:22]Now brothers and sisters, I encourage you to take to heart this brief[27] but challenging message[28] that I have written for you. [23]Note that our brother Timothy has been released. If he makes it to me soon, he will be with me when I come to see you. [24]Say hello to all of your leaders and all of the saints for me. Your friends from Italy say hello to you. [25]May grace be with all of you.

We have now arrived at the last paragraph in Hebrews. Arthur ends his passionate plea for his good friends with a few personal comments. He begins by calling them "brothers and sisters." His role as faithful brother to look after their spiritual health has been carefully demonstrated throughout these thirteen chapters. He knows he has stretched their faith as he challenged their walk with the Lord. He lets them know here that he is aware of that. He encourages them to accept his challenging words and let them make a difference in their lives. The words "encourage" and "challenge" are forms of the same Greek word, and he uses this dual meaning to capture the goal he has had in his letter. He means to encourage them with all the blessings they have presently in Jesus but also to challenge them to keep running the race ahead of them so they don't miss out on all the blessings still to come.

He moves on to tell them that Timothy has been released. It's probably safe to assume this is the same Timothy we know as Paul's traveling companion.[29] We know from Romans 16:12 that he was acquainted with the Roman church, but we don't know what he is released from. Some kind of imprisonment seems to be the reference, but it could be that he is released from some other obligation detaining him. Whatever it is, the audience didn't need to be told. Timothy's release is secondary to Arthur's point that he will come with him should he arrive before his departure to see his friends in person.

Arthur wraps up by asking his friends to say hello to all of their leaders and all of the saints. This showcases that the letter is to a specific community, or house church, within the larger church in Rome. This particular group is but a small subset of a larger community, and Arthur asks that they pass on his greeting to their brothers and sisters in Christ as well.

He also passes on the greeting of their "friends from Italy." These are mutual friends originally from or associated with the audience who are now with Arthur and his community. They send their greeting as those also rooting for them to run the race and focus on Jesus.

Arthur ends his letter just like so many other letters in the New Testament conclude, with a prayer for grace. He has previously connected grace to God (2:9), his throne (4:16), and the Holy Spirit (10:29). Now he prays for this grace to find his friends in their trying time. It is with this sentiment that I close the commentary as well. I pray that wherever you are and whatever trials you are going through, God's grace will find you.

I encourage you to check out the back matter that follows this chapter. There is an epilogue that concludes the story of Fidelis and his friends. This is followed by the complete translation of Hebrews and an afterword.

PIECE OF MIND

1. Literally, "bed." This a euphemism for the sexual relationship and, thus, its exclusive tie to biblical marriage, see BDAG 554.
2. The dramatic shift in tone from 12:29, "considering that our God is a consuming fire" to "continue to love each other like family" in 13:1, has led some scholars to question the integrity of the thirteenth chapter. Some suppose it was appended at a later date to make the sermon more suitable to a wider audience via a letter, and others suppose a more malicious intent. They suspect that chapter 13 was added in order to make the letter appear more like the other New Testament letters so that it could be snuck into the canon. There is no evidence supporting either approach. All evidence indicates that chapter 13 was a part of the original material and was written by the same person who composed the first twelve chapters. For a strong defense of this position, see Lane 495–496. The difficulty is eliminated when 13:1-6 are seen as a practical outworking of the pleasing service to God called for in 12:28 and when 13:7-17 is understood to summarize the prior discussion of Section 3 and 4 into the call to honor the community's leaders. The closing remarks that follow are a logical addition seeing that the "written sermon" is delivered remotely in the form of a letter being delivered through a courier and orator.
3. The most poignant example of an unexpected angelic visitor is Abraham and the three "men" from Genesis 18. Other Old Testament examples include the angelic visit to Gideon (Judges 6), Manoah (Judges 13), and the apocryphal Tobit (Tobit 5).
4. The literal Greek of 13:3 is "Remember those in prison as being imprisoned and those being mistreated as also being in the body." Some have interpreted the use of "body" as the church by understanding it to be a reference to "the body of Christ." This overlooks the balance between the two phrases. Arthur is urging them to care for those in prison and those being mistreated as though it was happening to them.
5. The connection between prostitution and idol worship is a challenging connection to make for the modern Western mind. The ancients easily connected sexual relations with religious expression. Ancient idol worship understood that the sexual activity of the gods empowered the earth's productive power in harvest time. Thus, prostitution created a visual demonstration for the gods designed to lure them into their sexual relations with the earth. This also helps to understand why Paul lists "sexual immorality" as the final entry in a list of idolatrous practices in Acts 15:29.
6. The injunction to "prevent the marriage relationship from being compromised" could also be a general warning against adultery within the community and not necessarily just a reference to use of cult prostitution. This command is also intrinsically connected to their circumstances as well. In the midst of life's hardships, one is most tempted to seek temporary solace in sin. Persecution doesn't prevent problems in marriage, it doesn't solve attractions. As the community is called to take care of each other, closer bonds will form. Arthur doesn't want to see this result in the breach of any marriage relationship.

7. Sexual immorality (13:4) and greed (13:5) are often connected in ancient Jewish and Christian literature. This probably stems from their proximity in the Ten Commandments, see Lane 517–518.

8. The command to "live without loving money; instead be satisfied with what you have" is especially relevant for our culture. When the U.S. government founded an internal regulatory body to protect from abusive financial practices, they named it the "Consumer Financial Protection Bureau." The government identifying individuals as "consumers" is extremely concerning, but probably not an unfair assessment within Western society. Arthur's challenge to rise above the love of money and to pursue satisfaction with what one has is more important now than ever before.

9. The estimation that the average American sees up to ten thousand ads per day is from Forbes, https://www.forbes.com/sites/forbesagencycouncil/2017/08/25/finding-brand-success-in-the-digital-world. For those interested in significantly reducing the number of advertisements seen, I highly recommend rethinking social media accounts.

10. I would be remiss not to mention the subject of minimalism when talking about being satisfied with what you have. Minimalism has developed into an internet subculture, and although, it was not started by Christians (at least as far as I can tell), it certainly should've been. Many Christians do inhabit the movement now, and I encourage everyone to evaluate the benefits for themselves of reducing possessions and simplifying the home.

11. The citation is difficult to identify with complete certainty. Arthur quotes it as "I will never abandon you and I will never give up on you," but no Old Testament reference exactly matches this wording. The challenge is intensified in that the verse is quoted the same way by Philo, the first century Jewish philosopher. Deuteronomy 31:6 fits the best and is what is defended above. Joshua 1:5 is also very close, but given Arthur's propensity for quoting Deuteronomy, it seems more likely. The adjustment to Deuteronomy 31:6 is probably to merge its wording with Genesis 28:15, see David M. Allen 68–71 and Pierce 190–193.

12. The use of Psalm 118 is not surprising given Arthur's persistent use of the Psalms. Numerous verses have a Messianic understanding, see 118:22 and 118:26.

13. The Greek word translated as "same" can also mean "himself." This carries the additional caveat that Jesus is always himself. He is always who he is. This invites another challenge to us. Am I myself or am I someone else? It is easy to fall into the trap of wishing we were someone else or pretending to be something we are not. Jesus is the supreme example of being himself and can challenge us to do the same.

14. The biblical support for Jesus always being the same is from Psalm 102, which Arthur quoted in 1:10–12.

15. For the notion that the "unfamiliar teachings" serve as a reference to idolatry, see Whitlark 119–121.

16. Other New Testament passages similarly condemn participation in sacrificial meats. The most telling is when Paul and the Jerusalem council set expectations for the Gentile believers in Acts 15:29 (ESV), "That you abstain from what has been sacrificed to idols, and from blood, and from what has been strangled, and from sexual immorality." See also Revelation 2:20.

17. Some scholars observe a reference to communion in 13:10, "We have an altar that those who serve in the Tabernacle aren't permitted to eat from." They understand the Christian "altar" as the eucharist and that we are permitted to eat from this altar but those who serve in the Tabernacle are not. This is an unfortunate misunderstanding of the verse since the entire argument hinges on the fact that we have an altar *no one is*

permitted to eat from. Arthur means to establish the utter sanctity of Jesus' sacrifice by comparing it to the holiest Levitical sacrifice, which also could not be eaten.

18. For more on this position, and references to Rome as the "eternal city," see Whitlark 104–108.

19. A more literal rendering of 13:15 would be, "Through him then, we should offer a sacrifice of praise to God continually, that is, the fruit of lips that confess his name." The expression "fruit of lips" is taken from the LXX version of Hosea 14:3. We observed above that the "sacrifice of praise" is from Psalm 50:14, but it is also found in Leviticus 7:13. The expression, "Confess his name" is drawn from Psalm 54:6. The word "continually" serves as a reference to the evening and morning daily sacrifices, see Lane 549–550.

20. For the concept that the "sacrifice of praise" as the remaining sacrifice in view of Jesus' definitive atonement, see Moffatt 237, "This tallies with the well-known rabbinic saying, quoted in Tanchuma, 55.2: 'in the time of messiah all sacrifices will cease, but the sacrifice of thanksgiving will not cease; prayers will cease, but praises will not cease.'"

21. The word has the general meaning of "persuaded" (this is its meaning in 6:9), and the passive voice would imply a passive of permission. This would yield a literal, "Allow yourselves to be persuaded by your leaders" and is thus simplified to "be influenced by your leaders." This further supports the relational and familial nature of the church emphasized throughout Hebrews.

22. The phrase "God of peace" used in 13:20, and also found elsewhere in the New Testament, probably originates from the pseudepigraphal work Testament of Dan 5:2.

23. The Greek word for peace occurs in 7:2, 11:31, 12:14, 12:11, and 13:20.

24. Paul also references Isaiah 63:11 in a similar context in Romans 10:7. Interestingly enough, Isaiah is himself referencing his Bible. He is commenting upon Psalm 78:52.

25. The phrase "by the blood of the eternal covenant" in 13:20 is a blending of three different Old Testament passages: Isaiah 55:3, Ezekiel 37:26, and Zechariah 9:11. All three passages share the theme of God's coming salvation for his people.

26. For the diverse range of meaning found in the Greek word translated as "equip" in 13:21, see TLNT vol. 2, 271–274.

27. Some challenge the accuracy of Arthur referring to his letter as brief. This is particularly relevant since Hebrews is longer than most of the New Testament letters. Arthur isn't referencing a specific length though. He is merely saying he spoke briefly in comparison to how long he could have spoken, see Koester 582–583.

28. The literal Greek is "word of exhortation." Note that this is the same phrase used in Acts 13:15 in reference to the synagogue sermon preached by Paul. Arthur wrote his letter to be presented as a sermon for his friends. The epistolary ending shows us that the letter served as the vehicle for him to preach it while being geographically separated from them.

29. The reference to Timothy could be a different Timothy since the Gospels and Acts regularly offer examples of different biblical figures with the same name (For example there are multiple Johns and Jameses). This is less likely in the case of Timothy since we know of no such other figure from the Scripture or early church history.

Epilogue

Copy and Paste

"Your friends from Italy say hello to you. May grace be with all of you."

Fidelis had done it. Arthur warned him that the letter would take about an hour to read, and he'd gone slightly over the mark. Fidelis took a deep breath. He prayed silently that the message would be received well. He was confident he had done everything he could. Whatever came next depended on God now.

He looked out at the stunned faces. How would they react? Camilla was still crying, but Florus flashed a half smile. Livia had the same expression of joy she always had, but Calvus was a closed door. What was he thinking? Fidelis wished Salvius was here; he could have counted on him to reinforce the message and support these challenging words.

The mystery soon ended as Fidelis saw a stir. Calvus stood to his feet. He hesitated, then he spoke the words everyone was thinking.

"Can we hear it again?"

Fidelis was stunned. He cleared his throat and stammered, "Can I get a drink first?" All sixteen people erupted in laughter. Florus was laughing harder than anyone, and Camilla somehow instantly converted her loud sobs into snorting bursts of joy. Livia skipped to the back and poured a small cup; she stepped with extreme care as she brought the cup to Fidelis. Fidelis took a large gulp and returned the scroll to the beginning.

"Wait," Calvus interjected as he started to sit down, "Read it slower this time; I had some questions I wanted to ask."

"Me too!" shouted Florus, more loudly than he had intended. Others joined in agreement.

Fidelis smiled. Another tear trickled down his cheek. He reread the letter, but this time much slower. Weary, Fidelis sat down to read. But the congregation bubbled over with newfound life. He could barely get a sentence out without being interrupted by their thoughts and questions. The second reading took over three hours to finish.

When Fidelis finally finished reading, Calvus stood up again. Fidelis sighed with weariness, "I'm so sorry; there is no way I have the strength to read it again."

"Actually, I have another question," said Calvus. "Can we copy it? I want to share this with everyone I can."

Fidelis smiled ear to ear and nodded, "Sure, let's start making copies tomorrow."

The Anonymous Letter

The complete Translation of the Letter to the Hebrews

God, who previously spoke in many different ways to our ancestors through the prophets, spoke to us at the end of these days through his Son. He appointed the Son as rightful owner of everything, after all it was through him that God created the universe. The Son is the tangible expression of his presence and the physical representation of his essence. Even now he sustains the universe by his powerful word. After purifying our sins, he sat down next to the Majesty in heaven. He has become superior to the angels to the same degree that the role he has received is more distinguished than theirs.

Did God ever say to an angel, "You are my Son; today I have crowned you king"? Or, "I will be his Father and he will be my Son"? On the contrary, when he presents the Firstborn into the heavenly world, he declares, "All of God's angels must worship him." When talking about the angels, God says, "He turns his angels into the wind and his ministers into fire." But he says to the Son, "God, your reign is forever and ever, and your rule is characterized by justice. You value what is right instead of what is wrong, and that's why God, your God, has crowned you Messiah with a joyous celebration rather than your partners." He also says to the Son, "Lord, in the beginning you established the earth, and you made the sky with your hands. They will both wear out like clothing and come to an end, but you will continue on. You will wad them up like an old shirt, and just like clothes, they will be replaced with something new. You, however, are the same, and your lifetime will never end." Has God ever said to an angel, "Sit next to me until I pile your enemies under your feet"? Aren't the angels just ministering spirits sent to serve those who are about to receive salvation?

This is why we must really pay attention to what we have heard so that we don't get distracted. After all, if the message God spoke through the angels became binding so that every violation received a rightful punishment, how will we escape punishment if we disregard such a great salvation? God initially spoke of this salvation through the Lord which was confirmed for us by those who had heard him. God verified their testimony with many powerful miracles and by distributing the Holy Spirit just like he wanted.

Now we are talking about the future world, which God did not subject to angels. On the contrary, one of them declared somewhere, "Why do you think about man and why do you care about the son of man? You ranked him lower than the angels for a little while; you crowned him with nobility, and you subjected everything under his feet." Now when it says he subjected everything to him, it means he left nothing unsubjected to him. But for right now, we don't see everything as being subjected to him. However, we do see Jesus, the one who was ranked lower than the angels for a little while because he suffered death and who is now crowned with nobility so that he could experience death for everyone as an expression of God's grace.

Now God is the source and goal of the universe so it makes sense for him to qualify the pioneer of their salvation through suffering, ultimately leading many sons and daughters to nobility. After all, the one who makes holy and those being made holy all come from a single ancestor, which is why he is not ashamed to call them his brothers and sisters. He says, "I will proclaim your name to my brothers and sisters and praise you in the middle of the family gathering." He also says, "I will depend on God." He then goes on to say, "I am here with the children God has entrusted to me."

So, given that the children are composed of flesh and blood, he took on the exact same condition. He did this so that, by dying, he could disarm the devil, who has the power of death, and liberate everyone who was enslaved to the fear of death throughout their lives. After all, it's obviously not angels that he helps, quite the contrary, he helps the descendants of Abraham. This being the case, he had to become exactly like his brothers and sisters so that he could become a merciful and faithful high priest to make atonement for the sins of the people in the service of God. Now he is able to help those in the midst of temptation because he was tempted when he suffered.

So, holy brothers and sisters, recipients of a heavenly invitation, contemplate Jesus the apostle and high priest whom we have sworn allegiance to. Contemplate how he was faithful to the one who appointed him just like Moses was faithful within his entire household. He deserves more glory than Moses to the same degree that the person who builds a house has more respect than the house itself. After all, every house is built by someone, but God built the entire universe. Now Moses was faithful within his entire household as a servant to put what God would say on record, but Messiah is faithful as a Son over his household. We are members of his household if we don't let go of the confidence that comes from our hope.

This is exactly why the Holy Spirit says, "Today if you hear his voice, don't let your hearts be resistant like on the day when your ancestors rebelled in the desert. This was where they skeptically tested me even though they saw my works for forty years. That's why I was provoked by this generation and said, 'Their hearts are constantly wandering off and they wouldn't learn my ways.' So, when I was angry, I swore, 'They will never enter my place of rest!'"

Brothers and sisters, make sure to prevent there from being in even one of you, a heart corrupted by unfaithfulness that causes you to turn your back on the living God. To prevent this, encourage each other every single day, as long as today lasts, so that you don't let a single heart among you be resistant due to the seduction of sin. After all, we have become Messiah's partners but only if we stick closely to our original plan all the way to the end. When it says, "Today if you hear his voice, don't let your hearts be resistant like when your ancestors rebelled," who was it that heard God, but then rebelled? Wasn't it everyone who left Egypt under the leadership of Moses? Who provoked him for forty years? Wasn't it those who sinned and fell down dead in the desert? If it wasn't those who disobeyed, who did he swear would not enter his place of rest? So, we see that they couldn't enter because they were unfaithful.

Since the promise to enter his place of rest remains open, we should take it seriously to prevent even one of you from missing out. After all, we received an invitation to enter his place of rest just like they did, but the message they heard didn't benefit them because they didn't join in with those who responded in faithfulness to what they heard. We will enter the place of rest because of faithfulness just like he said, "So, when I was angry, I swore, 'They will never enter my place of rest!'" Neverthe-less, his works have been finished since the beginning of the world considering he has declared somewhere about the seventh day, "God rested on the seventh day from all of his works." Yet in another place he says, "They will never enter my place of rest!"

So, given that it is reserved for some people to enter it, and those who were originally invited failed to enter because of disobedience, he has scheduled a new date. The new date is today, which he said much later through David as quoted above, "Today if you hear his voice, don't let your hearts be resistant." Now, if Joshua had offered them rest, God would not have spoken about another date after these days. Then a Sabbath rest must be reserved for the people of God. After all, those who enter his place of rest also rest from their own works just like God did from his works.

So then, we should give it all we've got to enter that place of rest so that no one goes down due to the same kind of disobedience. After all, the Word of God is alive and effective. It is sharper than any double-edged sword. It penetrates all the way down to the border between soul and spirit and the border between joints and marrow. It is qualified to judge the thoughts and feelings of the heart. Nothing created escapes his sight, quite the contrary, everything is naked and vulnerable in front of the one who will judge us.

So then, we should maintain our commitment to Jesus the Son of God since we have him as a great high priest who has gone beyond the sky. After all, we have a high priest who is more than capable of under-standing our limitations since he was tempted exactly like us except that he never sinned. So then, we should confidently approach God's throne, the source of grace, so that we can receive mercy and grace to help us in our time of need.

Now every human high priest is appointed to represent humanity so that he can offer sacrifices for sins in the service of God. He can be sensitive to the ignorant or wayward given that he is also burdened with limitations. This is why he has to offer sacrifices for his own sins just like he offers sacrifices for the sins of the people. Additionally, no one picks himself for this honored position, but he must be invited to it by God just like Aaron was.

This being the case, Messiah didn't promote himself to the position of high priest; quite the contrary; he was promoted by the one who told him, "You are my Son; today I have crowned you King." He goes on to say in another place, "You are a priest forever in the Melchizedek tradition." During his natural life, Messiah offered loud and tearful prayers to the one who could save him from death and God answered him because of his devotion. Despite the fact that he was his Son, he learned obedience from what he suffered. Since he was qualified, God named him high priest in the Melchizedek tradition, ultimately becoming the basis for eternal salvation to everyone who obeys him.

We have a lot to say about this but it's hard to explain given that you have become lazy listeners. You should be teachers by now, but you need someone to reteach you the very basics about what God has said. You have regressed to needing milk and can't handle solid food. After all, nursing babies are not prepared to discuss righteousness since they are just babies. Solid food is for grownups who have conditioned themselves to tell the difference between what is helpful and what is harmful.

This is why we should advance beyond the initial lessons about Messiah and carry on towards the destination. We shouldn't have to start from scratch by reteaching you about repentance from dead works, faithfulness to God, purification instructions, the laying on of hands, resurrection from the dead, and eternal judgment. Although we will help you carry on, assuming God allows.

Now for those who have already seen the light, tasted the heavenly gift, shared the Holy Spirit, tasted how good God's Word is, experienced the miracles of the future universe, and have fallen back, it is impossible to reinstate them to repentance again since they are recrucifying the Son of God and making a mockery of him. After all, soil that gets frequent rainfall and produces useful crops for those who tilled it, receives a blessing from God. However, if it produces thornbushes, it is worthless and in danger of being cursed. It is destined to be set on fire.

Beloved, despite the fact that we are talking like this, we are certain of a better outcome for you, one that includes salvation. After all, God is fair so he will not ignore your loving support which you have shown for his name when you cared for the saints both now and in the past. However, we want each of you to show the same level of effort towards the future fulfillment we hope for, all the way to the end. This is so that you can emulate those who inherit what is promised because they persevered faithfully instead of becoming lazy.

Now given that God had no one greater to swear by when he made a promise to Abraham, he swore by himself when he said, "I promise to bless you and give you many descendants." As a result, Abraham obtained what was promised after he persevered. After all, people swear by someone greater than themselves and an oath is used to confirm the end of any dispute they have. So, because God really wanted to prove to the beneficiaries of the promise that his plan is irreversible, he guaranteed it with an oath. God, who cannot lie, used two irreversible declarations so that we who rely on him could be strongly encouraged to hold on to the hope in front of us. This hope is an anchor for our soul, firmly secured behind the curtain. This is where Jesus our forward scout has entered; he has become high priest forever in the Melchizedek tradition.

Now Melchizedek, who was king of Salem and priest of the Most High God, blessed Abraham whom he had met while Abraham was returning from defeating the kings. Then Abraham gave him a tithe of everything. First and foremost, based on the meaning of his name, Melchizedek is the righteous king, but since he was king of Salem, he is also the peaceful king. Since he has no record of a father, mother, lineage, birth, or death, he simulates the Son of God and remains a priest permanently.

Do you see how important this man is? Even Abraham, the father of the whole nation, gave a tithe to him. The descendants of Levi, who have the right to be priests, are commanded in the Torah to collect tithes from the people even though the people are their own family since they also came from Abraham. However, Abraham has given a tithe to someone who doesn't share their lineage and he is the one who blessed Abraham, the recipient of the promises. Now it is undeniable that someone ranked lower is blessed by someone who is ranked higher. So, in the one case, men who are destined to die receive tithes, but in the other case, someone received a tithe who is on record as still being alive. Considering that, you could almost say that Levi, who normally receives tithes, has paid a tithe to Melchizedek since he would have been inside of his great-grandfather's body when Melchizedek met him.

The Torah, which governed the Levitical priesthood, was given to the people by God. However, if it was possible for that priesthood to reach the destination, why would we need a different type of priest to emerge in the Melchizedek tradition? Why wouldn't he just be chosen from the order of Aaron? So, when the priesthood is replaced, naturally an amendment is needed to the Torah as well, because the person this is all about is part of a different tribe—a tribe that has never served at the altar. After all, it is a fact that our Lord sprung from Judah, and Moses never said anything about priesthood for this tribe. This is even more blatant when a priest like Melchizedek emerges. He has become a priest because he has an unbreakable life and not because of a commandment governing his lineage. After all, God is on record as saying, "You are a priest forever in the Melchizedek tradition." Now the prior commandment can be rescinded because of its limitations so that a better hope can be commenced. This allows us to live in God's presence since the Torah didn't bring anything to this destination.

In all of this, God didn't fail to swear an oath. Now those who became priests were inducted without an oath being sworn, but he was inducted with an oath by the one who told him, "The Lord has sworn and will not reconsider it, 'You are a priest forever.'" This is why Jesus has become the cosigner to a better covenant. In addition to that, there have been many priests because death prevented them from continuing in their service. However, he holds his priesthood permanently because he lasts forever. This being the case, he offers an unlimited salvation to those who approach God through him since he will stay alive forever to advocate for them.

A high priest like this is exactly what we need, so loyal, virtuous, and flawless. God has exalted him to heaven and separated him from sinners. The other high priests have a daily requirement first to offer sacrifices for their own sins before they can offer sacrifices for the sins of the people. However, he has no need to do this because he sacrificed for their sins once and for all when he offered himself. After all, the Torah appoints men with limitations to be high priests, but the oath which came after the Torah appoints a Son who is qualified forever.

Now the main thing we are trying to get across is that we have a high priest who sat down next to the throne of the Majesty in heaven. He is a minister in the sanctuary, the original Tabernacle which God, not man, has built. After all, every high priest is appointed to offer sacrifices so it was necessary for him to have something to offer as well. Now, if he were on earth, he wouldn't even be a priest since there are already priests here offering the sacrifices from the Torah. They serve in a model of the heavenly version. This was proven to be the case when Moses was about to finish construction on the Tabernacle and God cautioned him, "Be sure you make everything exactly like the pattern you were shown on the mountain." So, he has obtained a ministry more distinguished than theirs to the same degree that the covenant he mediates is better. The covenant is better because God instituted it on the basis of better promises.

Now if that first covenant had been without issue, there would have been no reason to expect a second one. However, he identifies an issue with them when he says, "Pay attention; this is the Lord talking. The days are approaching when I will ratify a new covenant with the nation of Israel and the nation of Judah. This covenant will not be based on the covenant I made with their ancestors when I led them by the hand out of Egypt. This is because they refused to abide by the terms of my covenant so I disassociated myself from them. Pay attention; this is the Lord talking. Since that was the case, this is what the new covenant will be like that I will make with the nation of Israel after those days. Pay attention; this is the Lord talking. I will install my instructions in their minds and engrave them on their hearts. I will be their God and they will be my people. They will never have to teach any family member or fellow citizen to learn about the Lord because every single one of them will know me personally. This is because I will offer atonement for their wrongdoings, and I will never remind myself of their sins again." Now right when he said, "New," he made the first one outdated and what has become outdated is about ready to expire.

So, even the first covenant has procedures for service to be used in the sanctuary on earth. The first section of the sanctuary was furnished with the lampstand and the table for the sacred bread, and it was named the Holy Place. Past the curtain was the second section which was named the Most Holy Place. It included the golden incense altar and the ark of the covenant which was completely encased in gold. The ark contained the gold jar of manna, Aaron's staff that sprouted, and the stone tablets of the covenant. The cherubim, which represent the presence of God, were above it and cast their shadow where atonement is made. Now is not the time to discuss these things in detail though.

Once all of the furniture was arranged like this, the priests were granted access to the first section regularly to perform their services. However, only the high priest was granted access to the second section, but just once a year. He was required to take blood with him which he would offer for his mistakes and the mistakes of the people. The Holy Spirit uses this to show that the path into the Most Holy Place is not yet revealed as long as the first section is standing in the way, which is a metaphor for the present time. This is when sacrifices are offered that only focus on food, drinks, and various purification rituals. These external requirements can't rehabilitate the conscience of the servant and are only imposed until the time of restoration.

Messiah appeared to enter the superior Tabernacle as high priest of the better future. This is the Tabernacle beyond the created universe not the manmade one. He was granted access to the sanctuary once and for all to purchase an eternal redemption because of his own blood, not the blood of goats and calves. After all, he offered himself spotless to God through the eternal Spirit. So, if it's true that the blood of goats and bulls and the sprinkled ashes of a heifer can externally purify the impure, then isn't it certainly true that the blood of Messiah can purify your conscience from dead works to serve the living God? This is why he is the mediator of a new covenant so that those who have been invited can receive the promised eternal possession since he died to redeem them from the violations committed under the first covenant.

Now it is a requirement for the death penalty to be carried out against the party who broke the covenant since it is a binding covenant that has been broken. After all, a broken covenant is proven valid when the death penalty is delivered to those who broke it since it isn't being enforced as long as the one who broke it is allowed to live. This being the case, of course the first covenant was inaugurated with blood. So, when Moses had told all of the people every commandment in the Torah, he mixed the blood of bulls and goats with water, scarlet wool, and hyssop. Then he sprinkled the mixture on the book and all of the people and said, "This is the blood of the covenant which God established with you." Following that, he also sprinkled the Tabernacle and all of its utensils for ministry. In fact, nearly everything is purified with blood in the Torah since there can be no pardon without the offering of blood.

So, it was required for the models of the things in heaven to be purified with sacrifices like these, but the heavenly versions themselves required better sacrifices. After all, Messiah entered heaven itself to represent us now in the presence of God, not the manmade sanctuary which is a counterpart to the originals. He didn't offer himself over and over again like the high priest enters the sanctuary each year with animal blood or else he would have had to suffer repeatedly since the beginning of the world. Quite the contrary, he has appeared once at the culmination of history to expunge sin by sacrificing himself. In the same way that people are destined to die once and then face judgment, Messiah was offered once to bear the sins of many, and then he will come a second time, not to bear sin, but to save those who are ready to welcome him.

Now the Torah foreshadows the better future but doesn't achieve its realization. The same sacrifices are offered each year indefinitely which can't qualify those who approach. Otherwise, wouldn't the sacrifices have been discontinued since the servants would have already been purified and had no awareness of sins? However, there is a reminder of sins in the sacrifices every year because the blood of bulls and goats can't eradicate sins.

This is why, when he came into the world, he said, "You didn't want a sacrifice or an offering, instead you prepared a body for me. You didn't enjoy burnt offerings or sin offerings. Then I said, 'It's written about me on the pages of the book, I have come here to do what you want, God.'" The reason why he says, "I have come to do what you want" is because of when he said, "You didn't want or enjoy sacrifices, offerings, burnt offerings, and sin offerings," even though these are offered from the Torah. He repeals the first one so that he can establish the second one. We are being made holy because Messiah Jesus offered his body once and for all since that is what God wanted.

In addition to that, every priest must stand day in and day out as part of their ministry so that they can offer the same sacrifices repeatedly which can never eradicate sins. However, he sat down next to God after he offered a single and permanently effective sacrifice for sins. From now on, he is looking forward to when his enemies will be piled under his feet. After all, he has permanently qualified those who are being made holy by a single sacrifice.

Now the Holy Spirit testifies to us about this. After saying, "This is what the new covenant will be like that I will make with them after those days. Pay attention; this is the Lord talking. I will install my instructions in their hearts and engrave them on their minds," he goes on to say, "I will never remind myself of their sins or their defiance again." Where these are pardoned, there is no longer a need for a sin offering.

So, brothers and sisters, we have confidence to enter the sanctuary by the blood of Jesus. Because of his death we can use the new path he opened up for us through the curtain that leads to life. We also have him as a great priest over the family of God. That is why we should approach God with genuine hearts in complete faithfulness since our hearts have been purified from a corrupt conscience and our bodies have been washed with pure water. We should maintain our commitment to hope without hesitation because the one who promised is faithful. Let's also think of ways to motivate one another to be supportive and not give up on gathering together like some have the habit of doing. Quite the contrary, let's encourage each other even more as you see the day getting closer.

Now if we continue sinning on purpose after we learned the truth, there is no longer a sacrifice for sins that can be made. Quite the contrary, all that is left is a terrifying anticipation of judgment and a burning rage which will consume the opposition. Anyone who violates the Torah of Moses is sentenced to death without mercy based on the testimony of two or three witnesses. If that is the case, don't you think a much more severe sentence is warranted for the one who disparages the Son of God, who thinks the blood of the covenant that made him holy is ordinary blood, and who ridicules the Spirit of grace? After all, we know the one who said, "Justice is my job, and I will administer it," is also the one who said, "The Lord will avenge his people." It is terrifying to fall into the hands of the living God.

Let me remind you of the days gone by when you first saw the light; you endured a tough fight in your suffering. Sometimes you were publicly degraded and persecuted, and other times you banded together with those who were being treated like that. You were there for those in prison, and you joyfully accepted your possessions being seized since you realized you have a better possession that lasts longer.

So, you shouldn't throw away your confidence since it comes with a great reward. This is why you need endurance so that you can receive what God promised once you have done what he wants. After all, "in just a little while the one scheduled to arrive will get here and no longer delay. My righteous one will live because of faithfulness. However, if he retreats, I will not accept him." Now we are on the side of those who remain faithful and preserve their soul not those who retreat and end up destroyed.

Now faithfulness is the deed to the things we hope for; it is the guarantee for the things we don't see yet. It is because of faithfulness that God commended our ancestors. In faithfulness, we recognize that the universe was created by the word of God, meaning what we see originated from invisible things. In faithfulness, Abel offered a better sacrifice to God than Cain. Because of his faithfulness, Abel was commended as being righteous since God approved of his sacrifices. Because of his faithfulness, he is still speaking even after death. In faithfulness, Enoch was relocated to avoid death and no one could find him since God relocated him. Before he was relocated, he had been commended as having pleased God. Now it is impossible to please God without faithfulness because the one who approaches God must believe that he is faithful and will reward those who pursue him. In faithfulness, Noah built an ark to save his family as an act of devotion. He did this in response to being warned about what was not seen yet. Because of his faithfulness, he condemned the world and became the rightful owner of the righteousness that is based on faithfulness.

In faithfulness, Abraham obeyed God and departed for a place he was going to become the rightful owner of. He did this in response to being invited even though he didn't know where he was going. In faithfulness, he lived in the Promised Land as if he were a visitor in a foreign country. He lived there in tents with Isaac and Jacob who were co-owners of the same promise. After all, he was looking forward to an established city, which was founded by God. In faithfulness, Sarah received the ability to conceive, even though she was past childbearing years since she considered the one who promised was faithful. This is how a large number of descendants came from one man even though he was old enough to die. There are as many as the stars in the sky; they are countless like the sand on the beach.

Even though they were faithful they all died without having received what was promised. However, they perceived it a long way away despite the fact they were ready to usher it in. They even acknowledged that they were foreigners on the earth. Now those who say things like this show that they are yearning for a hometown. If they had reminisced about where they came from, they would have had a chance to return. However, they wanted something better, a heavenly home. That is why God is not ashamed to call himself their God. After all, he prepared a city for them.

In faithfulness, Abraham offered Isaac when he was put to the test. Abraham, the one who received the promises, was in the act of offering his one and only son. He concluded that God could raise him from the dead since he told him, "Your descendants will come from Isaac." Figuratively speaking, he essentially did get him back from the dead. In faithfulness, Isaac blessed Jacob and Esau regarding the future. In faithfulness, Jacob blessed both of Joseph's sons before he died and he worshipped God while leaning on his staff. In faithfulness, Joseph referenced the Exodus of Israel's descendants and left instructions for his burial at the end of his life.

In faithfulness, Moses was hidden by his parents for three months after his birth because they knew their baby was special and because they weren't afraid of the king's rules. In faithfulness, Moses refused to be called the son of Pharaoh's daughter after he grew up. He picked to be mistreated along with God's people instead of indulging in the momentary pleasure of sin. He considered being degraded for Messiah more valuable than all of the riches in Egypt because he was fixated on the reward. In faithfulness, he left Egypt because he was not afraid of the king's anger since he was focused on the one who is invisible. In faithfulness, he kept Passover by applying the blood so that the Destroyer couldn't hurt them.

In faithfulness, they crossed the Red Sea like walking on dry ground but when the Egyptians tried to cross, they were drowned. In faithfulness, the walls of Jericho collapsed after they walked around them for seven days. In faithfulness, Rahab the prostitute didn't die with the disobedient because she welcomed the spies peacefully.

What else can I say? There isn't enough time for me to tell you about Gideon, Barak, Samson, Jephthah, David, Samuel, and the prophets. Because of their faithfulness, they conquered kingdoms, enforced justice, and obtained promises. They shut lions' mouths, extinguished powerful fires, and avoided being killed by the sword. They were strengthened despite limitations, became dominant in battle, and forced foreign armies to retreat. Women received their family members back from the dead, yet others were tortured and refused to surrender so that they could obtain the better resurrection. Others faced beatings, ridicule, and imprisonment. Others were stoned to death, cut in half, and executed with the sword. Others were displaced and forced to wear sheepskin and goatskin, being destitute, persecuted, and mistreated. They were forced to take shelter in deserts, hillsides, caves, and ditches. The world didn't deserve them.

Although God commended all of them because of their faithfulness, they didn't receive what was promised. He had something better in store, to include us so that we could all reach the destination together.

So, since we are surrounded by such a great crowd of witnesses, we should remove every obstructive impediment and sin so we can run the race in front of us with endurance. We should run with our focus on

Jesus, the undisputed champion of faithfulness. He endured crucifixion for the joy that awaited him and disregarded the shame involved. He is now sitting next to the throne of God. Concentrate on the one who endured this level of animosity at the hands of sinners so that you don't get exhausted and give up.

In your struggle against sin, you have not yet resisted to the point of bleeding for it. Did you forget the encouraging words which address you as sons and daughters, "My son, don't underestimate the Lord's training or give up when he corrects you. After all, the Lord loves those he trains and welcomes every son he disciplines"?

You have to endure since God is training you like sons and daughters. After all, is there any child who doesn't receive training from his father? So, if you haven't received training, which all of us have experienced, then it means you are illegitimate children not sons and daughters. Besides we've had natural fathers who trained us and we respected them. If that is the case, shouldn't we accept the authority of our spiritual Father to live? Now they trained us briefly as they thought best, but he trains us for our benefit so that we receive his holiness. Training doesn't seem enjoyable at the time, sometimes it even seems painful, but later on it yields the peaceful result of righteousness for those who complete their training.

This is why, despite your arms and legs being worn out, you have to keep going and run straight towards the goal so that you get reinvigorated and don't get an injury. Aim to be at peace with everyone, and aim for holiness, because no one will see the Lord without it. Be careful that no one misses out on God's grace and that no poisonous weed sprouts up to cause trouble and ends up contaminating many. Also, be careful that no one is depraved like Esau, who traded his birthright for a single meal. After all, you're aware that later on, when he wanted to receive the blessing, he was denied because he didn't repent, even though he begged and cried for it.

Now you haven't approached something tangible, a raging fire, pitch blackness, a foreboding gloom, a violent storm, a deafening trumpet sound, and a voice so intense it made those who heard beg for it to stop talking. They couldn't handle the command that even if an animal touched the mountain it had to be stoned to death. In fact, the phenomenon was terrifying to the degree that even Moses was so scared he was shaking. Quite the contrary, you have approached Mount Zion, the city of the living God, heavenly Jerusalem, thousands of celebrating angels, the firstborn community who are registered in heaven, God who is judge of everyone, the righteous spirits who have reached the destination, Jesus the mediator of a new covenant, and the purifying blood that has something better to say than Abel.

Make sure you don't refuse to listen to the one speaking! After all, if they didn't escape punishment when they refused to listen to him when he warned them on earth, we have no chance of escaping punishment if we reject him when he warns from heaven. His voice shook the earth then, but now he has promised, "Next time I will not just shake the earth, I will also shake the sky." This quotation reveals that the earth and the sky are shakable things and will be replaced so that what is unshakable can prevail. We should be grateful because we are being welcomed into an unshakable kingdom. To show our gratitude, we should serve God in a way that pleases him with constant devotion considering that our God is a consuming fire.

Continue to love each other like family. Don't stop showing hospitality, because this is how some people hosted angels without realizing it. Take care of those in prison as you would if it were you in prison and those who are being mistreated as if it were you being hurt. Everyone should respect marriage and prevent the marriage relationship from being compromised, because God will judge those who sin sexually. Live without loving money; instead be satisfied with what you have. After all, God has told us, "I will never abandon you and I will never give up on you," which is why we can confidently respond, "The Lord supports me, so I won't worry; what can anyone do to me?"

Remember your leaders who taught you the Word of God. Reflect on the results of their lifestyle and emulate their faithfulness. Messiah Jesus is the same yesterday, today, and forever. Don't be led astray into any unfamiliar teachings because it is better for you to be nourished by grace than by food which hasn't benefited those who live by it. We have an altar that those who serve in the Tabernacle aren't permitted to eat from. After all, the high priest takes the animals' blood into the sanctuary as a sin offering but their bodies are burned outside the camp. In fact, this is why Jesus suffered outside the city walls so that he could make the people holy with his own blood. So then, we should go to him outside the camp and accept being degraded like he was because we don't have a lasting city here. Quite the contrary, we yearn for the future city. Because of Jesus, we should always swear allegiance to God's name which is like offering him a sacrifice of praise. Don't stop supporting each other, because sacrifices like this please God. Be influenced by your leaders and follow their guidance because they guard your souls knowing that they will be judged. Please let them enjoy doing this and don't make it difficult since that wouldn't be in your best interest.

Pray for us, because we believe our motives are sincere since we are trying to be helpful in all that we do. We specifically encourage you to pray that I can return to you sooner.

May the God of peace—who brought our Lord Jesus, the great shepherd of the flock, back from the dead by the blood of the eternal covenant—may he equip you with everything helpful to do what he wants and to make us into something that pleases him through Messiah Jesus. May all glory go to him forever and ever. Amen.

Now brothers and sisters, I encourage you to take to heart this brief but challenging message that I have written for you. Note that our brother Timothy has been released. If he makes it to me soon, he will be with me when I come to see you. Say hello to all of your leaders and all of the saints for me. Your friends from Italy say hello to you. May grace be with all of you.

AFTERWORD

I have stored up your word in my heart, that I might not sin against you. Blessed are you, O LORD; teach me your statutes! (Psalm 119:11–12 ESV)

These verses have been my heart's prayer as I wrote this book, and I can think of no one they better apply to than Dr. Dwight A. Pryor.

I met Dwight Pryor for the first time at one of his *Haverim* Schools in April of 2009. I had already been studying Hebrews for several months by that time, so when he mentioned his interest in the letter, I knew I had to talk to him about it. Our conversation lasted less than three minutes, but that was all it took to change my perspective forever. Dwight had a habit of doing that often. Ultimately, that conversation set me on a path that led to this book becoming a reality.

I hope that you have enjoyed our journey together to unpuzzle Hebrews. I pray that this has caused you to grow deeper in your faith and will be meaningful to you in your continued walk with the Lord. If you enjoyed this book, feel free to share it with me. You can reach me at tom@unpuzzlinghebrews.com. I'm available for speaking and teaching if you'd like to schedule me for an engagement with your local church or assembly.

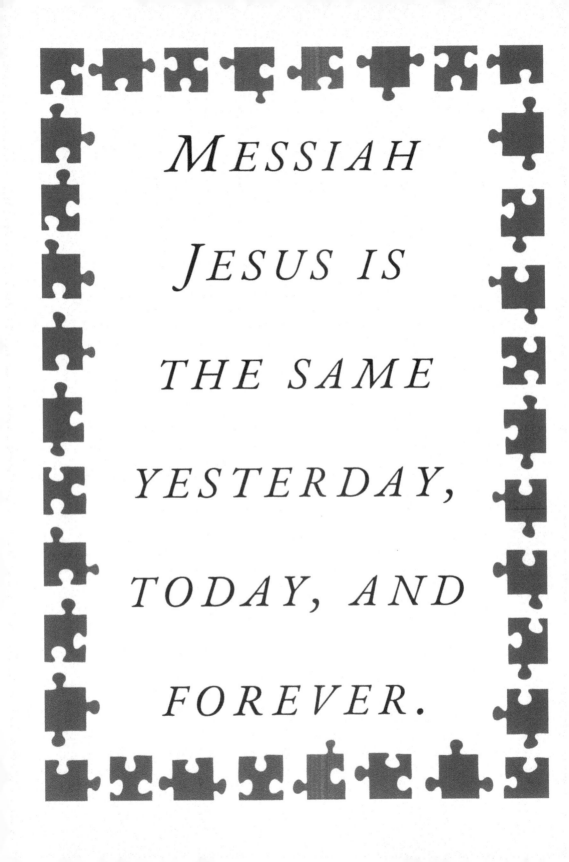

MESSIAH

JESUS IS

THE SAME

YESTERDAY,

TODAY, AND

FOREVER.

ACKNOWLEDGMENTS

There are so many people I want to thank who helped make this book a reality. I thank my lovely wife, Janine, for all of her support and for listening to me talk about Hebrews for over a decade. I thank my girls, Libby and Sadie, for being the best kids I could imagine.

I thank Lisa for encouraging me to set out on this path. Thanks to Ben for letting me teach early versions of the commentary. Thanks to Alex for early feedback on the translation. Thanks to Ben, Mark, and Scot for pastoral review and feedback. A big thanks to Angela and Dale Barthauer for volunteering to be the first readers and for providing helpful feedback on the first draft. Thanks to my editor and proofer for all of your expertise.

Thanks to Mom for being there for me. Thanks to Jake for sharing my passion for Hebrews. Thanks to Megan, New Mike, Mike Classic, Sarah, Paul, Kasey and the kids (Elodie, Isla, Nori, Shia, Knox) for being a great family.

Thanks to my spiritual mentors whom God has blessed me with over the years: Andre, Sid, Tsuma, Ahin, and Tim. I thank Cyndi for all the support she has been to me as well.

I thank Dr. Dirk Jongkind for taking the time to discuss textual criticism. I also thank Dr. Brian Small for his work starting and continuing the Polumeros kai Polutropos blog (www.polumeros.blogspot.com). I have read this blog since it started in 2009 and it is the hub for all things Hebrews.

Most of all, I thank the God and Father of our King, Messiah Jesus, who saved my life and has given me a purpose and a destiny.

BIBLIOGRAPHY

The following bibliography contains the resources cited in the text of this book. All resources are cited by the author's last name and relevant page number except where indicated differently below. The bibliography also contains key resources reviewed in the production of the translation and commentary.

Aland, Barbara and Kurt et al. *The Greek New Testament Fourth Revised Edition*. United Bible Societies, 1983.

Allen, David L. *Hebrews*. B & H Publishing Group, 2010.

Allen, David M. *Deuteronomy and Exhortation in Hebrews*. Mohr Siebeck, 2008. Referenced in the text of this book as "David M. Allen."

Asumang, Annang. *Unlocking the Book of Hebrews: A Spatial Analysis of the Epistle to the Hebrews*. Wipf and Stock, 2008.

Asumang, Annang. "Strive for Peace and Holiness: The Intertextual Journey of the Jacob Traditions from Genesis to Hebrews, via the Prophets." *Conspectus* 17 (March 2014): 1–52. Referenced in the text of this book as "Asumang2."

Attridge, Harold. *The Epistle to the Hebrews: A Commentary on the Epistle to the Hebrews*. Fortress Press, 1989.

Balz, Horst and Schneider, Gerhard. *Exegetical Dictionary of the New Testament*. William B. Eerdmans Publishing Company, 1990. Referenced in the text of this book as "EDNT."

Bateman IV, Herbert W. *Charts on the Book of Hebrews*. Kregel Publications, 2012.

Bates, Matthew W. *The Birth of the Trinity: Jesus, God, and Spirit in New Testament & Early Christian Interpretation of the Old Testament*. Oxford University Press, 2015.

BibleProject. "Overview: Hebrews." *YouTube*, 15 October 2015. https://www.youtube.com/watch?v=1fNWTZZwgbs.

Black, David Alan. "Origen on the Authorship of Hebrews." *DaveBlackOnline*, 5 February 2004. https://www.dave-blackonline.com/origen_on_the_authorship_of_hebr.htm.

Brennan Breed. "Hebrews, Session #4: Hebrews 6–7 with Dr. Madison Pierce." *YouTube*, 8 October 2021. https://www.y-outube.com/watch?v=Fgrbd6hDFRw.

Bruce, F.F. *The Epistle to the Hebrews*. William B. Eerdmans Publishing Company, 1990.

Center for Judaic-Christian Studies, The. *A Continuing Quest: The Dwight A. Pryor Legacy Collection, Edited by Keren H. Pryor*. Center for Judaic-Christian Studies, 2011.

Charlesworth, James H. *The Old Testament Pseudepigrapha Volume One: Apocalyptic Literature and Testaments*. Hendrickson Publishers, LLC, 1983.

Charlesworth, James H. *The Old Testament Pseudepigrapha Volume Two: Expansions of the "Old Testament" and Legends, Wisdom and Philosophical Literature, Prayers, Psalms, and Odes, Fragments of Lost Judeo-Hellenistic Works*. Hendrickson Publishers, LLC, 1983.

Cockerill, Gareth Lee. *The Epistle to the Hebrews*. Wm. B. Eerdmans Publishing Co., 2012.

Cohen, Abraham. *Everyman's Talmud*. Schocken Books, Inc. 1975.

Compton, Jared. *Psalm 110 and the Logic of Hebrews*. Bloomsbury T&T Clark, 2015.

Danker, Frederick W. *A Greek-English Lexicon of the New Testament and Other Early Christian Literature / revised and edited by Frederick Willian Danker.* — 3rd ed. The University of Chicago Press, 2000. Referenced in the text of this book as "BDAG."

Deibler Jr., Ellis W. *A Semantic and Structural Analysis of Hebrews.* SIL International, 2017.

Diggle, J. et al. *The Cambridge Greek Lexicon.* Cambridge University Press, 2021.

Dyer, Bryan R. *Suffering in the Face Of Death: The Epistle to the Hebrews and Its Context of Situation.* T&T Clark, 2017.

Easter, Matthew C. *Faith and the Faithfulness of Jesus in Hebrews.* Cambridge University Press, 2018.

Ellingworth, Paul. *The Epistle to the Hebrews: A Commentary on the Greek text.* Wm. B. Eerdmans Publishing Co., 1993.

Ellingworth, Paul and Nida, Eugene A. *A Translator's Handbook on the Letter to the Hebrews.* United Bible Societies, 1983.

Emmrich, Martin. "'Amtscharisma': Through the Eternal Spirit (Hebrews 9:14)." *Bulletin for Biblical Research* 12.1 (2002): 17–32.

Fudge, Edward William. *Hebrews: Ancient Encouragement for Believers Today.* Leafwood Publishers, 2009.

Gudorf, Michael E. "Through a Classical Lens: Hebrews 2:16." *Journal of Biblical Literature*, vol. 119, no. 1, Society of Biblical Literature, 2000, pp. 105–08, https://www.doi.org/10.2307/3267971.

Guthrie, George H. *Hebrews* in *Commentary of the Old Testament Use of the New Testament* edited by Beale, G.K. and Carson, D.A. Baker Academic, 2007.

Hahn, Scott W. "A Broken Covenant and the Curse of Death: A Study of Hebrews 9:16–22." *Catholic Biblical Quarterly* 66 (2004): 416–436.

Hahn, Scott W. "Covenant, Cult, and the Curse-of-Death: διαθήκη in Heb 9:15–22." Pages 65–88 in *Hebrews: Contem-*

porary Methods—New Insights. Edited by Gabriella Gelar-
dini. Biblical Interpretation Series 75. Society of Biblical
Literature, 2005.

Harris, Dana M. *Exegetical Guide to the Greek New Testament:
Hebrews.* B&H Academic, 2019.

Hartley, Donald E. "Heb. 11:6—A Reassessment of the Translation 'God Exists'" *Trinity Journal NS*, 27.2 (Fall 2006):
289–307.

Jewett, Robert. *Letter to Pilgrims: A Commentary on the Epistle
to the Hebrews.* The Pilgrim Press, 1981.

Jobes, Karen H. "The Function of Paronomasia in Hebrews
10:5–7." *Trinity Journal* 13 (1992): 181–91.

Johnson, Luke Timothy. *Hebrews: A Commentary.* Westminster
John Knox Press, 2006.

Johnsson, William G. *Defilement and Purgation in the Book of
Hebrews.* Fontes Press, 2020.

Jongkind, Dirk et al. *The Greek New Testament.* Crossway and
Cambridge University Press, 2017.

Josephus, Flavius. *The New Complete Works of Josephus/Flavius
Josephus; translated by William Whiston*; commentary by
Paul L. Maier. Kregel Publications, 1999.

Kaiser, Walter C. "The Old Promise and the New Covenant:
Jeremiah 31:31–34." *Journal of the Evangelical Theological
Society* 15.1 (1972): 11–23.

Ken Schenck. "Paul and the Temple Video." *YouTube*, 17
November 2018. https://www.youtube.com/watch?
v=rsl0DP9-0Zs.

Kibbe, Michael Harrison. *Godly Fear or Ungodly Failure:
Hebrews 12 and the Sinai Theophanies.* Walter de Gruyter,
2016.

Kittel, Gerhard. *Theological Dictionary of the New Testament.*
Wm. B. Eerdmans Publishing Co., 1964.

Koester, Craig R. *Hebrews: A New translation with Introduction
and Commentary.* Doubleday, 2001.

Kugel, James L. *Traditions of the Bible: A Guide to the Bible as it was at the start of the common era.* Harvard University Press, 1997.

Jongkind, Dirk. *An Introduction to the Greek New Testament, Produced at Tyndale House, Cambridge.* Crossway, 2019.

Lancaster, D.T. *Depths of the Torah.* First Fruits of Zion, 2006.

Lane, William L. *Hebrews 1–8, Volume 47A.* Zondervan, 1991.

Lane, William L. *Hebrews 9–13, Volume 47B.* Zondervan, 1991.

Lewis, C.S. *The Lion, the Witch and the Wardrobe.* Harper-Collins Publishers, 1994.

Love, Todd et al. "Neuroscience of Internet Pornography Addiction: A Review and Update." *Behavioral sciences* (Basel, Switzerland) vol. 5, 3 388–433. 18 Sep. 2015, doi: 10.3390/bs5030388.

Mackie, Scott D. "Visually Oriented Rhetoric and Visionary Experience in Hebrews 12:1–4." *Catholic Biblical Quarterly* 79, no. 3 (n.d.): 476–97. doi:10.1353/CBQ.2017.0128.

Martin, Michael Wade and Whitlark, Jason A. *Inventing Hebrews: Design and Purpose in Ancient Rhetoric.* Cambridge University Press, 2018.

McKee, J.K. *Hebrews for the Practical Messianic.* Messianic Apologetics, 2006.

Metzger, Bruce M. *A Textual Commentary on the Greek New Testament: Second Edition.* United Bible Societies, 1994.

Moffatt, James. *A Critical and Exegetical Commentary on the Epistle to the Hebrews.* T.&T. Clark, 1924.

Moffitt, David McCheyne. *A New and Living Way: Atonement and the Logic of Resurrection in the Epistle to the Hebrews.* Ph.D. diss., Duke University, 2010.

Montefiore, Hugh William. *A Commentary on the Epistle to the Hebrews.* Hendrickson Publishers, Inc., 1964.

Moulton, J.H. and Milligan, G. *Vocabulary of the Greek Testament.* Hendrickson Publishers, 1930.

Mounce, William D. *Basics of Biblical Greek Grammar.* Zondervan, 1993.

Nanos, Mark D. "New or Renewed Covenantalism?: A

Response to Richard Hays' 'Here We Have No Lasting City: New Covenantalism in Hebrews.'" The St. Andrews Conference on Hebrews and Theology. 2006.

Newman Jr., Barclay M. *Greek-English Dictionary of the New Testament*. German Bible Societies, 1993.

One For Israel Ministry. "Messiah Revealed in the First Murder! - Genesis 1–4 - Messiah in the Torah." *YouTube*, 11 March 2021. https://www.youtube.com/watch?v=hi_Etq3T0ak.

Pfitzner, Victor. *Abingdon New Testament Commentaries: Hebrews*. Abingdon Press, 1997.

Pierce, Madison N. *Divine Discourse in the Epistle to the Hebrews: the Recontextualizaion of Spoken Quotations of Scripture*. Cambridge University Press, 2020.

Pryor, Dwight A. "Jesus, Christians & the Law: Two Part Teaching Series." *The Center for Judaic Christian Studies*. https://www.jcstudies.store/jesus-christians-the-law.

Pryor, Dwight A. "Our Father, Our King, Who Is God, What Is His Name: Three Part Teaching Series." *The Center for Judaic Christian Studies*. https://www.jcstudies.store/our-father-our-king.

Pryor, Dwight A. "Paul, the Law and the Church: Four Part Teaching Series." *The Center for Judaic Christian Studies*. https://www.jcstudies.store/paul-the-law-and-the-church.

Pryor, Dwight A. "Wrestling with Hebrews: Six Part Teaching Series." *The Center for Judaic Christian Studies*. https://www.jcstudies.store/wrestling-with-hebrews.

Roberts, Alexander et al. *The Researcher's Library of Ancient Texts, Volume II: The Apostolic Fathers: includes Clement of Rome, Mathetes, Polycarp, Ignatius, Barnabas, Papias, Justin Martyr, and Irenaeus*. Defense, 2012.

Schenck, Kenneth. *Understanding the Book of Hebrews: The Story Behind the Sermon*. Westminster John Knox Press, 2003.

Schenck, Kenneth. *A New Perspective on Hebrews: Rethinking the Parting of the Ways*. Fortress Academic, 2019. Referenced in the text of this book as "Schenck2."

Schnittjer, Gary Edward. *The Torah Story: An Apprenticeship on the Pentateuch.* Zondervan, 2006.

Simpson, Jon. "Finding Brand Success In The Digital World." *Forbes*, 25 August 2017. https://www.forbes.com/sites/forbesagencycouncil/2017/08/25/finding-brand-success-in-the-digital-world.

Spicq, Ceslas. *Theological Dictionary of the New Testament translated and edited by James D. Ernest.* Hendrickson Publishers, 1994. Referenced in the text of this book as "TLNT."

Swetnam, James. "The Crux at Hebrews 5,7–8." *Biblica* 81 (2000): 347–61.

Swetnam, James. "The Context of the Crux at Hebrews 5,7–8." *Filologia Neotestamentaria* 14 (2001): 101–120.

Swetnam, James. "Εξ ενος in Hebrews 2,11." *Biblica* 88 (2007): 517–25.

Temple Institute. "The Holy of Holies" *Temple Institute*, 2020. https://www.templeinstitute.org/illustrated-tour-the-holy-of-holies

Thiessen, Matthew. "Hebrews and the End of the Exodus." *Novum Testamentum*, 2007.

Thiessen, Matthew. "Hebrews 12.5–13, the Wilderness Period, and Israel's Discipline." *New Testament Studies*, 55(03), 366. https://www.doi.org/10.1017/S0028688509000277. Referenced in the text of this book as "Thiessen2."

Tolkien, J.R.R. *The Fellowship of the Ring.* Houghton Mifflin, 1994.

Wallace, Daniel. *Greek Grammar Beyond the Basics: An Exegetical Syntax of the New Testament.* Zondervan, 1996.

Wheaton College. "Exegetically Speaking: The Last Days Are Not a But." *YouTube*, 1 March 2021. https://www.youtube.com/watch?v=-kIE-IkL2io.

Wheaton College. "Exegetically Speaking: Distributions of the Holy Spirit." *YouTube*, 28 June 2021. https://www.youtube.com/watch?v=-kIE-IkL2io.

Whitlark, Jason A. *Resisting Empire: Rethinking the Purpose of the Letter to "the Hebrews."* Bloomsbury T&T Clark, 2014.

Witherington, Ben III. *Letters and Homilies for Jewish Christians: A Socio-Rhetorical Commentary on Hebrews, James and Jude.* InterVarsity Press, 2007.

ABOUT AUTHOR

Tom graduated from Word of Life Bible Institute in 2007 and completed hundreds of hours of biblical training at Dwight Pryor's Haverim School of Discipleship from 2008 to 2009. Since then he has served as a youth pastor, teacher, and biblical consultant in churches throughout the United States. In addition to specializing his studies in Hebrews, he also loves studying the historical background of the Gospels, the new perspective on Paul, the character of God in the Old Testament, and ancient Jewish culture. Most of all, Tom enjoys telling the story of how God rescued a suicidal teenager and transferred him into the kingdom of his beloved Son. *Unpuzzling Hebrews* is his first book, but Lord willing, not his last. Tom lives in the Cincinnati area with his wife and daughters.